Ask Me Smarter!

Brain Questions for Kids that are **FUN**-da-men-tal
In Helping Them SOAR to Scholastic Success

SOCIAL STUDIES and CIVICS

Preschool – 5th Grade

By: Donna M. Roszak

Ask Me Smarter!

Brain Questions for Kids that are FUN-da-men-tal in Helping Them SOAR to Scholastic Success

SOCIAL STUDIES and CIVICS

Preschool – 5th Grade

Published in the United States by: Zebra Print Press, LLC

Cover Design by Donna M. Roszak
Cover Creation by www.jimandzetta.com
Interior layout and typesetting by www.jimandzetta.com
Ebook conversion by www.jimandzetta.com

Library of Congress Control Number: (I WILL SUPPLY THIS LATER WHEN I GET IT!)

ISBN: 978-0-9860801-7-3 (Trade Paperback)
(Hard Cover)

Printed in the United States of America

First Edition

Website: **www.askmesmarter.com**

To my son Lucas who has always believed in this book and is my biggest supporter, to my mother Dorothy, whom I hope would be proud, and to my-mother-in law Joan who has continued to encourage me throughout this endeavor.

Table of Contents

A Note to Parents, Guardians, and Teachers

This book is based on the premise that parents/guardians are their children's greatest and most influential teachers!

This book is designed as a **one-source tool** to help parents/guardians empower their children with a solid knowledge foundation, *based on traditional state content standards per grade level,* as they progress through their elementary school years. It is intended to enhance and reinforce the facts, ideas, and concepts that children are learning in school. This book serves to take away the guesswork, and to provide concrete questions that relate to the listed content standards per grade level. It is an oral approach to disseminating primarily rote information. It is a book based on the notion that learning is a life-long process, and that children learn differently and at different rates. Leaning is not always aligned with chronological age. It is a book that is sensitive to the fact that children come from diverse cultural upbringings and have diverse educational backgrounds and experiences.

What it is NOT: This book is *not* a school curriculum guide. It is *not* intended to be a quiz, a trivia game of random questions, or a competition venue. It is *not* a school textbook or workbook. It is *not* a manual for homeschoolers. It is *not* intended to be a substitute for fulfilling all school grade objectives and outcomes. It is *not* intended to promote the higher level thinking skills as outlined in Bloom's taxonomy. Further, it is *not* expected that children memorize and "master" all questions at any given grade level before proceeding to the next.

Knowledge gained by answering ***Social Studies and Civics*** content questions is a sound learning strategy in that it is:

Specific
Measurable
Attainable
Results oriented
Time framed by grade level
Empowering
Reinforcing

Preface

This book provides a **one-source** guide for parents/guardians/teachers to help their children learn important **SOCIAL STUDIES AND CIVICS** facts and concepts across the elementary levels that are child, grade, and age appropriate. All the grade levels are integrated together into one book to achieve a comprehensive approach that also accommodates different learning paces. It further allows for review and reinforcement based on child-readiness and retention capacity. Even though a child may learn one topic in one year does not guarantee the child will retain that same information and have the retention and recall capacity to build on that knowledge the following school year!

This oral approach is based on the premise that knowledge is acquired through the senses: sight, hearing, touch, smell, and taste. The more senses that are used in learning, the higher the retention rate will be. Children have different learning rates and different learning styles. If "speaking" is added to hearing and seeing, the learning will come even faster, and retention will be maximized. It can be concluded then, that learners have a higher retention of what they HEAR, and SAY than by what they *SEE* alone. Employing more than one sense in learning then, as this book aims to do, is what makes the learning permanent. When all is said and done, the key to long-term retention is sustained practice over time.

This book also provides a vacation or summer "bridge" tool for young learners when school is not in session. "Ask Me Smarter" may also prove to be a good companion during a long road trip!

Inherent in this simple question format is building a child's self-esteem with a *low-anxiety* verbal approach, empowering him or her with essential knowledge, facts, and insights.

This book is a result of my difficulty in comprehending my son's just published 5th grade social studies textbook that was so convoluted with facts and minute details that the understanding of the main idea was completely lost. After reading a particularly wordy passage on the Civil War, my son had no clue from that reading which leader was on which side and who ultimately won the war! It further stems from my frustration in locating a resource that did not read like a textbook, or one that was not specific to just one grade level or operate like a workbook. Further, many libraries and bookstores have an abundant selection of educational psychology books, how-to books, science experiment books, how to read books, colorful trivia decks, but I was not able to locate a single resource that provides a direct and comprehensive approach to asking specific questions to young learners across all core and non-core disciplines. Trivia cards and interactive websites while fun and educational, are somewhat random and hit or miss with regard to ensuring coverage of essential facts encompassing all the necessary academic subject areas. I felt compelled to write something that might help fill a niche I felt was lacking, and one that expands on current resources. To this end, it was my intent to compile several grade levels into one book.

How to Use This Book

It is important to use careful judgment in ascertaining which topics and how many questions should be asked of your child (children) at any one time. It is encouraged that questions be asked from different topics and questions that encompass different grade levels as appropriate. For example, a 1st grader may benefit from being posed "2nd grade" questions as well as being asked questions from the "kindergarten" section on any given topic. A 5th grader would similarly benefit from being asked a 3rd grade question! Some overlap with regard to the questions should be expected. Further, it is important to note that what may be deemed a "2nd grade" question in one state, may be regarded as a "3rd grade" question in another. In addition, some topics may be listed as a content standard in one state and not another. The question, "Why do you save money?" is posed as a pre-school question. That same question can be asked at any grade level. Theoretically, the older and more knowledgeable the child, the higher the level of response.

Core Questions: It is given that many questions in this book could represent a full week lesson, many worksheets, practice, application, and analysis. In many cases, a choice is offered after a question, but this choice could easily be eliminated if need be, or if the question is asked for the second or third time.

SOCIAL STUDIES: Many of the social studies questions encompass geography and history. While many elementary schools may focus on different early civilizations, most do cover units relating to early American heritage and history. Several of the questions related to specific states and countries are written as "mini-lessons." Further exploration of the names and places in those questions is also highly recommended!

CIVICS: The focus of this chapter is to prompt children to think about all levels of government, the role of the citizen, and the importance of becoming contributing members of the community, the state, and the nation. The 5th grade level also includes a common version of the Practice Citizenship Test.

IMPORTANT: It should not be expected that children ***master*** a grade level before proceeding to the next! The emphasis is on the questions, *not* the grade level. As both a mother and an educator, one of the best pieces of advice I ever received was, "teach the child, not the grade or subject."

Questions are somewhat sequential and are inherently progressive as students gain knowledge. The questions are aimed to serve as a *representation* of what is listed as the prescribed "standards" or learning outcomes for the elementary grade levels in most states.

Parents/guardians/teachers are encouraged to *re-word* questions, repeat questions, and improvise. For example, if on one occasion you ask your child: *"How many continents are there?"* Next time ask, "*What are the seven major land masses called?"* Further, many questions have an inherent challenge in that they are posed with a choice, something that can, and should be omitted at the discretion of the interrogator.

If questions are asked at bedtime, an ideal time for the brain to process information and store it for future retrieval, ask your child some of the **same** questions the next morning for further reinforcement and empowerment. If the question has a choice of two or more answers, leave out the choice when asking the question again.

Some questions listed as curriculum content standards will and should illicit further discussion. Many questions may be posed as yes and no or true and false questions, simply to suggest a specific learning objective. For many of the questions it is suggested that *similar* types of questions be asked to promote further competence and awareness. For example, a preschooler may be asked to name the state he or she lives in. You can follow up with, *"In what city, state, and country do we live in?"* A high level question posed may ask the learner to name as many states as he or she can that make up the United States.

The intention of the author is for this book to be used as an oral and auditory approach to learning and reviewing or discussing information, but it certainly would work well for a learner to read the questions and see how many questions he or she can answer correctly. It is intended to enhance and compliment what our children are already learning in school or at home. Its all-inclusive format and oral approach is what makes it unique, I believe.

If a child seems intrigued by a particular question or answer, I would highly encourage seeking out other resources from books, the Internet, pictures, etc. (See list of further resources.) We need to expand upon our children's great capacity to learn and feed their unwavering curiosity!

My hope is that your child will be engaged and challenged, and therefore empowered through this oral questioning format.

In assessing correctness, the answers are located in the appendix in numerical order.

Further Resources:
Library (School and Local)
Internet
Family Members
Field Trips
Field Experts
Authentic Learning Moments (Teaching fractions while cutting and serving pizza)
Real-time applications: (Conduct a science experiment: What time of day is your shadow longer; shorter? Follow a recipe.)
"Wonder" Questions (What do you wonder about?)
Have your child ask YOU a question! If you are unable to answer it, suggest that you seek out the answer together.

It needs to be stated that information expands exponentially every day. Any given topic in and of itself could easily fill a library. One war may be an entire semester of study at the University level! Neither an entire library, nor the nearly infinite information capacity of a computer could ever fit into one manageable book. Given the limits and constraints of time and space, the inclusion of any topic or question is frequently at the expense or exclusion of another. If I was remiss in any regard, I invite the reader to fill in any perceived missing questions, as you deem appropriate. What follows is a compilation of questions that encompass a wide array of essential knowledge questions aimed at children 12 and under based on traditional state learning standards. The questions loosely "cover" the learning objectives listed under the curriculum guidelines for each respective grade level. Variations and expanding upon the questions is encouraged and expected.

There is definite overlap between grade levels. Because this is a question format, this approach in no way is intended to promote and develop a mastery of grade-level *skills* (socialization, cooperative learning, reading, writing, spelling, vocabulary acquisition, story-telling etc.) Nor can this format measure a child's proficiency with technology and research skills that are an integral part of learning outcomes per grade level. Any omission or perceived bias is completely unintentional. Ideally, this question and answer approach will serve to empower our children with essential and meaningful knowledge through these fact-based questions, and provide them with a strong foundation as they continue to learn, grow, and prepare for higher learning. In so doing, our children will become informed citizens and future contributing members of our global community.

Research shows that children learn in different ways and at different rates. This book is formatted to compliment the brain networks that play a key role in learning. The "Spacing Effect" is a sound strategy in that facts are learned best when they are studied at frequent intervals over a long time span. Long-term retention of facts and information is maximized through repeated retrieval. "Ask Me Smarter" aims to provide the opportunity for optimal learning to occur in that the emphasis is on the knowledge, not the grade level.

As you use this book as a supplemental learning tool, it is important to keep in mind:

1) Many learners may certainly benefit from ***looking at maps, a globe,*** and venturing out and taking "field trips."

2) Many of the questions, especially in grades 3, 4, and 5 have a choice of answers after the colon. The degree of difficulty is inherent in these questions in that the choice can be read or not, at the discretion of the person asking the questions, and the readiness of the learner.

3) Many questions are yes or no questions that reflect a specific learning standard per grade level. These questions are given the answer "Yes" if only to suggest the learning goal.

4) Many of the questions asked in the higher grades are admittedly a "stretch," but they are purposely included to challenge and engage the young learner.

"Knowledge is ***potential*** power!"

Now go ahead, ask them smarter!

Chapter 1 – Social Studies

Social Studies – Pre-School

1. What is the name of the country that you live in?
2. Which state do you live in?
3. Which city do you live in?
4. What language(s) do you speak?
5. Do we have art, music, and dance as part of our culture?
6. What does an artist do?
7. What are the names of some musical instruments?
8. When do we celebrate America's Independence Day?
9. What holidays do we celebrate?
10. What is our nationality?
11. What is the name of the first people that lived in America?
12. Who came to America from England on the Mayflower, and met with the Native American Indians?
13. What holiday do we celebrate where we remember the first big feast that the Native American Indians and the Pilgrims had after a good harvest?
14. What is the name for the houses of the Indians: Totems or Teepees?
15. What is the name of our first President of the United States?
16. Can you name something that is named for George Washington?
17. Which American President is considered the "Father of our Country?"
18. What did President George Washington ask Betsy Ross to sew?
19. What colors are in our American flag?
20. What is the name of the American President that was born in a log cabin in Indiana and was often called "Honest Abe?"
21. During the time of President Lincoln there was a Civil war in which the North fought against whom: the South or the West?

22. What was a major cause of the Civil War pitting the North against the South: slavery or farmland?

23. What were the two main crops that were grown on the farms or plantations in the South: potatoes and tomatoes, or cotton and tobacco?

24. What is the name of the Nobel-Prize winning African American pastor who led the Civil Rights Movement in the 1950's, and gave a famous speech called, "I Have a Dream?"

25. Did Martin Luther King Jr. have a "dream" where all people of all races have equal rights?

Social Studies – Kindergarten

26. Are you a member of a family?

27. In what ways can a child become a member of a family?

28. Can you name the members of your *immediate* family?

29. What relatives outside of your immediate family can you name?

30. What is the name of the city or town we live in?

31. What is the name of the state we live in?

32. How many states are there in the United States?

33. What is the full name of the country we live in?

34. What is the name of the country above us to the north?

35. What is the name of the country below us to the south?

36. Do you think that Mexican culture is similar of different than our culture?

37. Do you think Canadian culture is similar of different than our culture?

38. Are all the people that live in America originally from America?

39. Do you think the Native Americans lived differently than we do today?

40. Does the word "native" refer to someone that was born here?

41. Are Native Americans also called American Indians?

42. How did Native Americans get their food?

43. What kinds of tools or weapons did Native Americans have?

44. What kinds of animals did Native Americans hunt for?

45. What is the name of the "house" that many Native Americans lived in, made of long poles and covered with Buffalo hide?

46. What shape are most teepees?

47. What kinds of things did Native Americans make?

48. What is the name of the shoes worn by many Native Americans?

49. What is the name of the dwelling that some early settlers like the Iroquois Indians lived in, made of wood and bark: longhouses or cliff houses?

50. What is the name of the dwelling built by Native Americans of the Southwest like the Hopi tribe, that were like small villages formed out of adobe clay bricks: cliff dwellings or pueblos?

51. What is the name of the dwelling built by Woodland Indians like the Ojibwa Tribe that were round houses with round tops made from poles, hide, and bark, and were either portable or permanent: teepees or wigwams?

52. What is the name of the boat that Native Americans carved from the bark of birch trees?

53. What is the name for the symbolic sculptures that Native Americans carved from large trees?

54. What is the nationality of our family?

55. Do all people have skin color that is the same or different?

56. What is our religion or belief system?

57. Does everyone have the same religion or belief, or can they be different?

58. Is it good to embrace and respect everyone's differences?

59. Why do you suppose the United States with its diverse population is called the "melting pot?"

60. On which continent is the United States located: North American or South America?

61. How many continents are there: six or seven?

62. Which continent is missing from the following: Asia, Europe, Africa, North America, South America, and Australia?

63. Which is bigger: a continent or a country?

64. Which continent is the largest continent in the world: Asia or Africa?

65. Can you name a large country in Asia?

66. In which continent are China, India, and Russia located: Asia or Africa?

67. What is the name of the second largest continent with 54 countries, the Sahara Desert, the Nile River, and is known for its abundant wildlife like elephants, giraffes, zebras, leopards, and cheetahs?

68. What is the name of the third largest continent with 23 countries that include the United States, Canada, Mexico, the Caribbean Islands, Bermuda, the Central American countries, and Greenland, the world's largest island?

69. What is the name of the fourth largest continent with 12 independent countries; the territories of the Falkland Islands, the Galapagos Islands, and French Guiana; where the Andes Mountains, the Amazon Rainforest, the Amazon River, Angel Falls, and the Atacama Desert are located; and is known for animals like llamas, alpacas, and parrots?

70. What is the name of the fifth largest continent that is located at the South Pole, is 98% solid ice, and is known for its abundance of glaciers, penguins, and seals?

71. What is the name of the sixth largest continent, part of the peninsula of Eurasia with 47 countries, and includes Germany, Austria, Switzerland, Spain, Italy, France, Norway, Sweden, Denmark, Finland, Belgium, England, Scotland, Ireland, Poland, Russia, Greece, and The Vatican?

72. What is the name of the smallest continent that includes an island where kangaroos, koalas and platypus live, New Zealand, many islands of the South Pacific, and is collectively known as Oceania?

73. What is the full name of the country we live in?

74. What are the two states that are located outside of the continent of North America?

75. What does the abbreviation U.S.A. stand for?

76. What is the common nickname for the symbol of our country, also called "the red, white, and blue:" Old Glory or the Stars and Stripes?

77. What are you drawing when you draw land and water shapes on a piece of paper?

78. What kind of map shows the locations of towns, cities, and highways: state or physical?

79. Can you locate where a relative lives, or where we go on vacation on a map?

80. What is a map representation called that is a three-dimensional scale model of the Earth?

81. What are the two main oceans on our planet?

82. What are the four cardinal directions that tell us where things are?

83. Which direction is the opposite of south?

84. Which direction is the opposite of east?

85. In which direction does the Sun rise: east or west?

86. In which direction does the Sun set: east or west?

87. In most cases, which direction is the top of the map: north or south?

88. In most cases, which direction is the bottom of the map: north or south?

89. Do you think Christopher Columbus used a map when he sailed here from Spain?

90. When Columbus landed after more than a month, what did he call the natives because he was so sure that he had reached the East Indies?

91. Did Columbus think that the world was flat or round?

92. What is the name of the country named for the Italian navigator Amerigo Vespucci?

93. What language or languages do you speak?

94. How do you think family life today is different now than many years ago?

95. What things do we have today that they didn't during pioneer days?

96. What kind of a school do you think that pioneer children attended?

97. Can you name some things that families of long ago had that we do not have today?

98. Which number president was George Washington?

99. Can you see George Washington's picture on a quarter and a dollar bill?

100. Who was the second president of the United States: John Adams or Thomas Jefferson?

101. Who was the third president of the United States: John Adams or Thomas Jefferson?

102. What is the name of the document that Thomas Jefferson drafted in 1776 that was written to explain to foreign nations why the colonies had decided to separate themselves from Great Britain that declared "All men are created equal: The Declaration of Independence or the Bill of Rights?

103. Who was the first to sign The Declaration of Independence: John Hancock or John Adams?

104. Did Thomas Jefferson want to declare independence from England or Spain in 1776?

105. Was Abraham Lincoln our 16th President or our 17th President?

106. Whose face is on the penny: Washington or Lincoln?

107. What was the nickname of our 26th President, Theodore Roosevelt?

108. What is the name of the stuffed animal that was named for "Teddy" Roosevelt?

109. What is the name of the famous monument in South Dakota carved in stone with the faces of Washington, Jefferson, Lincoln, and Roosevelt: Mount Rushmore or Mount Vernon?

110. Who is the President of the United States today?

111. What is the name of the house where the President of the United States lives?

112. Where is the capital and the White House located: Washington or Washington, D.C?

113. What does D.C. stand for in Washington, D.C: District of Colombia or District of Congress?

114. Are dance, theater, and music all part of American culture?

115. What is the name of a dance where the dancers wear pointed shoes?

116. What are the holidays that we celebrate?

117. What family *tradition* do we have when we celebrate Thanksgiving or some other holiday?

118. What foods are *custom* for Americans to eat on Thanksgiving Day?

119. Who were the two groups of people who gathered to eat a great feast at the first Thanksgiving?

120. Which month of the year do we celebrate New Year's Day?

121. Which month of the year do we celebrate Thanksgiving Day?

122. Which month of the year is Christmas celebrated in?

123. Do you think customs are the same or different in other countries?

124. When is America's Independence Day celebrated?

125. How would you describe the American flag?

126. Who was the first President of the United States?

127. Do we celebrate Presidents' Day in January or February?

128. Do we honor George Washington and Abraham Lincoln on Presidents' Day?

129. In which month do we honor Martin Luther King Jr: January or February?

130. What are the four seasons?

131. What holidays do we celebrate in winter?

132. What holidays do we celebrate in spring?

133. What holidays do we celebrate in summer?

134. What holidays do we celebrate in fall?

135. Do you think that other cultures have different holidays that they celebrate?

136. Do you think that there are different ways to celebrate a holiday?

137. Are homes here in America the same or different as homes in other countries?

138. Do you think we eat the same foods here as they do in other countries?

139. Is spaghetti and lasagna Mexican food or Italian food?

140. Are enchiladas and tacos Mexican food or Italian food?

141. Can you name other (ethnic) foods from another country?

142. Do you think that music is the same or different in other countries?

143. How is our family the same as other families that you know?

144. How is our family different than other families you know?

145. Do you think that each person in the world is special and unique?

146. Do people have different body shapes and sizes?

147. What are some qualities of being a responsible citizen?

148. What are some responsibilities that you have?

149. What do we use in order to buy goods and services?

150. Before money, what do you think that people long ago used in exchange for goods and services?

151. What do many people have to do in order to earn money?

152. Do we have to make choices with money?

153. Is buying food a want or a need?

154. Is buying a toy a want or a need?

155. What is the name for American currency?

156. Can you name some of the coins and bills we use as currency in the U.S?

157. Do you think that currency (money) is the same or different in other countries?

158. What do you do or can you do to earn money?

159. Is it important to save part of the money that you earn?

160. What is the name of a place that people use to keep the money that they earn?

Social Studies – 1st Grade

161. What is the difference between a map and a globe?

162. Why do we use a map?

163. Where is "North" on a direction compass: at the top or bottom?

164. Where is "South" on a direction compass: at the top or bottom?

165. Where is "East" on a direction compass: to the right or to the left?

166. Where is "West" on a direction compass: to the right or to the left?

167. Can you locate our city (town) on a map?

168. Can you locate our state on a map?

169. What is the name of the country you live in?

170. Can you locate our country on a world map?

171. Can you locate our continent on a globe?

172. How many states are in the United States of America?

173. What is the name of the state you live in?

174. Which two states are located outside the continental United States?

175. What is the capital city of the United States?

176. What is the name of the President of our country?

177. What is the name of the residence of the President and first family in Washington, D.C?

178. How do we elect the President and Vice-President to lead our country?

179. What is the capital of our state?

180. What is our state famous for?

181. What is the name of the ***county*** you live in?

182. Have you ever gone to the county fair?

183. Does our state have a state fair?

184. What is the name of the city we live in?

185. What is the name of the street we live on?

186. What types of things would you find in a city?

187. What types of things would you find in a small town or farm community?

188. What is the name for the total number of people living in a city, town, state, or country: residents or population?

189. How can communities around the world be different?

190. How can communities around the world be similar?

191. Do you live in a culturally diverse community with many different types of people?

192. What kind of a society do we live, whereby we follow laws and act as responsible citizens: libertarian or democratic?

193. Can you cite the Pledge of Allegiance?

194. What is the name of a song we can sing to honor our flag?

195. Does each country have its own National Anthem?

196. Can you describe how the American flag looks?

197. Do you know the colors of the Mexican flag?

198. What are the two colors in the Canadian flag?

199. What do you know about the culture (people, food, language, music, dance, holidays, Indian groups, currency, monuments, and landforms) of Mexico?

200. What do you know about the culture (people, food, language, music, dance, holidays, and wildlife) of Canada?

201. What language is spoken in Mexico?

202. What two languages are spoken in Canada?

203. What kind of wildlife is found in Canada?

204. Do you think that different countries celebrate different holidays?

205. What holiday do we celebrate the first Monday in September to honor workers and laborers?

206. What is celebrated on October 12th to remember this navigator that sailed the ocean blue on three ships from Spain?

207. What do we celebrate on October 31st when we decorate in black and orange, carve pumpkins, and wear costumes?

208. What is the name of the national holiday that falls on November 11th in which we honor military veterans, all who have served in the U.S Armed Forces: Veterans Day or Memorial Day?

209. What holiday do we celebrate on the fourth Thursday of November to give thanks, as the Native Americans and the Pilgrims did back in 1621 after a bountiful harvest?

210. How are our lives different today compared to the lives of the Pilgrims?

211. What is one of our family *traditions* for celebrating Thanksgiving?

212. What holiday is celebrated in December by many people?

213. What is a *custom* for Americans during the December holiday season?

214. Do you think all cultures share this same customs?

215. What holiday is celebrated on the first of January with food and music and parties?

216. What national holiday is celebrated the third Monday of January to honor this activist who preached to the nation in defense of the civil rights of African Americans?

217. Besides Valentine's Day, what important national holiday do we celebrate in February to honor former leaders of the United States?

218. Who was the first President of the United States whose face is pictured on the nickel: Lincoln or Washington?

219. Who was the 16th President of the United States whose face is pictured on the penny and was regarded as "Honest Abe?"

220. What is celebrated on March 17th that is a tribute to people of Irish descent?

221. Is there a holiday in spring that we celebrate as a family?

222. Do you know the name of the holiday that is celebrated in Mexico on a specific date at the beginning of May that celebrates the Mexican victory of the peasants of Puebla over the superior French army on May 5th, 1862?

223. What is the name of the national holiday at the end of May that is a day to remember and honor those who gave their lives in wars while serving in America's Armed Forces?

224. What is the date and month of America's Independence Day?

225. From where did the United States win its independence: the United Kingdom or France?

226. Do we have family photographs of holidays and celebrations?

227. What things do we have as symbols of a holiday?

228. What do many people do to earn money to purchase goods and services?

229. What is an example of a "want" that someone might purchase with the money he or she earns?

230. What is an example of a "need" that someone might purchase with the money he or she earns?

231. What are some basic needs that people have?

232. What denominations of coins are you familiar with?

233. What is the value of a penny?

234. What is the value of a nickel?

235. What is the value of a dime?

236. What is the value of a quarter?

237. What is the value of a fifty cent piece?

238. What denominations of bills or paper currency are you familiar with?

239. Can you name the currency of another country?

240. Do you think that the currency of other nations has the same value as our American dollar?

241. Why is it important to save money?

242. Before paper and coin money, how do you think people of long ago bought and sold goods and services?

243. In some shops or markets, is it possible to barter, or to go back and forth on a price for an item?

244. Who in the community do you visit when you are sick or need a check-up?

245. Who in the community wears a badge and a uniform, carries a gun and handcuffs, and can help you if you are lost or are in some kind of danger?

246. Who in the community wears a heavy coat, boots, a hard hat, and rides in a truck with ladders, water, hoses, gauges, and sirens?

247. Who in the community makes sure you have a beautiful and healthy smile by caring for your teeth and gums?

248. Who in the community delivers letters and packages to your home and wears a uniform?

249. Who in the community cares for the well-being of domestic or farm animals like dogs, cats, horses, and cows?

250. Who in the community helps young people learn in a school with their knowledge of different subjects?

Social Studies – 2nd Grade

251. What do the galaxies, stars, Sun, moon, planets make up?

252. What is the name of the galaxy we live in that also is a name for a chocolate candy bar?

253. What is the name of the planet we live on?

254. What other planets can you name?

255. What are the biggest bodies of water on the Earth called?

256. What are the names of the Earth's two biggest oceans, as referenced in the last line of the patriotic song *America the Beautiful*, from "Sea to Shining Sea?

257. Do the oceans make up most of our world?

258. Which ocean is the biggest on Earth?

259. Can you name another ocean or sea?

260. What is the name of the imaginary line that divides the Earth into the Northern and Southern hemispheres?

261. What are the pieces of land called between the oceans: regions or continents?

262. How many continents are there on the Earth?

263. What is the full name of the continent we live on?

264. Which continent are Mexico and Canada part of: North America or South America?

265. Is Mexico to the north or south of the United States?

266. Is Canada to the north or south of the United States?

267. Are the states of Alaska and Hawaii located in the *continental* United States?

268. What is the name of the spherical representation of the earth?

269. What are the two hemispheres that the Earth is divided into at the Equator?

270. Can the world be represented on a flat map?

271. Can agricultural products, languages spoken, or physical landforms be represented on a map?

272. On a physical map, what types of landforms might be indicated?

273. Can charts, graphs, and maps be used to provide specific data about a place?

274. Can symbols be used on a map?

275. What symbol does a star represent on a map: a capital or a large city?

276. What is the term for the ratio that compares a measurement on a map to the actual distance between locations: scale or legend?

277. What are the four cardinal directions located on a map compass?

278. What is the intermediate direction if a place is both north and east?

279. What is the intermediate direction if a place is both south and west?

280. In which direction does the Sun rise?

281. In which direction does the Sun set?

282. What are Northeast, Midwest, South, and West all considered: regions or areas?

283. What are regions divided into: areas or divisions?

284. What is the name of the region of the United States that you live in?

285. What is the name of the state that you live in?

286. What is the name of the city or town that you live in?

287. What is the name of the county that you live in?

288. Can you name other counties in our state?

289. What is the name of a resource book that shows different areas of the world along with facts and information about each continent: an atlas or an almanac?

290. Which of the following would likely not be included in an atlas: World map, United States map, State map, or a city map?

291. What is the name for the study of specific regions and locations: geography or geology?

292. What are Asia, Europe, Africa, North America, South America, Australia, and Antarctica the names of?

293. What is each continent is made up of: regions or countries?

294. Does each country of a continent have a name?

295. Are Canada, the United States, and Mexico located in the continent of North America or Central America?

296. Which continent are Afghanistan, Bahrain, Bangladesh, Bhutan, Brunei, Cambodia, China, East Timor, India, Indonesia, Iran, Iraq, Israel, Japan, Jordan, Kazakhstan, Korea North, Korea South, Kuwait, Kyrgyzstan, Laos, Lebanon, Malaysia, Maldives, Mongolia, Myanmar, Nepal, Oman, Pakistan, the Philippines, Qatar, Russia, Saudi Arabia, Singapore, Sri Lanka, Syria, Taiwan, Tajikistan, Thailand, Turkey, Turkmenistan, United Arab Emirates, Uzbekistan, Vietnam, and Yemen part of?

297. Does more than half of the world's population live on the continent of Asia?

298. Which is the smallest continent: Australia or Europe?

299. What is the name of the second largest continent known for its jungles, deserts, and wildlife, and includes the countries of Algeria, Angola, Cape Verde, Chad, Congo, Egypt, Equatorial Guinea, Ethiopia, Gambia, Ghana, Guinea, Kenya, Liberia, Libya, Madagascar, Malawi, Mali, Morocco, Mozambique, Namibia, Niger, Nigeria, Rwanda, Senegal, Somalia, South Africa, South Sudan, Swaziland, Tanzania, Togo, Tunisia, Uganda, Zambia, and Zimbabwe?

300. What is the name of the newest country in the world that is located in Africa: North Sudan or South Sudan?

301. What animals can you name that live in Africa?

302. Did many of our ancestors come from the continent of Africa?

303. How did many people from Asia and Africa arrive here in America, traveling between Asia and Alaska more than 12,000 years ago: on a land bridge or on a ship?

304. Do you know the names of the countries that our distant relatives or ancestors came from?

305. What is the nationality of our family?

306. What is the name of the largest non-polar desert in the world located on the continent of Africa: the Sahara or the Arabian?

307. What is the name of the longest river in the world located on the continent of Africa: The Nile or The Amazon?

308. What is the name of the third largest continent with the countries of the United States, Mexico, Central America, and Canada?

309. Which is the largest country of North America that was once covered with ice and glaciers and is divided into provinces where the people speak English and French?

310. What is the North American country that has 50 states and is covered with land, mountains, canyons, rivers, and five great lakes?

311. What is the North American country that is divided into states, is covered with mountains, lakes, volcanoes, jungles, ancient ruins and pyramids, and is Spanish-speaking?

312. What is the name for the region between Mexico and South America that includes the countries of Belize, Costa Rica, El Salvador, Guatemala, Honduras, Nicaragua, and Panama?

313. What is the name of the fourth largest continent with the countries of Argentina, Brazil, Colombia, Peru, Chile, Ecuador, Bolivia, Venezuela, Uruguay, Paraguay, Guyana, Suriname, French Guiana, and the Falkland islands, and covered with jungles and mountains and rivers?

314. What is the name of the longest mountain range in South America: The Andes or The Himalayas?

315. What is the name of the second longest river in South America that also runs through the rainforest: the Nile or the Amazon?

316. Do you know the name of the pack animal of South America that has soft fur that is sheared and made into rope, blankets, sweaters and textiles, and can even be known to spit at you?

317. What is the name of the fifth largest continent located in the polar region at the bottom of the world, is covered with ice sometimes one to two miles thick, and is the continent with an abundance of whales, penguins and seals?

318. What is the name of the sixth largest continent that includes the countries of Albania, Andorra, Armenia, Austria, Belarus, Belgium, Bosnia, Bulgaria, Croatia, Cyprus, Czech Republic, Denmark, Estonia, Finland, France, Georgia, Germany, Greece, Hungary, Iceland, Ireland, Italy, Kosovo, Latvia, Liechtenstein, Lithuania, Luxembourg, Macedonia, Malta, Moldova, Monaco, Montenegro, The Netherlands, Norway, Poland, Portugal, Romania, Russia, San Marino, Serbia, Slovakia, Slovenia, Spain, Sweden, Switzerland, Turkey, Ukraine, United Kingdom, and the Vatican City?

319. What is the name of the seventh and smallest continent that includes a mainland, New Zealand, several South Pacific islands, and is the known for the Sydney Opera House, the Great Barrier Reef, kangaroos, koala bears, and wombats?

320. What is the name for the piece of land surrounded by water?

321. What is the name of the ocean that is located south of Asia, and is the third largest ocean in the world: The Indian Ocean or the Arctic Ocean?

322. On which continent is China located?

323. What was the name given to the leader of the ancient Chinese government: king or emperor?

324. What is astronomy the study of, something the ancient Chinese and other civilizations were very advanced in?

325. Which Asian country is considered the biggest and most populated country of the world: China or India?

326. What is the capital of China: Beijing or Shanghai?

327. Are Asian countries sometimes regarded as the "far east" or the orient?

328. What language do they speak in China?

329. What do they eat in China?

330. Do they dress differently in China?

331. What is the name of the fabric that the Chinese developed made from the cocoons of worms?

332. What is the name of the only man-made object located in China that can be arguably be seen from space: the Great Wall of China or the Grand Buddha?

333. Are many items that we sell here in the United States made in China?

334. Do you think that family life is different in China than it is in the United States?

335. Is Japan a small country of Asia?

336. What is the capital of Japan: Tokyo or Osaka?

337. What language do they speak in Japan?

338. What do they eat in Japan?

339. Do they dress differently in Japan?

340. What is the name of the traditional Japanese dress: a sari or a kimono?

341. What article of clothing do the Japanese take off before entering a house: scarf or shoes?

342. Where do the Japanese and their guests sit when eating a traditional meal: on chairs or on the floor?

343. Do you think that school life is different in Japan than in our culture?

344. Which country is considered one of the most populated countries of the world after China: Indonesia or India?

345. What is the capital of India: New Delhi or Mumbai?

346. What is the principle language spoken in India: Hindi or Bengali?

347. What do you think they eat in India?

348. Do they dress differently in India?

349. What is the name of the garment that most Indian women wear: a sari or a kimono?

350. Do you think that the family life and school life is different in India than in our culture?

351. Can you name some countries on the continent of Africa?

352. What is one of the most widely spoken languages out of 2,000 in Africa: Swahili or French?

353. What are some foods they might eat in Africa?

354. What are some animals that live in the wild of Africa?

355. On which continent is Egypt located?

356. What is the name of the longest river located in Africa?

357. What is the name of the biggest desert in Africa: the Sahara or the Mojave?

358. What were built by the Egyptians that served as burial tombs in ancient Egypt?

359. What is the name for the alphabet used by ancient Egyptians: hieroglyphics or alpha beta?

360. What is the name of the plant what was used by the ancient Egyptians for paper: parchment or papyrus?

361. What is the name for the leader of the ancient Egyptian government: Emperor or Pharaoh?

362. Do they dress differently in Africa than in America?

363. Do you think that the family life and school life is different in Africa than in our culture?

364. What is the name of the continent we live on?

365. What is the name for the study that deals with the locations of places and features of the Earth?

366. Are continents, countries, states, mountain ranges, and rivers all part of geography?

367. In what area of the country is our state located?

368. Do you know the names of any states that border our state?

369. What is the name of the mountain range located in the state of Virginia that include the Allegheny Mountains and the Blue Ridge Mountains: Appalachians or Rockies?

370. What is the name of the longest river in the United States: Missouri or Mississippi?

371. What is the name of the largest salt water lake in the Western Hemisphere located in Utah: Great Salt Lake or Bear Lake?

372. What is the name of the mountain range that is located in the western part of the United States: the Rocky Mountains or the Appalachian Mountains?

373. What is the name of the 2000 mile long river that is located on the border between the United States and Mexico: the Mississippi or the Rio Grande?

374. In which the continent is Mexico located?

375. What language do they speak in Mexico?

376. What do they eat in Mexico?

377. Do they dress differently in Mexico?

378. What is the name for the type of dance from Mexico: Ballet Folklorico or Flamenco?

379. What is the name for a type of music of Mexico played with guitars, trumpets, and violins: Flamenco or Mariachi?

380. Which of the following was **not** an Indian civilization of Mexico: Aztec, Inca, or Maya?

381. What is the capital of Mexico, one of the biggest and most populated cities in the world?

382. What is the name of the country on the North American continent to the north of the United States?

383. What are Alberta, British Colombia, Manitoba, News Brunswick, Newfoundland, Nova Scotia, Ontario, Prince Edward Island, Quebec, and Saskatchewan considered: states or provinces?

384. What are Northwest Territories, Nunavut, and Yukon considered: provinces or territories?

385. What is the capital of Canada: Ottawa or Montreal?

386. What languages do they speak in Canada?

387. What do they eat in Canada?

388. Do they dress differently in Canada?

389. What types of fish and wildlife is Canada known for?

390. Do you think that the family life and school life is different in Canada than in our culture?

391. Can you name any countries in South America?

392. What language do they speak in South America?

393. Do you know of any foods that are eaten in South America?

394. Do you think that South America has its own unique music, musical instruments, and dances?

395. What language is spoken in Brazil: Portuguese or Spanish?

396. Do they dress differently in South America then here in the United States?

397. What type of clothing is South American known for: brightly-colored or dark-colored?

398. Do you know the name of an animal that is unique to South America?

399. What is the name of the ancient Indian civilization of Peru, South America: Inca or Aztec?

400. Can you name some countries on the European continent?

401. Are some countries considered part of Eastern Europe and other countries part of Western Europe?

402. Are the countries Germany, Spain, Portugal, Italy, France, Austria, and Switzerland, considered part of Eastern Europe or Western Europe?

403. What region are the kingdoms of Denmark, Sweden, and Norway collectively known as: Scandinavia or The Netherlands?

404. Are the countries Poland, the Czech Republic, Russia, Slovakia, Romania, Bulgaria, Belarus, and Ukraine considered part of Eastern Europe or Western Europe?

405. What is the name of the currency of most European countries: the Dollar or the Euro?

406. What is the currency "Euro" short for?

407. What is the official currency of England: the British Euro or the British Pound?

408. What is the official currency of Japan: the Euro or the Yen?

409. What is the official currency of China: the Yen or the Renminbi?

410. What is the capital of Germany: Berlin or Munich?

411. What language do they speak in Germany?

412. Can you name some foods that are considered German??

413. Do you think that German people dress similar to how we dress?

414. What do Lederhosen and Dirndl refer to: traditional German clothing or traditional foods?

415. Do you think Germany has music and dance unique to its culture?

416. Is Germany famous for composers like Bach, Beethoven, Schubert, and Brahms?

417. Do you think that the family life and school life is different in Germany than in our culture?

418. What is the capital of England: London or Winchester?

419. What language do they speak in England?

420. If you heard someone from England speak English, would you consider them to have an English accent?

421. What are Yorkshire pudding, Shepherd's pie, tea, and scones all considered: English cuisine or French cuisine?

422. Do you think people from England dress similar to Americans?

423. Do you think England has music and dance unique to its culture?

424. What country is also known as the "Emerald Isle:" Scotland or Ireland?

425. What is the capital of Ireland: Dublin or Waterford?

426. Does Ireland have music and dance unique to its culture?

427. Do you think that the family life and school life is different in Ireland than in our culture?

428. What is the capital of France: Marseille or Paris?

429. What language do they speak in France?

430. Can you name some foods that are considered French?

431. How do you think they dress in France?

432. Do you think France has music and dance unique to its culture?

433. Do you think that the family life and school life is different in France than in our culture?

434. What is the capital of Spain: Barcelona or Madrid?

435. What language do they speak in Spain?

436. What are churros: Spanish snacks or Spanish doughnuts?

437. What is the name of the saffron rice and seafood dish of Spain: Paella or chicken with rice?

438. Do you think that Spain has specific clothing unique to its culture?

439. Do you think Spain has music and dance unique to its culture?

440. What is the name of the traditional dance of Spain: flamenco or tango?

441. Do you think that the family life and school life is different in Spain than in our culture?

442. In which continent is Italy located?

443. What is the capital of Italy: Florence or Rome?

444. What language do they speak in Italy?

445. Can you name some foods that are considered Italian?

446. How do you think they dress in Italy?

447. Do you think Italy has music and dance unique to its culture?

448. Do you think that the family life and school life is different in Italy than in our culture?

449. What animals can be found on the continent of Antarctica?

450. What is the climate like in Antarctica compared to here in the United States?

451. Do you think anyone has ever made an expedition to Antarctica?

452. Is Australia considered both a continent and a country?

453. What is the capital of Australia: Sydney, Melbourne, or Canberra?

454. What language do they speak in Australia?

455. Do you think that Australians dress the same as Americans do?

456. Do you think Australia has music and dance unique to its culture?

457. What are some animals that live in Australia?

458. Do you think that the family life and school life is different in Australia than in our culture?

459. What cloth banner does every country of every continent have to represent their country?

460. What are the colors of our American flag and how would you describe it?

461. Can you describe out state flag?

462. What is the main city called of each state in the United States?

463. Do you know what the D.C. stands for in our capital city Washington, D. C?

464. Whom do you think our capital is named for?

465. What is the name of the study that tells a "story" of the people that lived long ago past to present: ancestry or history?

466. In our history, what is the name of some of our earliest settlers called Native Americans that hunted deer and buffalo, and lived in groups called tribes led by a chief?

467. What is the name of the first navigator to arrive here from Europe on his ship the Santa Maria?

468. What shape did Christopher Columbus believe the Earth to be?

469. What continent did Columbus sail to even though he thought that the New World he landed at was the continent of Asia?

470. What country of Europe did Columbus sail from: Spain or Italy?

471. What did King Ferdinand and Queen Isabella of Spain provide for Columbus in order for him to set sail for the New World?

472. What country did Columbus believe that he would be sailing to because he was not aware that North America existed: Africa or India?

473. What did Queen Isabella also want Columbus to bring back from the "Indies" and therefore agreed to help pay for Columbus's voyage: silk or spices?

474. Can you finish the saying: "In 1492 Columbus sailed the…?"

475. What were the names of Columbus's three ships?

476. What did Columbus call the people that he first came into contact with, thinking that he had reached the Indies?

477. What did Europeans call North and South America because it was "new" land to explore?

478. With whom did many Spaniards battle when they came here from Europe?

479. Were the Spanish successful in conquering the Indians with their superior weapons?

480. What is the name of the animal that was brought over from Spain: the horse or the cow?

481. What did the Spanish bring to the New World that included smallpox and measles: diseases or rashes?

482. What is the name for the study of peoples and cultures and their development: civilization or heritage?

483. What is the name of the Indian civilization that lived in the jungles of Central America and Mexico, and were extremely advanced in math and astronomy, the study of the universe: Maya or Aztec?

484. What were the buildings called that ancient civilizations built out of stone with tiers and steps?

485. What is the name of a later Indian civilization in Mexico, were considered great warriors, worshiped and made sacrifices to their gods, and built their capital city on a lake, Tenochtitlan?

486. Which Indian group in Mexico did the Spaniard Hernando Cortez steal gold from and ultimately conquer: the Aztecs or the Maya?

487. Which Indian group in South America lived high in the Andes Mountains and decorated everything with gold and silver: the Inca or the Zapotec?

488. What is the name of the Spanish conquistador that conquered the Inca civilization in South America in 1533: Francisco Pizarro or Vasco Nunez de Balboa?

489. What did many Indians do to provide food for their families?

490. From which continent did many of our ancestors come: Africa or Asia?

491. Did England and other European countries also want to claim some of the treasures of North America?

492. In which city in Virginia did the English colonists settle in the year 1607 right before the Pilgrims, the first important English settlement in our country: Jamestown or Williamsburg?

493. Which native people did the English continue to do battle with?

494. What is the name of the English settler who established the first permanent colony in Jamestown, Virginia in 1607: William Penn or John Smith?

495. What are groups of Indians called?

496. What do you call the leader of an Indian tribe?

497. What native Indian tribes can you name?

498. Who are the Apache, Navajo, Hopi, Potawatomi, and Sioux?

499. What is the name of the Indians of the southwest that lived in modular homes made of stone and adobe: Pueblo or Navajo?

500. What is the name for the rectangular dwellings built by some Eastern Woodland Indians like the Iroquois and Cherokee that were made from wood and bark: longhouses or wigwams?

501. What is the name of the Indians that travelled around the plains area of the U.S. following buffalo herds: Woodland Indians or Plains Indians?

502. What is the name of the poles carved and painted by Native American Indians of the Pacific Northwest that were made to represent a tribe and to tell a story?

503. What is the name for the 102 passengers that came over from England in the year 1620?

504. What were the Pilgrims seeking in the New World because they disagreed with the teachings of the Church of England?

505. What is the name for the ship that the Pilgrims sailed on from England?

506. Which ocean did the Pilgrims have to cross on the Mayflower to arrive here in America?

507. What is the name of the now famous boulder that the Pilgrims anchored their ship to, and the name for the colony that the Pilgrims established in 1620?

508. Who taught the Pilgrims how to hunt, fish, and plant crops?

509. What specific crop did the Wampanoag Indians teach the early settlers how to grow: corn or wheat?

510. With whom did the Pilgrims share their first big feast with, after a successful harvest that lasted for three days?

511. What food did the Wampanoag Indians and Pilgrims share at this first Thanksgiving feast: deer and pheasant, or turkey and stuffing?

512. Who do you think contributed the deer venison to the first Thanksgiving feast: the Wampanoag Indians or the Pilgrims?

513. What is the name of the holiday we celebrate in November to pay tribute to the union of these two important cultures?

514. What was the name of the colonist group that came after the Pilgrims and had very strict religious rules: the Puritans or the Quakers?

515. How many original English colonies were set up on the Eastern coast: 12 or 13?

516. What is the name of the American pioneer and trailblazer that led settlers to the west through the Cumberland Gap of the Appalachian Mountains, providing access to the western frontier: Davy Crockett or Daniel Boone?

517. What is the name of the famous explorer from Tennessee who was considered the "King of the Wild Frontier," and died at the Alamo in San Antonio helping the outnumbered Texans fight for their independence against the Mexican army: Davy Crockett or Daniel Boone?

518. What were early American settlers called in colonial times: pioneers or colonists?

519. Where did many early Americans settle for easy transportation and a water supply?

520. What kinds of things did pioneers have for food, shelter, work, and school?

521. Was there electricity in early colonial days?

522. What did pioneers use for light?

523. What is the name for the war that was a result of the conflicts between the thirteen colonies and the British because the colonies felt that they were not represented in the British government, a war that took place between 1775 and 1783?

524. Did the colonists have to resort to a "revolution" in order to claim their freedom from England?

525. Was one of the events that led to the Revolutionary War the French and Indian War in which the French and Indians fought against Great Britain?

526. Who won the French and Indian War 1754-1763: the French and Indians, or Great Britain?

527. After winning the French and Indian War in 1763, which country did the British win the right to keep along with several other possessions in the New World: France or Canada?

528. Which war did events like the French and Indian War, The Sugar Act, The Stamp Act, and the Boston Massacre in which 5 colonists were killed by British troops all contribute to: the Revolutionary War or the Civil War?

529. What was the name of the event in Boston, Massachusetts when the English colonists got tired of King George III and his numerous rules and new taxes, and decided to dump 342 full crates of tea into the Boston harbor on December 16, 1773?

530. Who published a pamphlet in 1776 entitled "Common Sense" that challenged the authority of the British government, and inspired the people of the thirteen colonies to declare their independence from Great Britain: Thomas Paine or Samuel Adams?

531. What was the name of the first congress that was established by the colonists who met secretly in Philadelphia in 1774 to discuss liberty from Great Britain: National or Continental?

532. What is the name of the document that came from the discussions of the Second Continental Congress, drafted in 1776 that declared the 13 American colonies independent from Great Britain?

533. Who is the principal author of the Declaration of Independence, a founding father who was also the third President of the United States: John Adams or Thomas Jefferson?

534. What did Thomas Jefferson write in the Declaration of Independence: "All men are…?"

535. Who was the second President of the United States: John Adams or Thomas Jefferson?

536. In what year did the people of the United States declare their independence from England and the King?

537. Was the Declaration of Independence signed by John Hancock, John Adams, George Washington, Ben Franklin, Thomas Jefferson, and Samuel Adams?

538. How many delegates of the Continental Congress signed the Declaration of Independence: 50 or 56?

539. What is the name of the delegate, then President of the Continental Congress, who was first to sign the Declaration of Independence: Benjamin Franklin or John Hancock?

540. What city in Pennsylvania was the site of the first reading of the Declaration of Independence, four days after it was signed in Independence Hall: Philadelphia or Harrisburg?

541. What is the name of the bronze bell in Philadelphia, Pennsylvania that serves as a symbol of American freedom?

542. What happened to the liberty bell after the first test ringing in 1752 in London, England?

543. Was the Liberty Bell rung during the first reading of the Declaration of Independence?

544. Did the British continue the war with the colonists even after the Declaration of Independence?

545. What is the name of one of the founding fathers of the United States of America; has his signature on The Declaration of Independence, The Treaty of Paris which marked the end of the Revolutionary War, The Treaty of Peace with Great Britain, and the United States Constitution; was the operator and editor of a newspaper called the "Pennsylvania Gazette;" was the publisher of "Poor Richard's Almanac;" and is credited for inventing electricity, the lightning rod, bifocal lenses, and a special stove: Thomas Jefferson or Benjamin Franklin?

546. What is the name of the famous officer who was the commander of the United States Navy during the Revolutionary War: John Paul Jones or George Rodney?

547. What is the name of the silversmith and American patriot during the Revolution who in 1775 rode on horseback to warn the American colonists that the "redcoats" or British soldiers were coming: John Hancock or Paul Revere?

548. What was Paul Revere's signal with lanterns placed in the steeple of the Old North Church in Boston to alert the colonists how the British were arriving: "One if by land, two if by…?"

549. What is the name of the Treaty that the British agreed to sign that ended the Revolutionary War on September 3, 1783: The Treaty of Versailles or The Treaty of Paris?

550. Who won the Revolutionary war in 1783: the British or the American colonists?

551. What is the name of the document that outlines America's form of government and the rights of its citizens, approved by American delegates in 1787: U.S. Constitution or the Magna Carta?

552. Which President from Virginia proposed the idea of a strong central government, and is regarded as the "father of the U.S. Constitution:" James Madison or James Monroe?

553. What kind of government do we have in America: a federal republic or a national republic?

554. What is the term that refers to the complete absence of rules and laws, a society without a publicly enforced government: democracy or anarchy?

555. What are the first 10 amendments to the United States Constitution called: the Preamble or the Bill of Rights?

556. What is the name of the purchase in 1803, considered one of the greatest real estate deals in history between the United States and France, and is regarded as one of Thomas Jefferson's greatest achievements?

557. How many millions of dollars did the United States agree to pay France in 1803 for 828,000 square miles of land west of the Mississippi: five or fifteen?

558. How much did the "Louisiana Purchase," organized by Thomas Jefferson, increase the size of the United States, expanding it by 15 states: doubled it or tripled it?

559. Who are the two explorers that were sent by Thomas Jefferson to explore and map the territory that was part of the Louisiana Purchase, and have a trail named for them?

560. Which European country still claimed the western states: England or France?

561. What name was given to the African American workers who had to work on tobacco, rice, and cotton farms in the south without pay, and were under the complete control of their masters?

562. From which continent did slaves come from that worked on the southern farms?

563. What is the term for the large farms where many slaves worked: haciendas or plantations?

564. What is the name of the war between the North or Union, and the South, known as the Confederacy, because the South wanted to break away and become its own country, and because it wanted the right to continue to use slaves on its southern plantations?

565. When did the Civil War take place: 1861-1865 or 1865-1869?

566. Who was the 16th President of the United States who saved the Union during the American Civil War, and whose face is on the penny and the five-dollar bill?

567. What was the nickname given to Abraham Lincoln because of his truthful nature?

568. What is the name of the brave woman and activist who led many slaves to freedom through a system known as the Underground Railroad: Harriet Tubman or Harriet Beecher Stowe?

569. Who become a free people as a result of the Civil War and President Lincoln?

570. Does our capital Washington, D.C. have many historical monuments?

571. What historical monument in Washington, D.C. can you name?

572. Where are the Lincoln Memorial, the White House, the Washington Monument, the Jefferson Memorial, the Pentagon Memorial, the World War II Memorial, the Vietnam Veterans Memorial, the Franklin Delano Roosevelt Memorial, the Martin Luther King Jr. Memorial, the Marine Corps Memorial known as Iwo Jima, the Korean War Veterans Memorial, and Arlington National Cemetery all located?

573. What is the name of the residence of the President of the United States?

574. Who lives at 1600 Pennsylvania Avenue in Washington D.C?

575. What is the name of the copper and iron statue in New York Harbor on Liberty Island that was a gift from France in 1886, and is recognized as a symbol of freedom and democracy?

576. What American banner is considered a historical symbol?

577. What is the Liberty Bell considered?

578. What is the name of the monumental sculpture and historical symbol in South Dakota with the faces of Presidents Washington, Lincoln, Jefferson, and Roosevelt carved into the granite?

Social Studies – 3rd Grade

579. What is the term for the study that includes history, geography, sociology, and government?

580. Does social studies include the study of geography or geology?

581. What is the name of the continent you live on?

582. What is the name of the geographic tool that is shaped like a sphere and shows all the continents and oceans?

583. What is the name for a bound collection of maps and graphs that gives detailed geographical information of different countries, continents and oceans: an atlas or an almanac?

584. What is the name of the book that is published every year that contains facts about astronomical events, the tides, weather, and includes a calendar: an atlas or an almanac?

585. What is the term for the imaginary lines that run north and south on a map or globe: latitude or longitude?

586. What is the term form the imaginary lines that run east and west on a map or globe: latitude or longitude?

587. What is the term for the imaginary east-west line that encircles the Earth midway between the North Pole and the South Pole?

588. Can you identify on a map the seven continents and the oceans of the world?

589. What are Asia, Africa, North America, South America, Antarctica, Europe, and Australia?

590. What are the Pacific, Atlantic, Indian, and Arctic?

591. Which ocean is the largest?

592. Which ocean is the smallest: the Indian or the Arctic?

593. What are the Alaska Range, the Appalachian, Blue Ridge, Alleghenies, Catskills, Coast Range, Sierra Nevada, and Rocky all considered?

594. What are the Andes, Himalayas, Alps, Pyrenees, and Ural all considered?

595. Which mountain range in the world is the tallest: the Andes or the Himalayas?

596. Which mountain is the world's longest: the Andes or the Himalayas?

597. What is the name for the tallest peak in the Himalayas standing over 29,000 feet tall: Mount Everest or Mount McKinley?

598. What is the name for the tallest peak in North America standing at just over 20,000 feet tall and located in Alaska: Mount Everest or Mount McKinley?

599. What is the name of the ancient city of the Inca high up in the Andes Mountains: Machu Picchu or Chichen Itza?

600. What are the Sahara, the Arabian, the Mojave, the Atacama, the Gobi, and the Sonoran all considered?

601. Which American desert is known for the saguaro cactus, a spiky cactus that can grow up to 50 feet tall and live for more than one hundred years: Sonoran or Mojave?

602. What are the two **polar** deserts in the world?

603. What is the term given for the region of the Earth surrounding the Equator: the tropics or the hemispheres?

604. What is the name for the type of forest characterized by very tall, densely growing trees, heavy annual rainfall, high humidity, and are located in tropical latitudes?

605. What is the name for the largest tropical rainforest in the world: the Amazon or the Congo?

606. Which country in South American has the largest tropical rainforest in the world?

607. In which habitat would you find many frogs, butterflies, birds, toucans, snakes, lizards, monkeys, ferns, orchids, waterfalls, and insects?

608. Can fire, drought, and volcanic activity have an effect on rainforests?

609. What type of storm are hurricanes, monsoons, and typhoons that may pose a threat and cause great damage to a rainforest?

610. What is the name for the piece of land that is completely surrounded by water?

611. What do Australia, Cuba, Iceland, Ireland, and the United Kingdom all have in common?

612. Are many islands part of some larger country?

613. What state are Maui, Kauai, Oahu, Molokai, and Lanai all part of?

614. What tropical storms are islands often affected by?

615. How many total states are there in the United States?

616. How many states are located in the continental United States?

617. What are the two states that are located outside of the continental United States?

618. What was the last state admitted into the union in 1959?

619. What is the name of the state you live in?

620. What is the capital of our state?

621. What state is Montgomery the capital of? Al

622. What state is Juneau the capital of? Al

623. What state is Phoenix the capital of? Ar

624. What state is Little Rock the capital of? Ark

625. What state is Sacramento the capital of? C

626. What state is Denver the capital of? C

627. What state is Hartford the capital of? C

628. What state is Dover the capital of? D

629. What state is Tallahassee the capital of? F

630. What state is Atlanta the capital of? G

631. What state is Honolulu the capital of? H

632. What state is Boise the capital of? I

633. What state is Indianapolis the capital of? I

634. What state is Des Moines the capital of? I

635. What state is Topeka the capital of? K

636. What state is Frankfort the capital of? K

637. What state is Baton Rouge the capital of? L

638. What state is Augusta the capital of? M

639. What state is Annapolis the capital of? M

640. What state is Boston the capital of? M

641. What state is Lansing the capital of? M

642. What state is Saint Paul the capital of? M

643. What state is Jackson the capital of? M

644. What state is Jefferson City the capital of? M

645. What state is Helena the capital of? M

646. What state is Lincoln the capital of? N

647. What state is Carson City the capital of? N

648. What state is Concord the capital of? N

649. What state is Trenton the capital of? N

650. What state is Santa Fe the capital of? N

651. What state is Albany the capital of? N

652. What state is Raleigh the capital of? N

653. What state is Bismarck the capital of? N

654. What state is Columbus the capital of? O

655. What state is Oklahoma City the capital of? O

656. What state is Salem the capital of? O

657. What state is Harrisburg the capital of? P

658. What state is Providence the capital of? R

659. What state is Columbia the capital of? S

660. What state is Pierre the capital of? S

661. What state is Nashville the capital of? T

662. What state is Austin the capital of? T

663. What state is Salt Lake City the capital of? U

664. What state is Montpelier the capital of? V

665. What state is Richmond the capital of? V

666. What state is Olympia the capital of? W

667. What state is Charleston the capital of? W

668. What state is Madison the capital of? W

669. What state is Cheyenne the capital of? W

670. What is the term for the administrative divisions of a state: districts or counties?

671. What is the name of the county you live in?

672. What city do you live in?

673. Is the city you live in near to or far from the capital of our state?

674. What is the name for the direction key that is located on a map: a direction legend or a compass rose?

675. What does the "N" stand for on a compass rose?

676. What does the "S" stand for on a compass rose?

677. What does the "E" stand for on a compass rose?

678. What does the "W" stand for on a compass rose?

679. What does the direction "NE" stand for?

680. What does the direction "NW" stand for?

681. What does the direction "SE" stand for?

682. What does the direction "SW" stand for?

683. Can you locate Canada on a world map or a globe?

684. What is Canada divided into: states or provinces?

685. Can you locate Mexico on a world map or a globe?

686. What is Mexico divided into: states or provinces?

687. Can you locate the United States on a world map or a globe?

688. Can you locate Central America on a world map or a globe?

689. Can you locate South America on a world map or a globe?

690. Can you locate Europe on a world map or a globe?

691. Can you locate Africa on a world map or a globe?

692. Can you locate Asia on a world map or a globe?

693. Can you locate Australia on a world map or a globe?

694. Can you locate Antarctica on a world map or a globe?

695. Can you locate the equator on a world map or a globe?

696. Can you identify the Northern Hemisphere on a world map or a globe?

697. Can you identify the Southern Hemisphere on a world map or a globe?

698. Can you locate the Pacific Ocean on a world map or a globe?

699. Can you locate the Atlantic Ocean on a world map or a globe?

700. Can you locate the Indian Ocean on a world map or a globe?

701. Can you locate the Arctic Ocean on a world map or a globe?

702. Can you locate the North Pole on a world map or a globe?

703. Can you locate the South Pole on a world map or a globe?

704. What is the name of the key on a map that explains the symbols and landmarks on a map: a compass rose or a legend?

705. What is the name of the key on a map that helps you determine distances: a legend or a scale?

706. What is the term for a large, natural stream of water that feeds into a larger body of water: a lake or a river?

707. What major rivers in the world can you name?

708. What are the Mississippi, the Missouri, the Ohio, the Colombia, the Arkansas, the Colorado, the Snake, the Hudson, and the Rio Grande?

709. What are the Ganges, the Danube, the Yangtze, the Nile, and the Amazon?

710. Which river is the largest in the world: the Amazon or the Nile?

711. Which river is the longest in the world: the Amazon or the Nile?

712. Is river water considered fresh water or salt water?

713. Is ocean water considered fresh water or salt water?

714. What is the term for the starting point of a river: source or tributary?

715. What is the term for the stream flows into another to form a river: a delta or a tributary?

716. What is the term for the landform that forms at the mouth of a river where it empties into an ocean or sea, and is often triangular in shape: a delta or a tributary?

717. What is the name of the river that has the largest delta in the world, and is located in both India and Bangladesh: Ganges or Nile?

718. What is the name of the river delta located in Africa flowing into the Mediterranean Sea, that was named by the Greek historian, Herodotus, who coined the term "delta" because the triangular shape of a river delta is similar to the Greek letter "delta:" Nile or Yellow?

719. What is the name of the river delta located in China that is known for its heavy sediment deposits and valuable arable land: Ganges or Yellow?

720. What river delta is found in the state of Louisiana, is known as the bird's foot delta, has millions of acres of wetlands, and is home to many birds and wildlife: Mississippi or Missouri?

721. What are the Missouri, Ohio, Minnesota, Wisconsin, St. Croix, Skunk, Rock, Ohio, La Crosse, and Des Moines rivers with respect to the Mississippi: deltas or tributaries?

722. What is the term for a collection of rivers and tributaries that flow together and empty into a bigger river, ocean, or sea: a river system or a river web?

723. What larger river does the Ohio River, the Tennessee River, the Arkansas River, and the Missouri River flow into: the St. Lawrence or the Mississippi?

724. What is the term for the section of land drained by a river system: a drainage basin or a reservoir?

725. Where does the Mississippi River drain into: the Pacific Ocean or the Gulf of Mexico?

726. What is the term for a narrow, navigable body of water that connects two larger bodies of water: a channel or a strait?

727. What is the name of the strait that separates Alaska from Siberia bordering on Russia, and connects the Arctic Ocean with another sea: Bering or Gibraltar?

728. What is the name of the narrow strait that connects the Mediterranean Sea with the Atlantic Ocean, and separates Spain in Europe and Morocco in Africa: Gibraltar of Magellan?

729. What is the name of the strait discovered and named for a Portuguese explorer in 1520 that separates South America from Tierra del Fuego and other islands, providing a short cut between the Atlantic and Pacific for commerce and exploration: Gibraltar or Magellan?

730. What is the term for a body of water that steams through two landmasses, or one that connects two seas: a strait or a channel?

731. What is the name of the channel separating southern England from Northern France, connects the Atlantic Ocean with the North Sea, and is one of busiest sea routes: English or French?

732. What is the name of the channel between Mexico and Cuba, connecting the Gulf of Mexico and the Caribbean Sea: Yucatan or Iberian?

733. What is the term for a man-made lake that is used for storing water like those built by the Egyptians that lived close to the Nile River: a reservoir or a channel?

734. What is the name for the large reservoir in central Missouri created by the Bagnell Dam on the Osage River that was built in 1931: Lake of the Ozarks or Lake Mead?

735. What is the name of largest reservoir in the United States located on the Colorado River in the States of Arizona and Nevada formed by the Hoover Dam: Lake of the Ozarks or Lake Mead?

736. What is the term for a high area of land with relatively flat terrain: a plain or a plateau?

737. What is the name of the highest and longest plateau in the world located in Tibet that is often referred to as the "roof of the world:" Tibetan or Andean?

738. What is the term for the long man-made waterway that is built to allow the passage of ships: canal or isthmus?

739. What is the name of the canal completed in 1825 that enabled the transportation of goods from the Great Lakes to New York City linking Lake Erie in the west to the Hudson River in the east: Panama or Erie?

740. What is the name of the waterway in Egypt completed in 1869 connecting the Mediterranean Sea and the Red Sea, separating the continents of Asia and Africa, and cutting thousands of miles from the routes of ships traveling between Europe and Asia: Panama or Suez?

741. What is the name of the 48 mile waterway completed in 1914 connecting the Atlantic with the Pacific oceans, cutting thousands of miles off voyages in that ships no longer had to sail completely around South America to reach the west: Erie or Panama?

742. What is the name of the Italian city known for its gondola boats and Italian architecture along its many canals: Florence or Venice?

743. What is the term for a narrow strip of land that connects two larger masses: isthmus or delta?

744. What is the name of the isthmus between the Caribbean Sea and the Pacific Ocean connecting North America and South America, and was first crossed by Vasco de Balboa in 1513 in his famous journey from the Atlantic to the Pacific: Panama or Erie?

745. What is the term for the piece of land that is bordered by water on three sides but connected to the mainland by an isthmus: delta or peninsula?

746. Which state is a peninsula: Texas or Florida?

747. Which state has an upper peninsula: Michigan or Wisconsin?

748. Which state has a peninsula stretching out in the northeastern part of the state having eight miles of Lake Michigan shoreline and named "Door:" Michigan or Wisconsin?

749. What is the name of the peninsula in northwest Mexico that is part of the state of California: Baja or Yucatan?

750. What is the name of the peninsula in southern Mexico that was once the home of the Maya: Baja or Yucatan?

751. What is the name of the European peninsula that includes Spain and Portugal: Iberian or Arabian?

752. What is the name of the European peninsula with the cities of Rome and Florence that makes up most of the country except for Corsica and Sicily: Greek or Italian?

753. What is the name of the peninsula in southwestern Asia that is home to many Arab people and the Islamic religion: Arabian or Iberian?

754. What is the name of the peninsula in East Asia that includes a North country and a South country, and is located between the East Sea and the Yellow Sea: Cambodian or Korean?

755. What is the term for an extension of land that extends out into a body of water like the sea: isthmus or cape?

756. What is the name of the cape on a rocky landmass in southern Africa's Cape Peninsula, first discovered by a Portuguese navigator in 1488, allowed for a route from Europe to Asia, and is known for its stormy weather and rough seas: Cape of Good Hope or Cape Horn?

757. What is the name of the cape that juts out into the Atlantic Ocean in the state of Massachusetts, and famous for its sandy beaches, rolling sand dunes, historic lighthouses, biking trails, fresh lobsters, and cranberry bogs: Cape Cod or Cape Horn?

758. What is the term for the piece of land that is completely surrounded by water: an island or a peninsula?

759. What is the largest island in the world: Greenland or Iceland?

760. What is the name of the state that is made up of many islands with Honolulu as its capital?

761. What is the name of the Polynesian island in the south Pacific, a territory of Chile, famous for its 887 Moai statues carved from solidified volcanic ash by the Rapa Nui people: Easter Island or Galapagos Island?

762. What is the name of the volcanic islands 600 miles off the western coast of Ecuador, South America famous for its tortoises, reptiles, plants, and birds and studied by Charles Darwin inspiring his theory of evolution and natural selection: Galapagos or Easter?

763. What famous rivers can you name?

764. In which Asian country can you find the Yellow river and the Yangtze River: China or India?

765. What is the name of the river that flows through India and Bangladesh, flows into the Indian Ocean, and is considered a holy river for many Hindus: the Ganges River or the Indus River?

766. What is the term for the fan-shaped deposit of sand and mud that forms at the mouth of a river, like the one located at Egypt's Nile River: channel or delta?

767. What is the name of the Asian river that flows through northern India and Pakistan and is one of the longest rivers in the world: the Indus River or the Nile River?

768. What is the name of the longest river in the world, over 4,000 miles long, located in Egypt that empties into the Mediterranean Sea: the Zaire River or the Nile River?

769. What was the Nile River often referred to as because it provided fertile soil, fresh water for drinking and bathing, provided raw materials, and was helpful to the Egyptians for trading and navigation: the Gifts of the Nile or the Presents of the Nile?

770. What is the name of the dam in southern Egypt that creates a reservoir and controls the flow of the Nile River: Hoover Dam or Aswan High Dam?

771. What is the name of the world's largest hydroelectric dam made of concrete and steel towering over the Yangtze River in China, and regarded as the world's largest power station: Three Gorges Dam or Gezhouba Dam?

772. What is the name of the river formerly called the Zaire River that flows through central Africa, is the second longest river after the Nile, and is considered the world's deepest river: the Congo River or the Niger River?

773. What is the name of the principle river that runs through western Africa, and is the third longest river in Africa after the Nile and the Congo: the Zaire or the Niger?

774. What is the name of the river that flows through four countries in western Africa: the Zaire or the Niger?

775. What is the name of the longest river in Europe that begins in Russia and flows into the Caspian Sea: the Danube or the Volga?

776. What is the name of the river that flows through Central and Eastern Europe that rises in the Black Forest Mountains of Germany and flows into the Black Sea: the Rhine or the Danube?

777. What is the name of the river that begins in the Swiss Alps, flows through several northern European countries, and empties into the North Sea: the Rhine or the Danube?

778. What is the name of the river in southern England that flows under the famous London Bridge and the Tower Bridge: the Thames or the Danube?

779. On which continent, considered the "outback," or the "land down under," are the Murray River and the Darling River located, that join together and flow into the Indian Ocean: Australia or Asia?

780. What is the name for the web-footed Australian animal that lives close to the banks of the Murray and Darling Rivers: the koala bear or the duck-billed platypus?

781. What is the name of the world's second longest river in the world located in South America that has the largest drainage basin in the world: the Orinoco River or the Amazon River?

782. What is the name of the South American river that flows through Venezuela into the Caribbean Sea and has the world's highest waterfall called Angel Falls: the Amazon River or the Orinoco River?

783. What is the name of the most famous waterfall in North America that can be seen in both New York and Ontario, Canada: Angel Falls or Niagara Falls?

784. What do Iguazu Falls in Argentina and Brazil, and Victoria Falls in Zambia and Zimbabwe have in common: are the biggest in the world, or both are located on a border?

785. Where is Yosemite Falls located in North America: Florida or California?

786. In which state is the subtropical swamp area called that is popular for its crocodiles, alligators, and tall grasses, and is commonly known as the Everglades: Florida or California?

787. What is the name of the biggest river in the United States?

788. How do you spell Mississippi?

789. What kind of boat do many people use to cruise along the Mississippi River: a canoe or a paddleboat?

790. What is the name of the river in Canada that flows north into the Arctic Ocean: the Mackenzie or the Yukon?

791. What is the name of the river that begins in the Canadian Rockies and stays frozen for nine months out of the year: the Mackenzie or the Yukon?

792. What is the term for the waterways that Venice, Amsterdam, and Panama are famous for: channels or canals?

793. What is the name of the type of boat that one may ride on in the Venice, Italy with over 150 canals: canoe or gondola?

794. How would you categorize all of the following: canoes, fishing boats, airboats, power boats, rowboats, fireboats, lifeboats, U-boats, hydrofoil boats, oil tankers, kayaks, paddleboats, pedal boats, speed boats, ships, barges, tugboats, ferries, galleons, ocean liners, submarines, gondolas, steamboats, steamships, riverboats, houseboats, rafts, cabin cruisers, vessels, yachts, jet skis, sail boats, windjammers, pontoon boats, and cruise ships?

795. What is the term that refers to the history of the world from the earliest civilization through the Roman Empire: pre-history or ancient history?

796. What is the meaning of the initials B.C. after a date that is used to refer to dates in history based on our calendar: Before Christ or After Christ?

797. What does the recent version of B.C. now written as B.C.E. mean: "Before the Common Era" or "Before the Common Epoch?"

798. What is the Latin meaning of A.D: "in the year of our Lord," or "After Christ?"

799. Is the recent version of A.D. the initials C.E. meaning Common Era?

800. If Rome was founded in the year 753 B.C.E., would that be considered 753 years before or after Christ?

801. Which ancient civilization came first: Greek or Roman?

802. Did Greek culture greatly influence Roman culture?

803. Which civilization dominated thousands of years ago in the Mediterranean, and provided the foundation for many things in Western culture today: Greek or Roman?

804. What were the time frames that include Archaic, Classical, and Hellenistic that ancient Greece was divided into: periods or eras?

805. What was ancient Greece divided into because it did not have a national government: provinces or city-states?

806. What were the two main city-states of ancient Greece: Athens and Sparta, or Corinth and Thebes?

807. Were Athens and Sparta allies or enemies?

808. Which Greek city-state was preoccupied with war and the military, and ruled by kings: Athens or Sparta?

809. Which Greek city-state was preoccupied with learning and the arts and believed in the rule of the people, or democracy: Athens or Sparta?

810. What is the name of the god of war, wisdom, and civilization that Athens is named for: Athena or Othello?

811. What is the name of the Greek fortress that was built as a retreat for the people in the event of an attack that is located high on a hill overlooking the city: the Acropolis or the Parthenon?

812. What is the name of the marble temple built as a shrine for Athena, located on a hill in the center of the city: the Acropolis or the Parthenon?

813. Which city-state was considered to have the best army and soldiers in Greece: Sparta or Athens?

814. What is the name of the series of wars between the Greeks and the Persians from 492 B.C. to 449 B.C: the Persian Wars or the Peloponnesian Wars?

815. Who did the city-states Athens and Sparta want to fight against as one force: the Persians or the Ionians?

816. Which Empire was conquered as a result of the Persian Wars: the Greek or the Persian?

817. What was the time called for the time of prosperity in Greece after winning the Persian Wars: the Golden Age or the Gilded Age?

818. What did the people of Athens watch in the theatres written by Aeschylus, Sophocles, and Euripides during the Golden Age: tragic plays or operas?

819. Were the Acropolis and the Parthenon constructed during the Greek Golden Age?

820. What artworks did many Greek artists create during the Golden Age: sculptures or portraits?

821. What do Doric, Ionic, and Corinthian refer to in Greek architecture: three types of columns, or three types of marble?

822. What is the name of the Greek General who was a leader of Athens during the Golden Age: Socrates or Pericles?

823. What is the name of the war that broke out between Athens and Sparta from 431 B.C because of conflicts regarding other city-states: the Persian Wars or the Peloponnesian War?

824. Who were Plato, Socrates, and Aristotle that became well respected after the defeat of Athens: Greek philosophers or Greek playwrights?

825. Which Greek philosopher was a student of Socrates: Plato or Aristotle?

826. Which Greek philosopher was a student of Plato: Socrates or Aristotle?

827. What is the name of the Greek poet who wrote the epic poems: the Iliad or the Odyssey: Homer or Aristotle?

828. What is the name of the King of Macedonia, a country north of Greece, who conquered vast regions of Europe and Asia and helped promote Greek culture even after his death: Alexander the Great or Peter the Great?

829. What is the name of the capital city of Egypt that is named for Alexander the Great?

830. Who were Zeus, Poseidon, Apollo, Athena, and Aphrodite in Greek mythology: Titans or Olympian gods?

831. Who were the first or elder gods who ruled during the golden age and included the parents of Zeus: the Titans or the Olympians?

832. Who was the king considered the most powerful of the Greek gods that lived at Mt. Olympus, is symbolized by a lightning rod, and rode on a horse name Pegasus: Zeus or Hercules?

833. What is the name of the mythological Greek hero who was the son of Zeus, half- man, half-god, and was famous for his strength and courage: Hercules or Apollo?

834. What is the name of the mythological Greek god of archery, light, and music, often symbolized with a bow and arrow, the Sun, and a lyre: Apollo or Artemis?

835. What is the name of the mythological Greek god of the ocean, earthquakes, and horses: Poseidon or Ares?

836. What is the name of the Greek goddess of wisdom, defense, and war, often symbolized with an owl or olive branch, and is regarded as the patron god of Athens: Aphrodite or Athena?

837. What is the name of the Greek goddess of love and beauty, often symbolized with a dove, a swan, or a rose: Aphrodite or Athena?

838. Who were Cyclopes, Medusa, Pegasus, Sphinx, and Typhon in Greek mythology: Greek monsters or Greek gods?

839. What is the name of the Greek monster that was a white horse that could fly: Minotaur or Pegasus?

840. What is the name of the Greek monster that was a one-eyed giant and was famous for making thunderbolts for Zeus: Cyclopes or Minotaur?

841. What is the name for Greek creatures that were half-man, half-horse: Centaurs or Cyclopes?

842. What ancient civilization is credited with the origins of the Olympic Games, beginning with competitions between the city-states: Greek or Roman?

843. What did the winners of the Olympic Games receive: olive branches or medals?

844. In which city were the Olympics held: Athens or Olympia?

845. Do you think the early Greek Olympics had all the events we have today?

846. What were two likely beginning Olympic competitions: running and chariot racing, or swimming and gymnastics?

847. How often are the summer and winter Olympics held?

848. Can you name an Olympic champion in a sport?

849. What did the Greeks develop for writing that includes 24 letters and symbols, begins with alpha, beta, gamma, delta, and is often used to refer to college sororities and fraternities: the Greek Numbers or the Greek Alphabet?

850. What word comes from the first two letters of the Greek letter system: alpha and beta?

851. What is the official language of Greece and Cyprus: Latin or Greek?

852. What is the name of the other ancient civilization after the Greeks: Italian or Roman?

853. How many hills was the city of ancient Rome built on: three or seven?

854. What civilization is evident in our calendar, our government, and in the design of our buildings: the ancient Roman or the ancient Mesopotamian?

855. Did Rome, Italy grow in power and go on to conquer other countries to spread its empire?

856. Who founded Rome: Romulus and Remus, or the Latins?

857. After whom is the city of Rome named after they built the city on the hills overlooking the Tiber River: Romulus or Remus?

858. In the year 753 B.C. was the city of Rome also known as "The Eternal City" and "The City of Seven Hills?"

859. Did the ancient Romans believe in several gods?

860. Who were Jupiter, Juno, Neptune, Pluto, Apollo, Diana, Mars, Venus, Cupid, Mercury, Minerva, Vulcan, Saturn, Bacchus, Janus, Uranus, and Flora: Roman Gods or Greek Gods?

861. Who did the Romans consider to be the king of all gods: Jupiter or Apollo?

862. Did the Romans engage in ceremonies and rituals to please their gods?

863. Where is Rome, Italy located: on a peninsula or on a river?

864. What is the name of the mountain range north of Rome that served to protect the Romans from invaders: the Alps or the Andes?

865. Who governed ruled Rome for hundreds of years: kings or gods?

866. What is the term for the early government of Rome after the era of kings that selected two principle leaders called consuls who were elected every year: a democracy or a republic?

867. What is the name of the Roman governmental group that gave advice to the consuls: the House of Representatives or the Senate?

868. What kind of social system did ancient Rome have which gave certain rights to certain levels: a class system or a feudal system?

869. What is the name of the land area that was conquered by the Romans: states or provinces?

870. What was the official language of the Romans: Italian or Latin?

871. What is the term for many languages spoken today that have a Latin base and include Italian, Spanish, French, and Portuguese: Germanic languages or Romance languages?

872. Do many English words have Latin roots?

873. What city located on the northern coast of Africa did the Romans want to invade and conquer in 265 B.C.E: Pompeii or Carthage?

874. Who founded Carthage: the Romans or the Phoenicians?

875. What areas of land did the Phoenicians fight to conquer: Northern Africa and Sicily, or Sardinia and Corsica?

876. What island did the Romans and the Carthaginians fight to win control of in a sea battle: Corsica or Sicily?

877. Which side was superior in winning battles at sea: Rome or Carthage?

878. What was the name of the wars between Rome and Carthage that were fought primarily at sea: the Punic Wars or the Italian Wars?

879. How many years did Rome and Carthage fight in the first Punic War: five or twenty?

880. What islands did Carthage offer Rome in a deal to end the war: Sicily, Corsica, and Sardinia, or only Corsica and Sardinia?

881. What other country did the Carthage General decide to fight in order to win back some land: France or Spain?

882. What is the name of the son that the Carthage General took with him to Spain, making him promise that he would continue the fight with the Romans as soon as he was old enough: Julius Caesar or Hannibal?

883. In which direction did Hannibal, a military genius at 26, decide to lead his 90,000 soldiers in a surprise attack against Rome: North across the Alps, or South across the Mediterranean?

884. What animal did Hannibal bring with him across the Alps that frightened the Romans: elephants or tigers?

885. Did the fight between the Romans and the Carthaginians continue for several years?

886. Who managed to win the Second Punic War in 203 B.C.E: Rome or Carthage?

887. Which side had to leave Spain, France, and Italy, reduce their warships, and pay war damages: Rome or Carthage?

888. Did Hannibal continue to spend the rest of his life fighting Rome?

889. Is Hannibal still regarded as a great military general?

890. Who won the Third Punic War winning control of Northern Africa, Spain, and the islands of Sicily, Corsica, and Sardinia: Rome or Carthage?

891. What did the Romans build to connect all the new territories, promote trade, and provide the means for transportation: canals and waterways, or roads and bridges?

892. What is the name of the man that is best known for being the leader of Rome and to ending the Roman Republic: Julius Caesar or Marc Antony?

893. Which country, now France, was Julius Caesar appointed the governor of: Gaul or Sicily?

894. What is the name of the Roman General that was a respected military leader, but soon become Julius Caesar's biggest rival: Pompey or Marc Antony?

895. Who won the civil war that came about between Caesar who had the support of the people, and Pompey who had the support of the Senate: Caesar or Pompey?

896. Who appointed Julius Caesar the dictator for life after the defeat of Pompey and his return to Rome: the Senate or the consuls?

897. What country did Pompey flee to where he was killed by King Ptolemy: Greece or Egypt?

898. Whom did Julius Caesar meet when he invaded Egypt: Ptolemy's sister, Cleopatra, or Isis?

899. Were Cleopatra and her brother Ptolemy the co-rulers of Egypt even though Cleopatra was many years older than her brother?

900. Did Ptolemy take over as the Pharaoh when he became older?

901. Whom did Cleopatra convince to help her win back the throne after she sneaked into the palace inside of a rolled carpet: Ptolemy or Julius Caesar?

902. Where did Julius Caesar defeat Ptolemy and his army making Cleopatra the ruler once again: the Battle of Alexandria or the Battle of the Nile?

903. Who uttered the famous words "I came, I saw, I conquered" after a victory in a military battle: Marc Antony or Julius Caesar?

904. Why did the Romans plot to kill Julius Caesar: they wanted a return to a republic, or they did not want to be controlled by Cleopatra and Egypt?

905. How was Julius Caesar killed on March 15th in the year 44 B.C.E on the Senate floor, in a hall next to the Pompey Theater: gunshots or stab wounds?

906. What are the names of the two men that shared control of Rome after the death of Julius Caesar: Marc Antony and Octavian, or Ramses and Caesarion?

907. Whom did Cleopatra meet in the city of Alexandria, the capital of Egypt: Octavian or Marc Antony?

908. Who came to power and ruled Rome after Marc Antony and Cleopatra lost all power and died by a sword and a snake: Octavian or Caesarion?

909. What name did the Roman Senate give to Octavian when he became the first emperor of Rome: Augustus Caesar or Emperor Octavian?

910. What month of the year is named for Augustus Caesar?

911. What month of the year is named for Julius Caesar?

912. Who is credited for making up the calendar we use today, with each month named for a god, a Latin translation, or a number: the Romans or the Greeks?

913. Which month is translated as number "7" in Latin: October or September?

914. Which month is translated as number "8" in Latin, and is similar to the words octopus, octave, and octagon?

915. Which month is translated as number "9" in Latin: November of October?

916. Which month is translated as number "10" in Latin, and is similar to the words decimal, decade, decimeter, and decathlon?

917. What is the name for the letters that the Romans used to represent cardinal numbers like I, V, X, L, C, D, and M that are still used today for outlines, Super Bowl numbering, and after kings' names: Roman numerals or Binary Numbers?

918. What was the name for the time of peace and prosperity during the 40-year rule of Emperor Augustus Caesar, and the 200 years beyond his rule: Pax Romana or Bellum Romana?

919. Were there several Roman emperors after Augustus?

920. What is the meaning of Pax Romana: Roman King or Roman peace?

921. What is the name of the downtown area in ancient Rome with its pottery, clothing shops, spice shops, markets, and temples: the Coliseum or the Forum?

922. What is the name for the temple that was built during the reign of Augustus for all the gods of ancient Rome: the Coliseum or the Pantheon?

923. What is the name for the stone structures that the Romans built that brought water from a river or stream into the city, and provided water for the public fountains and baths: aqueducts or irrigation canals?

924. Who built the famous Pont du Gard aqueduct in France and the Segovia aqueduct in Spain: the Greeks or the Romans?

925. What is the name of the largest Baroque fountain in Rome, Italy, one of the most famous in the world: the Trevi Fountain or the Tivoli Fountain?

926. Are the Romans regarded as good engineers with all their roads, bridges, aqueducts, and the Colosseum?

927. What is the name for the one-piece outer garment worn by male citizens in ancient Rome: the cape or the toga?

928. What is the name for the one-piece outer garment worn by women in ancient Rome: the stola or the tunic?

929. What was considered typical food in *ancient* Rome: spaghetti, pizza, and pasta, or bread, fish, and cheese?

930. What is the name for the open-air round arena with tiers of seats for 55,000 spectators that the Romans built for gladiator combats and other sporting events: a theatre in the round, or an amphitheater?

931. What is the name of Rome's most famous amphitheater, built over 2,000 years ago, where spectators would sit on marble seats to watch gladiators battle or animals fight, and is still the biggest landmark in Rome: the Pantheon or the Coliseum?

932. What is the name for the Roman horse races around a track called the Circus Maximus with the racer driving a team of horses several times around the track: gladiator races or chariot races?

933. What catastrophe occurred in 64 A.D. that destroyed nearly half of Rome under the reign of the unpopular Emperor Nero: the great fire or the great earthquake?

934. What is the name of the gladiator slave that led a slave revolt in 73 B.C.E: Spartacus or Olympus?

935. What is the name of the man that inspired a new religion and believed that there was just one God: Moses or Jesus?

936. What religion did many follow honoring one God, a religion that was opposed to the Romans believing in many gods: Christianity or Catholicism?

937. What is the name of the ancient city and vacation destination outside of Rome that was nearly destroyed and buried in ash after the eruption of Mount Vesuvius in 79 A.D: Sicily or Pompeii?

938. What did archaeologists discover in 1748 that they believe preserved the ancient city of Pompeii, and gave them information about the people and their way of living: sand or molten lava?

939. Under which emperor did the Roman Empire reach its peak in 117 A.D: Nero or Trajan?

940. What was the end result of Rome's excessively big empire, the plague, a weakened army, the economy, civil wars, and invasions from other tribes all contribute to over three hundred years: a divided Roman Empire or the decline and fall of the Roman Empire?

941. What is the name of the man who became the Roman emperor in 310 A.D., became the first to convert to Christianity after he had a vision, captured and ruled a united Rome, and established the new capital of Constantinople: Constantine the Great or Maxentius?

942. What artwork is Constantinople famous for that is found in many of its palaces and churches: murals or mosaics?

943. What is the modern name for Constantinople, Turkey that was the capital city of the Roman Empire in 330 A.D: Istanbul or Ankara?

944. What was the name of the western half of the Roman Empire under Constantine in 395 A.D: the Western Roman Empire or the Byzantine Empire?

945. What was the name of the eastern half of the Roman Empire under Constantine in 395 A.D: the Roman Empire or the Byzantine Empire?

946. What warrior groups invaded and conquered Rome in the 400's that marked the end of the Western Roman Empire: the Visigoths and Germans, or the Huns and the Spanish?

947. Did the eastern Byzantine Empire continue to flourish after the fall of the Roman Empire?

948. Who ruled the Byzantine Empire for forty years, is credited with compiling the laws of the Romans into ten books called a code, and now serves as a basis for our modern system of civil law: Justinian the Great or Byzantine the Great?

949. What is the name of the people that lived in Northern Europe in the Scandinavian countries of Norway, Sweden, and Denmark during the Middle Ages: the Vikings or the Visigoths?

950. What is the geographical term for a deep inlet of the sea between steep slopes in a valley that was carved by a glacier that Norway is famous for: fjord or channel?

951. Did Medieval Norway have many farming communities?

952. What were the Viking people also known as because of their numerous invasions of Northern and Western European countries and islands: imperialists or raiders?

953. What is the name of the place on the northern coast of France that was settled by the Vikings: Brittany or Normandy?

954. What is another name for Vikings: Raiders or Norsemen?

955. What did the Vikings or Norsemen wear on their heads when raiding a village or city: a horned helmet or a horned mask?

956. What things did the Vikings often steal in the late 700's when they invaded places like Iceland, Greenland, Scotland, Ireland, and England: gold and silver, or copper and steel?

957. What defenseless places, home to Christian monks, did the Vikings often burn down after they attacked and looted them: temples or monasteries?

958. What mode of transportation were the Vikings most noted for: Viking ships or Viking wagons?

959. What is the name for narrow ships that the Vikings made that were used for exploration and raiding, and were propelled by sails and oars: galleons or longships?

960. What is the name of the red-haired Viking man who fled Norway with his father to Iceland and then went on to discover and name Greenland: Eric the Red or Eric the Outlaw?

961. What is the name of Eric the Red's oldest son, a Norseman who was known as the first European explorer to arrive in North America 500 years before the arrival of Christopher Columbus: Leif Ericsson or Eric Jacobson?

962. What is the name of the large, Canadian island off the eastern coast of North America that Leif Ericson landed on early in the 11th century after a storm caused him to lose his way on his journey from Norway to Greenland: Newfoundland or Labrador?

963. What did Leif Ericson call the Canadian province where he landed because of the wild grape vines that grew there: Finland or Vinland?

964. What is the name for the strip of land that connected the continents of North America and Asia during the Ice Age that Native Americans and animals crossed: land bridge or Bering Strait?

965. What is the accepted name of the early people that made their home in the cold tundra climate of Alaska, Canada, Siberia, and Greenland: the Inuit or the Eskimos?

966. What is the Inuit name for the homes they built out of snow and ice: igloo or ice shanty?

967. What did the Inuit make their clothing from: linen cloth or animal skins?

968. What is the name for the warm boots made and worn by the Inuit: mukluks or moccasins?

969. What is the name for the warm coats with fur-lined hoods worn by the Inuit: Parkas or Minks?

970. Would the Inuit make many clothing items from the fur of rabbit, polar bear, and foxes, as well as sealskin and caribou?

971. What is the staple of the Inuit diet: corn or meat?

972. What kind of weapon would the Inuit use to hunt seals, walruses, otters, and whales: a bow or a harpoon?

973. What dog did the Inuit breed to pull their sleds: Alaskan Malamute dog or Inuit Eskimo dog?

974. What kind of boat did the Inuit often use for hunting: kayaks or canoes?

975. What is the largest state in the United States: Texas or Alaska?

976. What is the capital of Alaska: Juneau, Anchorage, or Fairbanks?

977. What is the nickname for the state of Alaska that refers to areas in the north where, during the summer, the Sun never completely disappears below the horizon, and the Sun is visible at midnight?

978. What is the common name for aurora borealis, the colorful lights that can be seen in Alaska and other places in the Northern Hemisphere: the Northern Lights or the Alaskan Lights?

979. Was Alaska known for having gold?

980. What is the name of the Alaskan gold rush that attracted more than 100,000 prospectors between 1896 and 1899, also known as the Yukon Gold Rush: the Klondike or the Skagway?

981. What other gem is abundant in Alaska besides gold: ruby or jade?

982. Is Alaska known for its wildlife like salmon, moose and bear?

983. Does Alaska have many mountains, glaciers, and fjords?

984. What kind of pipeline runs 800 miles in Alaska from wells at Prudhoe Bay to the Port of Valdez: gas or oil?

985. What is the name of the highest mountain peak in North America located in Alaska: Mt. Everest or Mt. McKinley?

986. What bears are found in Alaska besides polar bears and grizzly bears: Black or Kodiak?

987. What is the main sport in Alaska: dog sledding or snowmobiling?

988. What is the name of the famous Alaskan sled dog race: the Iditarod or the Birkebeiner?

989. What is the name of a breed of dog often used for Alaskan sled racing: Labrador or Husky?

990. What are huskies and malamutes?

991. What did some Native Americans build thousands of years ago as burial places: mounds or pyramids?

992. What is the name of the North American cliff dwellers that are regarded as the Ancient Pueblo people of Utah, Colorado, Arizona, and New Mexico: the Apache or the Anasazi?

993. What did the Anasazi use to build their multi-room homes, and built them so the overhanging cliff would serve as the roof: adobe bricks or dry rocks?

994. What is the Spanish term for the town or village that the Anasazi lived: pueblo or barrio?

995. Did the Anasazi homes have doors or windows?

996. How did the Anasazi move from level to level in their dwellings: stairs or ladders?

997. Did the Anasazi die out naturally, or did they disappear mysteriously, leaving behind their elaborate cliff dwellings?

998. What is the name of the brick that the Pueblo Indians built their houses out of in the 1500's that is a mixture of sand, clay, and straw: cement or adobe?

999. What was the name of the dance performed by the Pueblos to attract rain and good crops: the Wheat Dance or the Corn Dance?

1000. What is the name for the carved dolls of the Pueblo Indians that represent different spirits: Kachina dolls or Ancestral dolls?

1001. What is the term for the Native American tribes like the Navajo and the Apache that moved from place to place in search of food, water, and good land: wanderer or Nomad?

1002. What is the name of one kind of house built by the Apache with animal hides stretched over poles: a hut or a teepee?

1003. What is another name for a wickiup, a permanent house built by the Apache: a teepee or a wigwam?

1004. What did the Apache make many of their clothing items from: rabbit fur or buckskin?

1005. Did the Apache often decorate their clothing with beads, feathers, and fringes?

1006. What is the name for the shoes the Apache wear on their feet: moccasins or mukluks?

1007. What are the staples of the Apache diet: corn and buffalo meat, or wheat and pig meat?

1008. What weapon did the Apache use to hunt with: hatchets or bows and arrows?

1009. What did the Apache use to make the tips of their spears: flint or arrowheads?

1010. Was Geronimo the chief of an Apache tribe or a Navajo tribe?

1011. What were the Navajo Indians also known as: the Diné or the Hogans?

1012. What is the name of the dwelling built by the Navajo built with logs and clay: a wigwam or a longhouse?

1013. Which group of Native Americans are the largest in the nation: the Navajo or the Apache?

1014. What is the general term used to refer to Native American Indians that live east of the Mississippi River like the Mohican and the Iroquois: the Woodland tribes or the Mississippi tribes?

1015. What is the most important crop for the Woodland tribes: wheat or maize, a type of corn?

1016. What is the name of the language spoken by many Native American tribes: Algonquin or Cherokee?

1017. What is the name for a Native American infant or young child: a papoose or a bambino?

1018. What is the name of the structure that was built to safely carry the Native American babies: a cradleboard or a papoose?

1019. What is the modern day version of the game using sticks, balls and nets played by the Algonquin, the Iroquois, and the Huron: Cricket or Lacrosse?

1020. What did the Native Americans often cover their skin with to protect them from mosquito bites: mud and bear fat, or sand and seal fat?

1021. What is the name of the narrow boat with narrow ends that the Native Americans often built from birch trees: a kayak or a canoe?

1022. What is the name for the houses built by many Woodland Indians: teepees or longhouses?

1023. What is the name often used for the Native American religious or spiritual leader: the Medicine man or the healer?

1024. Are chiefs, headdresses, tribes, drums, dancing, war paint, jewelry, singing, and peace pipes all a part of Native American culture?

1025. What is the name for the Native American meeting and dance ritual: a powwow or a tribal dance?

1026. What is the name for the small axe used by Native Americans that is similar to a hatchet, and used as both a weapon and a tool: a tomahawk or a picket?

1027. What is the name of the symbolic wooden post carved out by the Native Americans: obelisk or totem pole?

1028. What is the name for the beads that were made from shells and used for money by many Woodland tribes: wampum or wontons?

1029. What is the name for a group of Native American families that have a common culture, language, and religion: a nation or a tribe?

1030. What is the name for the area of land that the U.S. government has set aside that is managed by a particular Native American Indian Nation or tribe: a reservation or a homestead?

1031. Which Italian explorer is remembered for his discovery of the "New World?"

1032. In what year did Columbus "discover" America?

1033. What is the name of the island that Christopher Columbus landed on in the Caribbean: San Salvador meaning "Holy Savior," or Puerto Rico?

1034. What did Columbus call the Taino natives that he met after he landed because he thought he had reached the East Indies?

1035. Who sponsored Columbus's voyages to America: Italy or Spain?

1036. What are the names of Christopher Columbus's three ships?

1037. What are the names of the Spanish monarchs who paid for Columbus's four voyages to the New World: King George and Queen Victoria, or Kind Ferdinand and Queen Isabella?

1038. What is the name of the explorer and mapmaker from Florence, Italy after whom our country is named, and because of his mapping skills, recognized that our continent truly was the "New World:" Amerigo Vespucci or Martin Waldseemuller?

1039. What is the name of the Italian explorer who sailed across the Atlantic in 1497 backed by King Henry VII of England, crossed the Atlantic with his small crew, and landed in Newfoundland, Canada: Henry Hudson or John Cabot?

1040. What is the Spanish word for "conqueror," like Hernando Cortez, Francisco Pizarro, and Vasco Nuñez de Balboa: conquistador or explorador?

1041. What were the Spanish Conquistadors searching for in the New World: gold or oil?

1042. What is the name of the Spanish Conquistador who claimed Mexico for Spain in 1519 after he conquered the Aztec Empire and killed the Aztec Emperor Montezuma: Hernando Cortez or Francisco Pizarro?

1043. What is the name of the Spanish explorer who is known for establishing the first European settlement in South America in 1511, and was the first European to see the Pacific Ocean after crossing the Isthmus of Panama in 1513: Vasco Nuñez de Balboa or Juan Ponce de León?

1044. What is the name of the Spanish conquistador who explored South America, conquered the Inca Empire in Peru in 1532, took over the Inca city of Cuzco, and established the new capital of Lima: Ferdinand Magellan or Francisco Pizarro?

1045. What is the name of the Spanish conquistador who sailed with Columbus on his second voyage, was appointed as the Governor of Puerto Rico by King Ferdinand, and led an expedition to discover the fountain of youth but somehow ended up in the state of Florida: Juan Ponce de León or Hernando de Soto?

1046. What is the translation of *Puerto Rico* in English, because of the all the gold, silver, and other minerals that are found on this island?

1047. What was Juan Ponce de León in search in the West Indies besides more gold: the fountain of youth, or silver mines?

1048. Which state did Ponce de León land on during the springtime, named this state a Spanish word that translates "place of flowers," and claimed this state for Spain: Florida or Louisiana?

1049. What is the name of the warm ocean current of the northern Atlantic Ocean, discovered by Ponce de León that helps ships sail at a higher speed: the Gulf Stream or the trade winds?

1050. On which Caribbean island did Ponce de León die because of a wound he received while fighting the Native Americans: Puerto Rico or Cuba?

1051. What is the name of the Spanish conquistador who arrived in Florida in 1539, was appointed the Governor of Florida and Cuba by the King of Spain, and was the first European to explore the territory west of the Mississippi River: Hernando Cortez or Hernando de Soto?

1052. What was Hernando de Soto main quest in exploring Florida: finding gold, or finding the fountain of youth?

1053. What animal did the Spanish bring with them to the New World: the chicken or the horse?

1054. What did the Spanish have that helped them overpower the Native Americans in the state of Florida: guns and horses, or longbows and mules?

1055. What is the name of the first permanent European settlement located on the eastern coast of Florida that Spaniard Pedro Menéndez de Avilés named for a saint: St. Angel or St. Augustine?

1056. What is "Castillo de San Marcos" that was built by the Spanish to protect the land against other invading Europeans: a fort or a castle?

1057. What is the name of the Spanish conquistador who was appointed the Governor of Spanish territories in Mexico, and traveled through the southwestern United States in 1540 in the hopes of finding the mythical Seven Cities of Gold: Francisco de Goya or Francisco Vásquez de Coronado?

1058. What natural wonder did Coronado's soldiers stumble upon in their quest to find the cities of gold: the Badlands or the Grand Canyon?

1059. What is the name of the river that the Spanish explorers discovered between the United States and Mexico that translates as "big river?"

1060. What religion did the Spanish explorers want to share with the Native Americans?

1061. What is the word used to refer to the schools and churches that the priests built close to Indian villages: cathedrals or missions?

1062. What diseases did the Spanish bring with them from Europe to the New World that many Native Americans died of during and after Coronado's exploration years?

1063. What is the name for the faster sea route that the Europeans would spend several years searching for through the icy Arctic Ocean that would lead them to Asia with all its desirable trade products like spices, tea, and silk: the St. Lawrence Seaway or the Northwest Passage?

1064. What is the name of the English explorer who sailed three times for the English and once for the Dutch in the early 1600's in his quest to discover the Northwest Passage, a shorter route between Europe to Asia by way of the Arctic Ocean: Henry Hudson or John Cabot?

1065. From which country are the Dutch: the Netherlands or Belgium?

1066. What country is regarded as a country of the Netherlands: Scandinavia or Holland?

1067. What area do Norway, Sweden, and Denmark make up: the Netherlands or Scandinavia?

1068. Which country do the Danes or Danish people call home: Denmark or Holland?

1069. What is the name of the sweet pastry that has become a specialty of Denmark?

1070. What famous explorer has a strait named for him, linking the Atlantic Ocean to a bay in Canada as well as a river in New York: St. Lawrence or Hudson?

1071. What is the name of the country, north of the United States, that extends from the Atlantic to the Pacific, and North to the Arctic?

1072. What is the largest country in the Western Hemisphere: Canada or the United States?

1073. What languages are spoken in Canada?

1074. What kind of leaf is featured on the red and white Canadian flag: oak or maple?

1075. What kind of syrup is produced from the sap of trees in Canada: maple or corn?

1076. What is Canada divided into: states or provinces?

1077. How many provinces does Canada have: eight or ten?

1078. What are Manitoba, Saskatchewan, Alberta, Ontario, British Colombia, Nova Scotia, Prince Edward Island, Quebec, New Brunswick, and Newfoundland: provinces or territories?

1079. What are Nunavut, Northwest Territories, and Yukon: Canadian provinces or territories?

1080. What is the capital of Canada, located in the province of Ontario: Montreal or Ottawa?

1081. What language is spoken in the province of Québec: French or English?

1082. What is the name of the French navigator, considered the "founder of New France," credited as the founder of the first permanent settlement and trading post near the St. Lawrence River that is now known as Québec: Henry Hudson or Samuel de Champlain?

1083. What was Champlain searching for when he came from France to Canada on his first voyage in 1603: gold mines, or animal furs?

1084. What is another name that refers to Québec: French Canada or Champlain Canada?

1085. What mountain range located in the United States extends to western Canada: the Smoky Mountains or the Rocky Mountains?

1086. What is the name of the territory where Canada connects with Alaska: Northwest Territories or Yukon Territory?

1087. Where are Québec, Toronto, Vancouver, and Montreal located: northern or southern Canada?

1088. Are moose, caribou, beaver, bear, and Canada Geese among the many animals that live in Canada?

1089. What industry and recreational sport in Canada include the following: muskellunge, salmon, and trout?

1090. What kind of hunting did the Inuit engage in while in Canada that is still a major industry today: caribou hunting or seal hunting?

1091. What are two popular sports played in Canada: lacrosse and hockey, or cricket and basketball?

1092. What age were the 1400's, 1500's and 1600's considered because it was a time when many Europeans were exploring and making new discoveries in the New World: Exploration and Discovery or conquest and invention?

1093. Where did many of the early European explorers of the 15th century come from: France and Spain, or Italy and Portugal?

1094. Which European country wanted to share in the wealth of the New World and find gold, silver, and other riches in the New World: Germany or England?

1095. What is the name of the document that was issued by King James I of England in 1606 that assigned land rights to the colonists to settle in North America: treaty or charter?

1096. Was the first journey from England to North America in 1607 an easy voyage or a difficult one?

1097. What is the name of the English navigator who founded the first English Colony in Virginia in 1607 and named it for the King of England: Captain John Smith or Captain John Cook?

1098. What is the name of the colony that the English settlers established on May 24th, 1607 that is regarded as the first permanent English settlement: Georgetown or Jamestown?

1099. Who was appointed as the leader of the Jamestown Colony: King James I or Captain John Smith?

1100. What did many settlers in Jamestown die of that first winter: starvation and disease, or frostbite and enemy attacks?

1101. What is the name of the Native Americans that Captain Smith and the settlers befriended and traded with: the Powhatan or the Patawomeck?

1102. What staple in the Powhatan diet was introduced and shared with the early English settlers: wheat or corn?

1103. What is the nickname of the Indian woman Matoaka who is credited with saving Captain Smith's life after he was visiting her village near Jamestown and captured by the Powhatan Indians: Sacajawea or Pocahontas?

1104. What is the name of the English settler that Pocahontas married, returned to England with him for a short time, and became known as the Indian Princess: John Smith or John Rolfe?

1105. Did the Native Americans and colonists have both peace and war with one another?

1106. What is the name for the period of starvation in Jamestown during the winter of 1609-1610 in which only sixty colonists survived out of five hundred: The Starving Time or The Famine?

1107. What crop did colonists raise in order to sell for profit in 1614 that helped the Jamestown economy: corn or tobacco?

1108. Who arrived on a ship in Chesapeake Bay for the first time in 1619, and paved the way for the family unit in Jamestown: slaves or women?

1109. Was Jamestown allowed to make its own laws under the governor?

1110. Who arrived on Dutch ships in Chesapeake Bay for the first time in 1619: Africans or Swedes?

1111. What is the term for the African people that came to America to work on the settlement for others for a specific period of time: slaves or indentured servants?

1112. What is the name of the 102 passengers who boarded a ship and arrived here from England in 1620 to escape religious restrictions and separate themselves from the Church of England: Puritans or Pilgrims?

1113. What is the name of the ship that the Pilgrims sailed on for sixty-six days to reach the New World?

1114. What is the name for the agreement that was signed by 41 Pilgrims that became the basis for their government in Plymouth Colony: the Pilgrim Pledge or the Mayflower Compact?

1115. What did the Pilgrims call the place where they landed in Massachusetts in 1620: Plymouth Rock or Jamestown II?

1116. What is the name of the leader of the Pilgrims that established Plymouth Colony and governed there for thirty years: John Smith or William Bradford?

1117. What did many Pilgrims die of that first harsh winter: malnutrition and exposure, or disease?

1118. What is the name for the Native American Indians that the Pilgrims met and signed a peace treaty with: the Wampanoag or the Powhatan?

1119. What is the name of the Chief of the Wampanoag: Samoset or Massasoit?

1120. What is the name of the Native American Indian who spoke English and helped to establish a treaty between the Pilgrims and local Native Americans: Powhatan or Squanto?

1121. What is the name of the three-day celebration of the first harvest in 1621 that the Pilgrims had with Chief Massasoit and ninety Native American men, organized by Governor William Bradford: the Harvest Festival or Thanksgiving?

1122. When did the Pilgrims and the Native Americans call this feast and celebration a "Thanksgiving:" the first gathering in 1621, or two years later in 1623?

1123. Did the Pilgrim and Indian Thanksgiving include goose, venison, duck, corn bread, singing, and dancing?

1124. What is the name of the people from England who started coming to the New World after the Pilgrims: the Puritans or the Calvinists?

1125. What leader guided 1,000 Puritans to America and established the Massachusetts Bay Colony in 1630: James Winthrop or Roger Williams?

1126. Why did King Charles I, the son of King James, charter the Massachusetts Bay Company, giving the Puritans the right to settle in New England: he wanted the Puritans to leave England, or he wanted the Puritans to promote the teachings of the Church of England?

1127. Who built Salem and Boston, and established more colonies in New Hampshire, Rhode Island, and Connecticut between 1630 and 1640: the Wampanoag or the Puritans?

1128. What did the Puritans build in several colonies to promote reading and knowledge for all children?

1129. Which Massachusetts University was founded by the Puritans: Boston University or Harvard?

1130. What is the name of the Puritan minister who wanted to establish a colony in Providence, Rhode Island, and believed in the separation of government and religion, commonly known as the separation of church and state: Roger Williams or John Winthrop?

1131. Did the Native Americans approve or disapprove the many Puritans that arrived here from England and claimed more and more of their land?

1132. What happened to the population of the Native Americans as more and more of them were exposed to diseases brought over by the Europeans?

1133. Did Europeans seeking religious freedom establish many English Colonies?

1134. What is the name of the religious group, known as the Society of Friends, who came to Pennsylvania to practice their faith because they were loyal to only God and not the English King: Quakers or Calvinists?

1135. What is the name of the Quaker who founded the Colony of Pennsylvania to promote religious freedom, and the Quaker belief that all men and women are created equal in the eyes of God: William Tell or William Penn?

1136. Did Pennsylvania welcome people of all religions, or only Quakers?

1137. What city did William Penn establish as the capital of Pennsylvania close to the Delaware River: Philadelphia or Pittsburgh?

1138. What is the name of the colony named for the King's wife, Queen Henrietta Maria, that was settled by many Puritans in 1634: Maryland or Maine?

1139. What was the name of the New York area and the island of Manhattan in the 1600's because for a time it was a colony of the Dutch: New Netherland or New Holland?

1140. Which English King is the colony Carolina named for: King Carlos II or King Charles I?

1141. What did many farmers in Carolina rely on to help with the crops before the 1680's: slaves or indentured servants?

1142. What two smaller colonies did Carolina divide into in the early 1700's?

1143. What new colony in the south did King George II of England in 1674 name for himself?

1144. What reached its height during colonial times with millions of slaves being transported to the European colonies in the Americans to work on the plantations: slave trade or African trade?

1145. What religious group believed in equal rights for all people and wanted to end slavery: the Amish or the Quakers?

1146. What are Judaism, Christianity, and Islam?

1147. What is the name of the monotheistic religion of the Jews, believing in only one God: Judaism or Hebrewism?

1148. What is the name of the Jewish language: Hebrew or Arabic?

1149. What is the name of the first five books of the Hebrew Bible: the Old Testament or the Torah?

1150. Who were the first two human beings, according to the Book of Genesis in the Hebrew Bible, who were driven out of the Garden of Eden when they ate the fruit of a forbidden tree?

1151. What is the name of the man that is regarded as the father of the Jewish people: Moses or Abraham?

1152. Who led the Hebrews away from the Egyptians and the Pharaoh: Moses or Abraham?

1153. What ten religious rules did God communicate to Moses on a mountaintop: the Ten Laws or the Ten Commandments?

1154. What name did the Hebrew give to the land of Canaan after they managed to conquer the whole country: Israel or Jerusalem?

1155. What is the name of the king who ruled Israel for several years: David or Abraham?

1156. What is the capital city of Israel: Canaan or Jerusalem?

1157. Who did the Jews surrender to in 66 A.D. and were shut out of Israel for nearly 2,000 years: the Romans or the Greeks?

1158. When did Israel become an independent nation again: 1848 or 1948?

1159. What is the name of the religion that is based on the life and teachings of Jesus who was believed to be the Messiah or the "anointed one:" Catholicism or Christianity?

1160. What did the Christians call the Hebrew Bible: the Old Testament or the New Testament?

1161. Do both the Old Testament and the New Testament make up the Christian Bible?

1162. What is the name for the first four books of the New Testament: the Prophets or the Gospels?

1163. Were Matthew, Mark, Luke, and John evangelists of whom the gospels were based on?

1164. What is the name of the Jewish prophet who baptized Jesus: John or Matthew?

1165. Was Jesus put to death by crucifixion because some did not believe in his teachings?

1166. Did Christianity start to spread as Christians were eager to share the gospel?

1167. What is the name given for people that are non-Jews: Prophets or Gentiles?

1168. Did the Jew Paul of Tarsus believe that Jesus was the son of God as well as the Messiah?

1169. What eventually replaced polytheism, the worship of many gods, in the Roman Empire: Judaism or Christianity?

1170. Which religion has the most followers of the three religions today: Christianity, Judaism, or Islam?

1171. Do some Christian denominations include Baptists, Catholics, Lutherans, and Orthodox?

1172. What is the dominant religion in Italy today: Roman Catholicism or Italian Polytheism?

1173. Is it a good ethic to always accept and respect religions and beliefs that are different from our own?

Social Studies – 4th Grade

1174. What is the name of the planet we live on?

1175. What is the name for the spherical representation of the Earth?

1176. How many continents are on planet Earth?

1177. What are the two main oceans on planet Earth?

1178. Which of the seven continents can you name?

1179. Can you read a map?

1180. What are climate, economic, physical, road, political, and topographic all considered?

1181. What is the name of the imaginary line that divides the globe in half and runs east to west?

1182. What is the name of the imaginary line that divides the globe in half and runs north to south: the equator or the prime meridian?

1183. What is the name for the top sphere and the bottom sphere of the Earth: pole or hemisphere?

1184. How many hemispheres is the Earth divided into?

1185. What is the geographical term given for everything above the equator: Northern Hemisphere or Southern Hemisphere?

1186. What is the geographical term given for everything below the equator: Northern Hemisphere or Southern Hemisphere?

1187. What is the geographical term given for everything to the right of the Prime Meridian: Eastern Hemisphere or Western Hemisphere?

1188. What is the geographical term given for everything to the left of the Prime Meridian: Eastern Hemisphere or Western Hemisphere?

1189. What is the name of the imaginary line that divides the globe down the middle at the poles: the equator or the prime meridian?

1190. What two hemispheres does the prime meridian divide: Northern and Southern, or Eastern and Western?

1191. What is the name for the lines that run parallel to the equator: parallels or meridians?

1192. What is the name for the lines that run from pole to pole: parallels or meridians?

1193. What is the name of the geographic coordinate that runs north to south: latitude or longitude?

1194. What is the name of the geographic coordinate that runs east to west: latitude or longitude?

1195. Do lines of latitude run north or south or east to west?

1196. Do lines of longitude run north to south or east to west?

1197. What is the name for the point where lines of longitude are measured from: the prime meridian or the equator?

1198. What is the name of the place in England that measures zero degrees longitude: London or Greenwich?

1199. Do all parallels and meridians have a number?

1200. What is the name of the unit of measurement for longitude and latitude: coordinate or degree?

1201. What is the degree number of the equator at the eastern most point and the western most point, and at the intersection with the Prime Meridian: 0 or 90?

1202. What is the degree number of the Prime Meridian from North Pole to South Pole: 90 or 180?

1203. What is another name for the 180th meridian, halfway around the globe: the prime meridian or the International Dateline?

1204. What is the name for where meridians and parallels intersect: an axis or a coordinate?

1205. How would you read the coordinates 30 degrees North 20 degrees east: 30 degrees north of the equator and 20 degrees east of the prime meridian, or 30 degrees north of the prime meridian and 20 degrees east of the equator?

1206. When given the exact coordinates of a place, can you find the location of that place on a map?

1207. Can you identify several states while looking at a map of the United States?

1208. Can you identify your city and several others on a state map?

1209. Can you follow a map inside a building?

1210. What is the term for the proportion between the distance on a map and the real distance on the Earth's surface: scope or scale?

1211. Do most maps include scales on the bottom or in the corner?

1212. What kind of map might you be looking at if the scale reads one inch equal one hundred miles: a city map or a state map?

1213. What kind of map might you be looking at if the scale reads one inch equals one mile: a state map or a city map?

1214. What kind of map might you be looking at if the scale reads one inch equals 1,000 miles: a state map or a country map?

1215. What is the name for the type of map that shows the outlines of the 48 states with their capitals in the continental United States: a political map or a relief map?

1216. What is the name for the type of map that shows the landscape like hills, mountains, and rivers: a political map or a relief map?

1217. What is the name for the type of map that shows the original 13 colonies or battles of the Civil War: a political map or a historical map?

1218. What is the name for the type of map that shows hills and valleys with contour lines, and is often three-dimensional: a relief map or a physical map?

1219. What is the name for the type of map that shows the distribution of natural resources: a physical map or a resource map?

1220. What is the name for the type of map that shows pictures of cheese in the state of Wisconsin and pictures of oranges in the state of Florida: a relief map or a product map?

1221. What is the name for the type of map that shows highways, airports, railroad tracks, cities, and points of interest: a guide map or a road map?

1222. What is the name for the type of map that shows information about the temperatures and precipitation of a region: a climate map or a topographic map?

1223. What is the name for the type of map that shows the elevations of different areas by using lines drawn close together to indicate steep terrain, and lines drawn far apart to indicate flat terrain, a political map or a topographic map?

1224. What is the name for the type of map that indicates the locations of the major mountain ranges: a relief map or a topographic map?

1225. What is the name of the mountain range in North America stretching 3.000 miles from New Mexico through Colorado and Canada, and north to Alaska: the Rockies or the Appalachians?

1226. What is the name of the tallest mountain peak in Alaska: Mount Everest or Mount McKinley?

1227. What is the name of the mountain range in North America stretching 1,800 miles from Alabama to the Gulf of Saint Lawrence that include the White Mountains, the Allegheny Mountains, the Blue Ridge Mountains, and the Great Smoky Mountains: the Rocky Mountains or the Appalachian Mountains?

1228. Which mountain range has taller peaks: the Appalachians or the Rockies?

1229. Which mountain range is older: the Appalachians or the Rockies?

1230. What may explain why the Appalachians, over 280 million years old, are shorter and have less jagged peaks than the Rockies, over 130 million years old: erosion or weathering?

1231. What does the state of *Montana* translate to from Spanish to English?

1232. What is the name of the mountain range in South America, the longest mountain range in the world, stretching 4,500 miles from the Caribbean coast to the southern tip of the continent: the Andes Mountains or the Ural Mountains?

1233. What is the name of the highest mountain in the Andes that measures over 22,000 feet above sea level: Mount Everest or Mount Aconcagua?

1234. What ancient Indian civilization settled in the Andes of Peru with Cusco as their capital city: the Aztec or the Inca?

1235. What is the name of the city built by the Incas high in the Andes Mountains, 8,000 feet above sea level that was re-discovered by Hiram Bingham in 1911: Tenochtitlan or Machu Picchu?

1236. What is the name of the mountain range located along the northwest coast of Africa stretching 1,500 miles: the Atlas Mountains or the Eastern Highlands?

1237. What is the name of the mountain range located in Eastern Africa: the Atlas Mountains or the Eastern Highlands?

1238. What is the name of the tallest volcanic mountain in Africa: Mount Kilimanjaro or Mount Kenya?

1239. What is the name of the mountains that cover the European countries of Switzerland, Austria, France, and Italy: the Rockies or the Alps?

1240. In which mountain range was a frozen human body, estimated to be 5,000 years old, discovered by hikers in 1991 and named "Otzi," the Ice Man: the Rockies or the Alps?

1241. What is the name of the highest mountain in the French Alps in Europe meaning "White Mountain" in English: Mont Blanc or Mont Fuji?

1242. What is the name of the mountain range in Russia extending from the Arctic to the Caspian Sea: the Atlas Mountains or the Ural Mountains?

1243. What is the name of the highest mountain in Japan: Mount Fuji or Mount Kilimanjaro?

1244. What is the name of the tallest mountain range in the world: the Rockies or the Himalayas?

1245. What is the name of the world's tallest mountain, measuring over 29.000 feet tall that is located between Nepal and Tibet in the Himalayas: Mount McKinley or Mount Everest?

1246. What mountain peak was first conquered by Edmund Hillary and Tenzing Norgay in 1953: Mount McKinley or Mount Everest?

1247. Is there more oxygen or less oxygen is you climb higher above sea level?

1248. What are the two major mountain ranges in the continental United States?

1249. Can the United States be divided into geographic regions?

1250. What is the name of the region that refers to the states of Delaware, the District of Colombia, Maryland, New Jersey, New York, and Pennsylvania: Mid-Atlantic or Midwest?

1251. What is the name of the region that refers to the states of Illinois, Iowa, Indiana, Kansas, Michigan, Minnesota, Missouri, Nebraska, North Dakota, Ohio, South Dakota, and Wisconsin: the Midwest or the Northwest?

1252. What is the name of the region that refers to the states of Alaska, California, Hawaii, Oregon, and Washington: Northwestern States or the Pacific Northwest?

1253. What is the name of the region that refers to the states of Arizona, Colorado, Idaho, Montana, Nevada, New Mexico, Utah, and Wyoming: Rocky Mountain or Pacific Northwest?

1254. What is the name of the region that refers to the states of Connecticut, Maine, Massachusetts, New Hampshire, Rhode Island, and Vermont: Atlantic States or New England?

1255. What is the name of the region that refers to the states of Florida, Georgia, North Carolina, South Carolina, and Virginia: South Atlantic States or Mid-Atlantic States?

1256. What is the name of the region that refers to the states of Arizona, California, Colorado, Nevada, New Mexico, and Utah: the Southwest or the Pacific Northwest?

1257. What is the name of the country north of the United States?

1258. What is the name of the country south of the United States?

1259. What are the two states that are located outside the continental United States?

1260. What type of map can you find landforms such as rivers, channels, deltas, and peninsulas: a political map or a relief map?

1261. What is the geographical term for a wide waterway between two landmasses like the one that is located at the Columbus River in Oregon: a strait or a channel?

1262. What is the geographical term for the navigable narrow waterway between two landmasses like the Bering located between Alaska and Siberia that connects the Pacific with the Arctic, or Gibraltar connecting the Atlantic with the Mediterranean: a delta or a strait?

1263. What is the geographical term for a landform that is formed at a mouth of a river form the deposition of sediment like the one in Northern Egypt where the Nile River spreads out and drains into the Mediterranean Sea: a channel or a delta?

1264. What is the geographical term for a large expanse of grassland and flowers: a mesa or a prairie?

1265. What is the geographical term for a tableland or high plain that is relatively level, like those located in Tibet, Antarctic, and Colorado: a mesa or a plateau?

1266. What is the geographical term for a hill with steep sides and a flat top like those found in Colorado and New Mexico: a mesa or a tableland?

1267. What is the geographical term for a steep face of rock, ice, or Earth: a hill or a cliff?

1268. What is the term for a deep valley with steep cliffs cut into the terrain by running water: a basin or a canyon?

1269. What is the name of the famous canyon, considered by many to be one of the seven wonders of the natural world, located on the Colorado River in the state of Arizona?

1270. What is the geographical term for a landform in the ocean or on land that is lower in the center than at the edges: a canyon or a basin?

1271. What is the geographical term for a piece of land stretching out into water as a peninsula or a point: a cape or a gulf?

1272. What is the name of the famous cape in the state of Massachusetts: Cape Cod or Boston Cape?

1273. What is the geographical term for a large area of ocean that is partially enclosed by land: a gulf or a bay?

1274. What is the name of the largest gulf in the world that is surrounded by Mexico, the United States, and Cuba?

1275. What is the name of the gulf located between Saudi Arabia and Iran where petroleum is transferred on oil tankers: the Middle Eastern Gulf or the Persian Gulf?

1276. What is the geographical term for a small body of water that is set off from a larger body of water where the land curves like San Francisco, Chesapeake, and Hudson: a bay or a gulf?

1277. What is the geographical term for a dry, sandy area where cactus grow, tumbleweeds roll, and has very little rainfall?

1278. What is the name of the biggest desert in the world that stretches across most of North Africa: the Sahara or Death Valley?

1279. What is the name of the continent that is also considered a polar desert: Antarctica or Arctic?

1280. What is the name of the desert that is named for a Native American tribe that stretches across California, Utah, Arizona, and Nevada and includes the area known as "Death Valley:" the Sonoran or the Mojave?

1281. What is the name of the driest desert in the world that is located in Argentina and Chile in South America: the Atacama or the Arabian?

1282. What is the name of the second largest desert in the world, located in Western Asia: the Arabian or the Atacama?

1283. What is the geographical term for a part of land that extends into the water and is connected to the mainland by an isthmus, and include the Iberian, Yucatan, Italian, and the states of Florida and Alaska: a delta or a peninsula?

1284. What is the geographical term for a narrow piece of land that connects two larger land masses like the bridge located in Panama that connects Central America with South America: a fjord or an isthmus?

1285. What is the geographical term for an inlet in the sea between steep slopes carved out by a glacier, like those found in Iceland, Norway, New Zealand, and the state of Alaska: an isthmus or a fjord?

1286. What is the geographical term for a relatively still body of water that is surrounded by land: a river or a lake?

1287. What is the geographical term for a flowing body of water that typically feeds into another body of water: a river or a lake?

1288. What famous lakes can you name?

1289. What are the names of the five great lakes in the United States whose initials spell out H-O-M-E-S?

1290. What is the name of the shallow, salty lake in the state of Utah: Utah Lake or Great Salt Lake?

1291. What famous rivers can you name in the world?

1292. What famous rivers can you name in the United States?

1293. What is the name of the 1,900 mile long river that translate "Big River" in Spanish, and flows along the border between Texas and Mexico into the Gulf of Mexico?

1294. What is the name of the second largest river in the world that is 4,000 miles long, located in South America: the Nile or the Amazon?

1295. What is the name of the longest river in the world that is 4,150 miles long, flowing northward through Eastern Africa into the Mediterranean: the Yellow or the Nile?

1296. What is the name of the second longest river in that is 2,800 miles long, located in China: the Ganges or the Yellow?

1297. What is the name of the longest river in Asia that flows from Tibet into the East China Sea at Shanghai: the Ganges or the Yangtze?

1298. What river located in Asia is 1,550 miles long, flows from the Himalayas into the Bay of Bengal, and is regarded as sacred by the Hindus: the Ganges or the Yangtze?

1299. What is the name of the longest river in Europe and one of Russia's most important rivers: the Volga or the Yellow?

1300. What is the second longest river in Europe that is 1,725 miles long, borders ten countries, and flows from Southeastern Germany into the Black Sea: the Yellow or the Danube?

1301. What is the name of the major river in Germany besides the Danube: the Yellow or the Rhine?

1302. What is the name of the principle river in France: the Seine or the Thames?

1303. What is the name of the principle river in England: the Seine or the Thames?

1304. What is the name of the principle river in the United States that is 2,320 miles long and flows from Northern Minnesota to the Gulf of Mexico: the Missouri or the Mississippi?

1305. What is the name for a stream or river that flows into a main river or lake, like those found at the Colorado River and the Mississippi River: a delta or a tributary?

1306. Does the Mississippi River have several tributaries or deltas?

1307. What is the term for a landform that forms at the mouth of a river, where the river flows into an ocean or sea, like the one found on the Nile River: tributary or delta?

1308. What is the name of the continent that you live on?

1309. How many of the seven continents can you name?

1310. Which continent has the highest population in the world: North America, Asia, or Africa?

1311. Which country in Asia has the largest population?

1312. Which continent has the lowest population in the world: Australia, Antarctica, or Asia?

1313. On which continent do Spaniards, French, Italians, and Germans live: Europe or Asia?

1314. In which area of Europe do Danes, Swedes, and Norwegians live: Scandinavia or the British Isles?

1315. In which area of Europe do Irish, Scottish, and English live: Scandinavia or the British Isles?

1316. On which continent do Egyptians, Nigerians, and Moroccans live: Africa or Asia?

1317. On which continent do Chinese, Japanese, and Koreans live: Africa or Asia?

1318. On which continent do Peruvians, Argentineans, and Chileans live: North America or South America?

1319. What is Canada divided into: states or provinces?

1320. Which continent is Canada part of: North America or Asia?

1321. What are the two languages that are spoken in Canada?

1322. What is Mexico divided into: states or provinces?

1323. Which continent is Mexico part of: North America or South America?

1324. What language is spoken in Mexico?

1325. How many states is the continental United States divided into: 48 or 50?

1326. Which two states are located outside the continental United States?

1327. Which state is the "Aloha" state known for volcanoes, palm trees, Waikiki Beach, the Pearl Harbor Memorial, hibiscus flowers, pineapples, floral leis, grass skirts, luau parties, coconuts, sugar cane, has Honolulu as its capital, and was the last state to join the Union?

1328. Which state is considered the "Land of the Midnight Sun," is known for the Klondike Gold Rush, Eskimos, polar bears, forestry, wildlife, game fish, wooly mammoth fossils, husky dogs, sled-dog racing, the Northern Lights, glaciers, an oil pipeline, Mount McKinley, has Juneau as its capital, and was the 49th state to join the Union?

1329. Which state is the "Grand Canyon" state, known for Native Americans, deserts, the Saguaro cactus flower, copper mines, the Petrified Forest, Hoover Dam, London Bridge, the Painted Desert, Fort

Apache, the gunfight at the O.K. Corral, has Phoenix as its capital, and was the 48th state to join the Union?

1330. Which state is called the "Land of Enchantment," is known for the Carlsbad Caverns, mining, roadrunners, adobe buildings, Navajo and Apache tribes, hot air balloons, the yucca flower, the Gila National Forest, turquoise, has Santa Fe, the oldest capital city in North America as its capital, and was the 47th state to join the Union?

1331. Which state is called the "Sooner State," was bought as part of the Louisiana Purchase, is known for oil and coal, tornados, man-made lakes, farming, mistletoe, the "Five Civilized Tribes" (Choctaw, Cherokee, Chickasaw, Creek and Seminole), the National Cowboy Hall of Fame, the Will Rogers Memorial, four mountain ranges including the Wichita Mountains, has Oklahoma City as its capital, and was the 46th state to join the Union?

1332. Which state is called the "Beehive State," is known for its mountains, skiing, prehistoric caves and ruins, rock formations, Dinosaur National Monument, mining and farming, Mormons, lilies, seagulls, Rainbow Bridge, Great Salt Lake, has Salt Lake City as its capital, and was the 45th state to join the Union?

1333. Which state is called the "Cowboy State" or the "Equality State" because it gave women the opportunity to vote in 1869, is known for sheep, cattle, bison, coal, oil, rodeos, cowboys, dude ranches, Yellowstone and Grand Teton National Parks, Old Faithful Geyser, Jackson Hole, Devil's Tower, Flaming Gorge, has Cheyenne as its capital, and was the 44th state to join the Union?

1334. Which state is called the "Panhandle State," is known for potatoes, elk, mining, the Shoshone Falls, Craters of the Moon National Monument, Hells Canyon, Sun Valley Ski Resort, the Appaloosa horse, has Boise as its capital, and was the 43rd state to join the Union?

1335. Which state is called the "Evergreen State," is known for its rain forests, apples, farming and lumber, the ferry system, rhododendron flowers, orca mammals, Mount Rainier, Mount Saint Helens, the Space Needle, the Boeing Aircraft Company, has Olympia as its capital, and was the 42nd state to join the Union?

1336. Which state is called the "Treasure State" and is also nicknamed "Big Sky Country," is known for hunting, grizzly bears, mountain goats, fresh water springs, mining for gold, silver, agate, and sapphire and oil, the Rocky Mountains, forestry, cattle, sheep farming, Ponderosa pines, Custer's Last Stand at Little Bighorn, Glacier National Park, has Helena as its capital, and was the 41st state to join the Union?

1337. Which state is called the "Coyote State," is known for the Black Hills, Black Hills Gold, Homestake Gold Mine, the Badlands, Wounded Knee, Mount Rushmore, wooly mammoth bones, prairie dogs, bison, has Pierre as its capital, and was the 40th state to join the Union?

1338. Which state is called the "Peace Garden State," is known for wheat, sunflowers, farming, Theodore Roosevelt State Park, rodeos, the Sioux Indians, has Bismarck as its capital, and was the 39th state to join the Union?

1339. Which state is called the "Centennial State," is known for Native Americans, bighorn sheep, skiing, aquamarines, Rocky Mountain National Park, Great Sand Dunes, the Grand Mesa flattop mountain, Pike's Peak, the Mesa Verde Ancestral Pueblo, the highest paved road in North America, the world's largest rodeo, has Denver, the mile-high city as its capital, and was the 38th state to join the Union?

1340. Which state is called the "Cornhusker State," is known for underwater water reserves, mammoth fossils, cottonwood trees, Chimney Rock, Agate Fossil beds, the Lewis and Clark Trail, has Lincoln as its capital, and was the 37th state to join the Union?

1341. Which state is called the "Silver State," is known for its gambling magnets Las Vegas, Lake Tahoe, and Reno, gold and silver mining, the Comstock Lode Silver Deposits, sagebrush, wild mustangs, the Sierra Nevada Mountain Range, Hoover Dam, has Carson City as its capital, and was the 36th state to join the Union?

1342. Which state is called the "Mountain State," is known for black bears, timber and coal mining, folk music, fine glass, forests, the Golden Delicious apple, Greenbrier Resort, Harper's Ferry, the Cass Scenic Railroad, has Charleston as its capital, and was the 35th state to join the Union?

1343. Which state is called the "Sunshine State," is known for "amber waves of grain" (wheat) production, sunflowers, cattle, dust-bowls, plane-manufacturing, was the home of Dorothy in "The Wizard of Oz," has Topeka as its capital, and was the 34th state to join the Union?

1344. Which state is called the "Beaver State," is known for timber and lumber, grape flowers, thunder-egg geodes, Sea Lion Caves, Mount Hood Volcano, The Carousal Museum, ghost towns, Crater Lake, the deepest lake in the United States, the Columbia River, Tillamook Cheese Factory, the largest cheese factory in the world, has Salem as its capital, and was the 33rd state to join the Union?

1345. Which state is called the "Gopher State" or the "North Star State," is known as the "land of 10,000 lakes," boating, The Mall of America," lady's slipper orchids, loons, Green Giant vegetables, skyways, Tonka Trucks, has St. Paul as its capital, and was the 32nd state to join the Union?

1346. Which state is called the "Golden State," is known for redwood and giant sequoia trees, poppy flowers, the Gold Rush, Death Valley desert, rodeos, wine, oranges, cheese, raisons, turkeys, Disneyland, Spanish missions, The Golden Gate Bridge, The Pacific Coast Highway, the movie industry, has Sacramento as its capital, and was the 31st state to join the Union?

1347. Which state is called the "Badger State," is known for dairy, cows, fishing, 14,000 lakes, Summerfest Music Festival, robins, deer, cheese, cranberries, Muskellunge, snowmobiling, Harley Davidson motorcycles, the American Birkebeiner cross-country ski race, Noah's Ark Water Park, the Ringling Brothers Circus, the House on the Rock, the very first kindergarten, has Madison as its capital, and was the 30th state to join the Union?

1348. Which state is called the "Hawkeye State," is known for agriculture, corn, roses, Buffalo Bill, Quaker Oats, Nordic Fest, Effigy Mounds National Monument, Winnebago Motor Homes, has Des Moines as its capital, and was the 29th state to join the Union?

1349. Which state is called the "Lone Star" state, is known for The Alamo, Davy Crockett, oil, cotton, cattle farming, sheep farming, pecan trees, rodeos, cowboys, the Space Center, Dell Computers, the first hamburger, President Kennedy's assassination, has Austin as its capital, and was the 28th state to join the Union?

1350. Which state is called the "Sunshine" state, is known for oranges, grapefruit, beaches, the Everglades, the Kennedy Space Center, Disney World, Epcot Center, Sea World, Cypress Gardens, Universal Studios, the Daytona 500 auto race, Gatorade, crocodiles, pumas, the "Keys," has Tallahassee as its capital, and was the 27th state to join the Union?

1351. Which state is called the "Wolverine" state, is known for having two peninsulas, Mackinac Bridge, automobiles, Ford Motor Company, the Great Lakes, Sault St. Marie Canal, boating, navy beans, Kellogg Cereal, Petoskey Coral Stones, lighthouses, ginger ale, the world's largest weather vane, has Lansing as its capital, and was the 26th state to join the Union?

1352. Which state is called the "Land of Opportunity," is famous for its Diamond Mine, Hot Springs National Park, the Ozarks, explorer Hernando de Soto, Crater of Diamonds State Park, the first Wal-Mart, quartz crystal, spinach, duck-calling competitions, apple blossoms, has Little Rock as its capital, and was the 25th state to join the Union?

1353. Which state is called the "Show-Me" state, is known for the St. Louis Gateway Arch, Branson Country Music Shows, Bass Pro Shops, the Pony Express mail service, lead production, the Anheuser-Busch brewery, the first ice cream cones, Aunt Jemima pancake flour, Dr. Pepper, barbecue sauce, Mark Twain, caves, the Ozarks, has Jefferson City as its capital, and was the 24th state to join the Union?

1354. Which state is called the "Pine Tree" state, is known for lighthouses, lobsters, sardines, blueberries, sawmills, paper-making, moose, tourmaline stones, Acadia National Park, has Augusta as its capital, and was the 23rd state to join the Union?

1355. Which state is called the "Yellowhammer" state, is known for wild turkeys, cotton, timber, peanuts, Talladega National Forest, the Confederacy, Rosa Parks and the Montgomery Bus Boycott, the beginning of the Civil Rights Movement, the Racking Horse, cast-iron production, rocket production, the world's first electric trolley system, Gulf Coast beaches, has Montgomery as its capital, and was the 22nd state to join the Union?

1356. Which state is called the "Prairie" state or the "land of Lincoln," is known for the Willis Tower skyscraper, John Deere machinery, the tallest man in the world (8'11"), the Dairy Queen franchise, the Windy City, the Chicago Fire, Wrigley Field, Wrigley gum, Navy Pier, The Art Institute, The Chicago Theatre, The Museum of Science and Industry, corn, pigs, has Springfield as its capital, and was the 21st state to join the Union?

1357. Which state is called the "Magnolia" state, is known for its southern magnolia trees, river boats, "Old Man River," the largest river in the United States, Theodore Roosevelt's "Teddy Bear," catfish, cotton, tree farms, "Blues" music, Pine-Sol cleaner, the first 4-H club, the International Checkers Hall of Fame, Coca-Cola, has Jackson as its capital, and was the 20th state to join the Union?

1358. Which state is called the "Hoosier" state, is known for the Indianapolis 500 auto race, corn, the first gasoline pump, basketball, the "Brain Bank of the Midwest" with many colleges and universities located there, the first Raggedy Ann Doll, interstate highways, the Saturday Evening Post, has Indianapolis as its capital, and was the 19th state to join the Union?

1359. Which state is called the "Pelican" state, is known for pelicans, Breaux Bridge, the "crawfish capital of the world," farming, frogs, alligators, tall cypress trees, Mardi Gras in New Orleans, the French quarter, jazz, the first Tarzan movie, the Superdome, Cajun descendants, "parishes" instead of counties, has Baton Rouge as its capital, and was the 18th state to join the Union?

1360. Which state is called the "Buckeye" state, is known for its buckeye trees, farming, the Pro Football Hall of Fame, the Rock and Roll Hall of Fame, rubber and bicycle tires, greenhouse plants, the first chewing gum, first cash register, first professional baseball team, first traffic light, first airplane by the Wright brothers, first police, fire, and ambulance service, has Columbus as its capital, and was the 17th state to join the Union?

1361. Which state is called the "Volunteer" state, is known for the Grand Ole Opry, Elvis's former home Graceland, Great Smoky Mountains National Park, the Country Music Hall of Fame, Bluegrass music, horses, salamanders, turtles, aluminum, zinc, caves, whitewater rafting, has Nashville as its capital, and was the 16th state to join the Union?

1362. Which state is called the "Bluegrass" state, is known for the blue grasses on the prairie, covered bridges, tobacco, whiskey, pickles, a horse derby, Mammoth Cave National Park, the long rifle, the largest amount of gold stored in the world, the Chevrolet Corvette, the first Mother's Day, has Frankfort as its capital, and was the 15th state to join the Union?

1363. Which state is called the "Green Mountain" state, is known for ski resorts, autumn colors, Morgan horses, maple syrup, Ethan Allan and his revolutionary Green Mountain Boys, dairy farming, granite and marble mines, the first Ben and Jerry's Ice Cream Store, having the lowest crime rate in the nation, the Von Trapp Family of Austria made famous in the musical "The Sound of Music," the Bing Cosby Christmas classic, "White Christmas," has Montpelier as its capital, and was the 14th state to join the Union?

1364. Which state is called the "Ocean" state, is known for red chickens, red maple trees, Newport's summer tourism, the first circus, Arkwright's "Spinning Jenny," cotton mills, textiles and electronics, silverware and jewelry, the Tennis Hall of Fame, the first National Lawn Tennis Tournament, the oldest school house in the United States, The Flying Horse Carousal, being the smallest state in the nation, has Providence as its capital, and was the 13th state to join the Union?

1365. Which state is called the "Tar Heel" or "Old North" state, is known for being the "barbecue capital of the world," the Cherokee Native Americans, Great Smokey Mountains National Park, Whitewater Falls, Pepsi, Krispy Kreme doughnuts, the Venus Fly- Trap, sweet potatoes, emeralds, furniture-making, tobacco and brick production, the first miniature golf course, Biltmore Estate, the nation's largest home, the Wright Brothers as the "First in Flight" at Kitty Hawk, has Raleigh as its capital, and was the 12th state to join the Union?

1366. Which state is called the "Empire" state, is known for Niagara Falls, the Catskill Mountains, the Adirondack Mountains, Long Island, Ellis Island, Staten Island and the Staten Island Ferry, Coney Island and the Coney Island Cyclone rollercoaster, Manhattan, Queens, the Bronx, the Bronx Zoo, Yonkers, Brooklyn, the Brooklyn Bridge, the Erie Canal, orchids, dairy farming, jazz, Yankee Stadium, Babe Ruth, The Statue of Liberty, Central Park, Radio City Music Hall, The Apollo Theatre, Times Square, Radio City Music Hall and the Rockettes, Madison Square Garden, Rockefeller Center, Lincoln Center, Broadway, The Empire State Building, The Metropolitan Museum of Art, The Museum of Modern Art, Saks 5th Avenue, Macy's Thanksgiving Day Parade, Tiffany's jewelry store, St. Paul's Cathedral, The Baseball Hall of Fame, The United Nations, the stock exchange, the first license plates, the first toilet paper, marshmallows, Jell-O, the first pizzeria, the longest running newspaper, the nation's largest public library, subways, being the most populated city in the nation, has Albany as its capital, and was the 11th state to join the Union?

1367. Which state is called the "Old Dominion" state, is known as the "birthplace of a nation" as well as for the first Colonial settlement at Jamestown, was the site of thousands of Civil War battles, the state of surrenders from both the Revolutionary and the Civil Wars, the site of Patrick Henry's speech, "Give Me Liberty or Give Me Death," home of the Blue Ridge Mountains, oysters, tobacco, the first peanuts, ship-building, Robert E. Lee, Arlington National Cemetery, the tomb of the Unknown Soldier, Chesapeake Bay Bridge Tunnel, the Pentagon, NATO headquarters, Thomas Jefferson's home Monticello, George Washington's home Mount Vernon, has Richmond as its capital, and was the 10th state to join the Union?

1368. Which state is called the "Granite" state, is known for its autumn colors, logging, leather work, farming, White Mountain National Forest, maple syrup, the first public library, the oldest pipe organ, the center for covered wagon-building, the longest covered bridge crossing 460 feet over the Connecticut River, is the home of the Clydesdales horses, poet Robert Frost, the first alarm clock, has Concord as its capital, and was the 9th state to join the Union?

1369. Which state is called the "Palmetto" state, is known for being the first state to break away from the Union at Fort Sumter, palmetto trees, the Blue Ridge Mountains, tobacco, peaches, ginkgo farms, furniture-making, basket-making, Myrtle Beach, Hilton Head Resorts, golf courses, the Thoroughbred Racing Hall of Fame, has Columbia as its capital, and was the 8th state to join the Union?

1370. Which state is called the "Old Line" state, is known for the Annapolis U.S. Naval Academy, shipping, Chesapeake Bay oysters, crabs, tobacco, John Hopkins University, the first school, the first refrigerator, the Mason-Dixon Line marking the boundary between this state and Pennsylvania, the first telegraph, wild ponies, sailing, Baltimore Oriole birds, has Annapolis as its capital, and was the 7th state to join the Union?

1371. Which state is called the "Old Colony" state, is known for the Pilgrims' arrival on the Mayflower at Plymouth, the first Thanksgiving with the Native Americans, the Revolutionary War battles at Lexington, Concord, and Bunker Hill, Boston Harbor, the Boston Tea Party, the Freedom Trail, Beacon Hill, the Old North Church, Paul Revere's House, Copley Square, Faneuil Hall, Bunker Hill Monument, the Old State House and the first reading of the Declaration of Independence, the Boston Pops, the Charles River Esplanade, Cape Cod, Nantucket Island, Martha's Vineyard, the first college now called Harvard University, the Boston Terrier, Boston baked beans, Boston Cream Pie, clam chowder, cranberries, the first Toll House chocolate chip cookies, the first Dunkin Donuts, Johnny Appleseed, Fenway Park, the John F. Kennedy Library, the John Hancock building, has Boston as its capital, and was the 6th state to join the Union?

1372. Which state is called the "Constitution" state, is known for providing goods to George Washington's Continental Army during the Revolution, the invention of Eli Whitney's cotton gin, Charles Goodyear's tire, Linus Yale's lock, Yale University, the first law school, nuclear submarine production, the first telephone book, cattle and pig branding, the first color television, the first Polaroid Camera, the first car insurance, has Hartford as its capital, and was the 5th state to join the Union?

1373. Which state is called the "Peach" state, is known for the production of peanuts, cotton, and peaches, chickens, the Okefenokee Swamps, Stone Mountain Park, the carvings of Stonewall Jackson, Jefferson Davis, and Robert E. Lee on the side of Stone Mountain making it the largest granite sculpture in the world, the Blue Ridge Scenic Railway, Ante-Bellum pre-war houses, was the location for the classic move, "Gone With the Wind," has Atlanta as its capital, and was the 4th state to join the Union?

1374. Which state is called the "Garden" state, is known for its garden vegetables, horses, the longest boardwalk in the world, seaside resorts, casinos, Princeton University, the chemical industry, shopping malls, the original "Miss America" pageant, the first Indian Reservation, Edison's inventions of the light bulb, movie projector, and phonograph, the first drive-in movie theatre, has its cities featured on the "Monopoly" board game, is home to "Lucy the Elephant" six-story building, is the most densely populated state, is almost completely surrounded by water, has Trenton as its capital, and was the third state to join the Union?

1375. Which state is called the "Keystone" state, is known for its Quaker founder William Penn, Independence Hall, the signing of the Declaration of Independence, the writing of the United States Constitution, the Liberty Bell, first American flag, Gettysburg, Valley Forge, farming, coal production, steel production, mushroom production, Hershey's chocolate, Christmas trees, the first public zoo, the world's first oil well, the first piano, the first computer, a high concentration of Amish, has Harrisburg as its capital, and was the 2nd state to join the Union?

1376. Which state is called the "First" state, is known for being the first state to ratify the U.S. Constitution, the Chesapeake and Delaware canal, chemical production, chicken farming, the blue hen chicken, ladybugs, horseshoe crabs, nylon production, processed foods, historic churches, Finnish log cabins, has Dover as its capital, and was the 1st state to join the Union?

1377. What is the largest state in the continental United States after Alaska?

1378. What is the smallest state in the continental United States?

1379. What is the capital of the United States?

1380. What do the letters "D.C." stand for as part of our capital's name?

1381. Which ocean borders the United States on the eastern coast: the Atlantic or the Pacific?

1382. Which ocean borders the United States on the western coast: the Atlantic or the Pacific?

1383. What is the name of the country that borders America to the North?

1384. What is the name of the country that borders America to the South?

1385. What are the other states that border the state you live in?

1386. Can you name any of the *counties* (or *parishes* if you live in Louisiana) that border the county (parish) you live in?

1387. Does the United States of America have symbols that represent it?

1388. What national symbol has red and white stripes, and fifty white stars on a blue background?

1389. How many stripes are there on the American Flag, representing the number of original colonies that declared independence from Great Britain and became the first states in the Union?

1390. What national oath do U.S. citizens recite while facing the flag that shows their loyalty to the United States?

1391. What is the name of the lady that is credited with making one of the original American flags: Betsy Ross or Martha Washington?

1392. What is the name of the American symbol located in Independence Hall in Philadelphia, Pennsylvania that cracked soon after it was rung?

1393. What is the national bird of the United States: the bald eagle or the hawk?

1394. What is the name of the American symbol located in New York Harbor on Liberty Island that was a gift from France, and depicts a lady holding a torch high above her head?

1395. What American national symbol is a document proclaiming the independence of the thirteen original colonies from Great Britain?

1396. What American document was approved at a Convention in Philadelphia in 1787, includes the Bill of Rights and several amendments, and is considered the supreme law of the land?

1397. What is the name of the patriotic song that was based on a poem written by Francis Scott King during the War of 1812, was adopted by Congress in 1931, and is the official national song of the United States: God Bless America or The Star-Spangled Banner?

1398. What kind of symbols do states have that represent that state?

1399. What American landmark located in South Dakota has four American presidents carved in into a mountain: Mount Rushmore or Mount Blanc?

1400. Who is the fourth president besides Washington, Jefferson, and Lincoln that is carved into the granite face at Mount Rushmore: Adams or Roosevelt?

1401. Where are the Lincoln Memorial, Jefferson Monument, National Mall, Washington Monument, World War II Memorial, Vietnam Veterans Memorial, Korean War Veterans Memorial, FDR Memorial, the Capitol Building, and the White House all located?

1402. What is the name of the memorial located at 1600 Pennsylvania Avenue in Washington, D.C?

1403. Are the following national monuments and memorials located in Washington D.C. or Virginia: Arlington National Cemetery, Washington's home Mount Vernon, Jefferson's home Monticello, Booker T. Washington Memorial, Pentagon Memorial, and Iwo Jima Memorial?

1404. What is the name of the memorial located in the National Mall that is the world's tallest stone obelisk towering 555 feet high: The Washington Monument or The Space Needle?

1405. What is another name for the memorial U.S. Marine Corps War Memorial in Virginia that honors the marines that defended America during World War II in a battle with the Japanese, and is a statue of four marines raising the American flag: Hiroshima or Iwo Jima?

1406. What is the name for the international landmark that is the collective name for three waterfalls called Horseshoe, American, and Bridal Veil that border the Canadian province of Ontario and the state of New York: Niagara Falls or Yosemite Falls?

1407. What kind of American landmark are all of the following: Rocky Mountain, Mammoth Cave, Glacier, Crater Lake, Yosemite, Badlands, Great Smokey Mountains, Everglades, Acadia, Death Valley, Grand Teton, Yellowstone, Hot Springs, Mesa Verde, and Redwood?

1408. What landmarks or monuments can you name in your state?

1409. Can history be divided into different periods?

1410. Did the Stone Age, Bronze Age, and Iron Age occur in ancient history or modern history?

1411. Does the civilization of Mesopotamia in the region in Southeast Asia fall under prehistory or modern history?

1412. Which country is referred to as the "cradle of civilization:" China or Mesopotamia?

1413. What is the name of the current country where Mesopotamia once was: Iraq or India?

1414. What ancient civilization translates in Greek as, "Land between the Rivers:" Mesopotamia or Egypt?

1415. What are the names of the rivers located in Mesopotamia: the Tigris and Euphrates, or the Nile and Danube?

1416. What type of societal system did Mesopotamia have: a class system or an estate system?

1417. What was the name of the ancient capital of the country of Babylonia, located along the banks of the Euphrates River in Mesopotamia: Babylon or Baghdad?

1418. What is the name of the ruler of Babylon, considered the greatest ruler of the first Babylonian dynasty, credited for developing a Code of Laws: Hammurabi or Herod?

1419. Which civilization was the first to develop the entity of the city, writing, government, the calendar, glass, the wheel, the potter's wheel, the aqueduct, astronomy, the 60 minute hour, the sundial, irrigation systems, and agriculture: Greece or Mesopotamia?

1420. Were Mesopotamians known for developing agriculture, government, religion, and city-states?

1421. What is the term for the first writing system of the Mesopotamian using a chisel and a clay tablet: cuneiform or hieroglyphics?

1422. Where did the empires of Sumerian, Babylonian, and Assyrian exist: Greece or Mesopotamia?

1423. What is the name for the earliest inhabitants of Mesopotamia: the Babylonians or the Sumerians?

1424. What is the name for the last race of Mesopotamia, and the first to develop iron weapons and use chariots: the Babylonians or the Assyrians?

1425. What is the name of the earliest inhabitants of Mesopotamia that invented the wheel: the Sumerians or the Assyrians??

1426. What farming machine was first invented in Mesopotamia: the seed plow or the tractor?

1427. What number did the Mesopotamians use to calculate the minutes in an hour that was based on astronomy and the moon: 24 or 60?

1428. What is the name for the sacred Sumerian structures built to honor the main god of the city, were the highest structures in the area, and resembled a step pyramid: ziggurats or temples?

1429. What is the name of one of the Ancient Wonders of the World located in Babylon: The Great Pyramid or The Hanging Gardens?

1430. What is the name given for the historical time period between Ancient and Modern: The Early Modern Era or The Middle Ages?

1431. What is the name given for the time that is associated with castles, knights, armor, King Arthur, and Joan of Arc that began after the fall of the Western Roman Empire: renaissance or medieval?

1432. What is the name for the last major group in the feudal system of people during medieval times after the king, the bishops, the barons, and the lords: the commoners or the peasants?

1433. What is the term that refers to the medieval farmer who worked the land for his lord and paid him dues in exchange for the use of the land: peasant or serf?

1434. What is the name given to the people that took control over the Western Roman Empire after Germanic tribes ruled it for a short time: the Barbarians or the Greeks?

1435. What is another name for the Eastern Roman Empire that included Greece, Turkey, and the Middle East: Byzantine or Barbarian?

1436. What is the former name of the capital of the Eastern Roman Empire: Constantinople or Istanbul?

1437. Who were the nomadic herdsmen from Mongolia, a country north of China, that destroyed much of Europe and Asia between the 3rd and 5th centuries: the Visigoths or the Huns?

1438. What is the name for the most successful king of the Huns: Herod or Attila?

1439. What is the name for what is attached to the bottom of a horse saddle that gave the Huns an advantage when fighting on horseback with their enemies: reins or stirrups?

1440. What is the name for the group of Germanic people regarded as Barbarians that are most known for conquering Rome with destruction and looting: the Vandals or the Visigoths?

1441. What is the name for the nomadic tribe who took most of southern France from the Romans but were later forced out by the German Franks, and eventually settled in Spain: the Huns or the Visigoths?

1442. What is the name of the group that England is named for that took over Britain in the Middle Ages: the Angles or the Jutes?

1443. What is the name of the group of people who merged with the Angles in Britain that the Old English language originated from: the Visigoths or the Saxons?

1444. What is the term that was created by an Italian poet that refers to the Middle Ages after the fall of the Western Roman Empire, characterized by intellectual darkness, social chaos, warfare, and poverty: Medieval Times or Dark Ages?

1445. What is the name of the official religion of the Roman Empire that experienced significant growth during the Middle Ages: Judaism or Christianity?

1446. What is the name of the leader of the Christian church in Rome: the Pope or the Bishop?

1447. What is the other main religion besides Roman Catholicism that was formed in the Middle Ages: Orthodoxy or Judaism?

1448. What is the name for the men who devoted their lives to the church in the Middle Ages and lived in monasteries: monks or friars?

1449. What is the name for the women who devoted their lives to the church in the Middle Ages and studied the writings of the ancient Romans and Greeks: postulants or nuns?

1450. Who was the King of the Franks of Germany, expanded the Frankish Empire, and was also a former Roman Emperor whose name means "Charles the Great:" Charlemagne or Carlos?

1451. What is the term given for the legal and social system in medieval times in which service was exchanged for land: feudalism or serfdom?

1452. What were the three major groups of people during medieval times: nobility, church, and commoners, or lords, ladies, and serfs?

1453. Who was more powerful: the lord or the king?

1454. Who was the person that received a piece of land, acted as a servant, and promised loyalty to the lord: the serf or the vassal?

1455. Who was the person that owned the land in a feudal system: the lord or the vassal?

1456. What was the term used for the land grant contract that a lord provided to a vassal: a contract or a fief?

1457. Could vassals promise their loyalty to more than one lord?

1458. What is the medieval term for fighters supplied to the king by the lord: warriors or knights?

1459. What is the name of the lowest member of a feudal class that performed labor on the farms and manors owned by a lord: a serf or a knight?

1460. What is the name of the medieval stone structure where the lords and kings lived that provided protection form raids and attacks: a labyrinth or a castle?

1461. What is the medieval term for a traveling musician that entertained the children: a jester or a minstrel?

1462. What is the medieval term for a clown that entertained the children: a jester or a minstrel?

1463. What is the name of a game played on the lawn that many adults and children played during the Middle Ages: croquet or lacrosse?

1464. What is the medieval term for a young boy who did simple things like waiting on tables for noblemen and knights: a page or a servant?

1465. What could a medieval page become after seven years of faithful service to a nobleman, and was considered a trainee to a knight: a squire or a page?

1466. What is the name of the poem about a squire written by the English poet Geoffrey Chaucer during the Middle Ages: "The Canterbury Tales," or "Knights at the Roundtable?"

1467. Who might have a horse, weapons, and armor: a knight or a squire?

1468. Could Noble girls train to be knights, or were they typically trained to sew, weave, and spin?

1469. What is the medieval term for battles on horseback using lances: bullfighting or jousting?

1470. What is the medieval term for the code of conduct of a knight that included bravery, courtesy, and honor: chivalry or loyalty?

1471. Did many medieval towns have craftsmen, farmers, and traders?

1472. Did merchants and craftsmen hold power in medieval towns?

1473. What is the term for the association of medieval craftsmen that regulated prices and trace: a union or a guild?

1474. What is the term for a person that is learning a new trade: a master or an apprentice?

1475. What could an apprentice be promoted to after working for a master at least seven years: a master or a journeyman?

1476. What could a journeyman be promoted to after learning the trade at an expert level: an apprentice or a master?

1477. Was religion important in medieval days?

1478. Did medieval England become stronger when the Angles and the Saxons united under King Edward the Confessor and converted to Christianity?

1479. Was Normandy, France under Duke William a weak or a strong kingdom?

1480. Where did Duke William travel to in 1066 with several hundred ships and thousands of Knights in order to defeat and conquer King Harold and his Anglo-Saxon army: England or Spain?

1481. What was the other name of the newly-crowned King William I: William the Conqueror or William the Great?

1482. Did the Anglo-Saxons object when King William promoted his Norman knights to English noblemen, built castles in England, and collected taxes from them?

1483. What is the name of the person who became the King of England after the death of William the Conqueror: William II or Henry I?

1484. Did King Henry I and King Henry II inherit the throne after William II?

1485. Did Henry II establish a strong government and new law system that is the basis of court procedures as we know them today?

1486. Is King Henry II credited for establishing English Common Law?

1487. Did King John, King Henry's son, add to England's kingdom, or did he manage to give up much of England's land to France?

1488. Who were the wealthy people of England that had to give up some of their power to King John and pay more in taxes: counts, dukes, lords, and earls, or peasants, journeymen, serfs, and knights?

1489. What is the name of the document that was created initially in 1215 to limit the rights of King John, guaranteed the rights of the average citizen from the King of England, and helped lay the groundwork for English Common Law and, later, the U.S. Constitution: the Magna Carta, the Declaration of Independence, or The Bill or Rights?

1490. What did King John's grandson Edward I create to make the royal government stronger, consisting of knights and nobles who approved the laws of the king: a Parliament or an Assembly?

1491. What was the name given for the mysterious disease, now known as the Bubonic plague that killed millions of people in Europe in the 1300's, and showed up as dark patches on the skin: Yellow Fever, Black Death, or Measles?

1492. What is the name for the string of conflicts in France between the armies of the kings of France and England that lasted between 1337 and 1453, and ended when King Edward's son, "The Black Prince," captured King John II of France: The Hundred Years' War or The French and English War?

1493. What is the name of the peasant girl from medieval France who felt that she had a calling, led a French army to several victories during The Hundred Years War, forced the English out of Orleans, and was burned at the stake at the age of nineteen: Joan of Arc or Lady Antoinette?

1494. Do many people consider the end of the Middle Ages in 1453 the same as at the end of The Hundred Years War?

1495. What major empire ended in 1453 after Turkish invaders captured the capital of Constantinople: the Byzantine Empire or the Ottoman Empire?

1496. What are Christianity, Judaism, Buddhism, and Islam all regarded as: world races or world religions?

1497. What is the name of the religion that is practiced by over one billion Muslims, believing that there is one God, and that Mohammad is the prophet: Islam or Buddhism?

1498. What is the name of the holiest place in Saudi Arabia where Muslims believe that Mohammad received the word of God whom they call Allah, and is the pilgrimage for all Islam believers: Fatima or Mecca?

1499. What is the name for the shrine and the most sacred site in Mecca where Muslims go to pray: Kaaba or Quran?

1500. What is the name of the first domed shrine to be built in Jerusalem, Israel where Mohammad is said to have begun his rise to Heaven from the top of a rock: Dome of the Rock or The Great Mosque?

1501. What is the name of the city that Mohammad and his followers moved to after being forced out of Mecca due to conflicts with traders: Medina or Jerusalem?

1502. What is the Islamic name for the journey of Mohammad and his followers from Mecca to Medina that also marks the beginning of the Muslim calendar: Hijra or Quran?

1503. What is the general term for the Muslim place of worship that has towers from which worshippers are led in prayer five times a day: a Temple or a Mosque?

1504. What is the name of the Mosque in Mecca: The Grand Mosque or the Mosque of the Prophet?

1505. What is the name of the Mosque in Medina: The Grand Mosque or The Prophet's Mosque?

1506. What is the Islamic term for a Muslim war waged by those in defense of the Islamic faith, like that led by Mohammad against non-believers in Mecca: Hijra of Jihad?

1507. What is the name of the holy book of the Islamic religion written in Arabic that Muslims believe to be the word of God: the Quran or the Makkah?

1508. What is the term for the five rules that represent the five primary obligations of Muslims that include a profession of faith, prayer, giving alms to the poor, fasting during the holy month of Ramadan, and a pilgrimage to Mecca: The Five Islamic Rules or The Five Pillars of Islam?

1509. Did the Muslims conquer other places in the Middle East, Africa, and Spain after the death of Mohammad in order to spread the Islam religion?

1510. Did the Muslims live in Spain and build many mosques and palaces there?

1511. What is the name of the Moorish palace located in Granada, Spain and named for King Alhamar with its renowned Court of the Lions, and is regarded as an elaborate example of Arabic architecture: The Alcazar or the Alhambra?

1512. What is the name of the southern Spanish city that become a center of Muslim culture and further study of the Quran: Seville or Córdoba?

1513. Do Muslims consider Jerusalem a holy city?

1514. What was the name of the military conflicts between European Christians in the 11th, 12th, and 13th centuries who wanted to win back Jerusalem (the Holy Land) from the Muslims: The Crusades or The Holy Wars?

1515. What is the term for the numbers like 1, 2, and 3 that were first introduced by the Muslims and then taught these symbols to Europeans: Roman numerals or Arabic numerals?

1516. What is the name of the people of both Arab and Berber descent from northern Africa that occupied Spain and Portugal for several hundred years: The Moors or The Moroccans?

1517. What is the second largest continent in the world: Asia or Africa?

1518. What is the name of the largest desert in the world in northern Africa: Sahara or Kalahari?

1519. What is the name of the mountain range in northern Africa: Atlas or Pyrenees?

1520. What is the geographical term for a flat area of grass in a tropical region with tall grasses and only a few trees that is the habitat for many African animals: woodlands or savanna?

1521. What is the name of the world's deepest river located in Africa that is a big economic resource for the continent, and provides parts of Africa with hydroelectric power: the Nile or the Congo?

1522. On which continent are Egypt, Ethiopia, Nigeria, and Morocco located?

1523. Which country in Africa is known for its pyramids, tombs, and kings: Egypt or Morocco?

1524. What name did Egyptians use for *king* meaning supreme ruler: Pharaoh or Chariot?

1525. Did the ancient Egyptians regard the Pharaoh as a God?

1526. Did Pharaohs have a hierarchy of rulers under them?

1527. Were the wives of the Pharaohs second or third in power?

1528. What is the term for the leader of the Egyptian government: the Vizier or the Monarch?

1529. Did citizens pay taxes to support the government?

1530. What is the term for the period of rule when Kings or Pharaohs come from the same family for several generations: dynasty or regime?

1531. Was Egypt ruled by several dynasties?

1532. Was ancient Egypt divided into Upper and Lower Egypt, or Upper, Middle, and Lower Egypt?

1533. What is the name of the first pharaoh that united Upper Egypt and Lower Egypt into one single country: King Tut or King Menes?

1534. What was the capital of Egypt during the Old Kingdom era: Memphis or Thebes?

1535. What was the capital of Egypt during the New Kingdom era: Memphis or Thebes?

1536. What is the current capital of Egypt: Cairo or Thebes?

1537. What is the name of the Great Pyramids that were built during the Old Kingdom: Giza or Sphinx?

1538. Is the Great Pyramid of Giza known as the Pyramid of Cheops or the Pyramid of Khufu?

1539. Which pyramid in Egypt is the oldest and largest of three limestone pyramids that has a perfectly square base, and is the oldest of the Seven Wonders of the ancient world: the Pyramid of Teotihuacan or the Great Pyramid of Giza?

1540. What is the name of one of the greatest monumental limestone sculptures in the ancient world from 2500 B.C. that has a lion's body and the head of a Pharaoh, is near Giza, and is a national symbol of Egypt: the Great Pyramid or the Great Sphinx?

1541. What was the purpose of the Sphinx: to honor Pharaohs or to guard the temples and tombs?

1542. How long is the Great Sphinx: 240 feet long or 20 feet long?

1543. What feature of the Sphinx's face has been mysteriously knocked off: the nose or the ear?

1544. What is the name for the natural weathering that has affected the appearance of the Sphinx thousands of years later: erosion or sand storms?

1545. What is the name for the tall, narrow monument that the Egyptians built two of near the entrance of a sacred temple: obelisk or pillar?

1546. What is the name of the Queen of Egypt, wife of King Akhenaton that reigned between 1353 and1336 B.C., played an active role in religious life, and has a symbolic painted bust of her face because of her great beauty that is now located in Berlin's Egyptian Museum: Nefertiti or Cleopatra?

1547. What Egyptian Pharaoh became king at the age of 9, ruled Egypt between 1334 and 1325 B.C, and is known today primarily because of the 1922 discovery of his tomb in The Valley of the Kings: King Menes or King Tutankhamen?

1548. What is the name of the Pharaoh that is considered the greatest Pharaoh of Ancient Egypt that ruled from 1279 B.C. to 1213 B.C., was regarded as a great military leader, and built many temples during his reign: Ramses II or Menes?

1549. What is the name for the image on the crown of an Egyptian headdress worn only by pharaohs: cobra goddess or python goddess?

1550. Where is King Tutankhamen's tomb located in Egypt: The Valley of the Kings or The Valley of the Gods?

1551. Who discovered King Tut's tomb with over 5,000 artifacts including gold, chariots, statues, boats, jewelry, and his golden coffin: Howard Carter or Hiram Bingham?

1552. What was often found on the walls of tombs: paintings or carvings?

1553. What is the name of the book that many Egyptians wanted in their tomb that was written on papyrus or on the walls of the tomb, empowering them in the after-life and offering them protection through magic spells: the Book of Life or the Book of the Dead?

1554. Who has taken much of the valuable art and artifacts that had been buried inside Egyptian tombs: archeologists or vandals?

1555. What is the word for the Egyptian process of preserving or embalming a pharaoh or a person of wealth by wrapping the body with many layers of linen cloth in order to prepare it for the after-life: cremation or mummification?

1556. Did the Egyptians use arithmetic, algebra, geometry, and fractions in their calculations?

1557. What mathematical system did the Egyptians use to help build their pyramids and tombs, calculate time, land area, and cooking using the numbers 1, 10, and 100: the binary system or the decimal system?

1558. What is the term for the system of writing using pictures and symbols during one of the earliest dynasties: cave drawings or hieroglyphics?

1559. Did hieroglyphics use consonant sounds or vowel sounds?

1560. What is the name for the people of Egypt that could read and write hieroglyphics after years of practice, and typically came from rich families: pages or scribes?

1561. Could all ancient Egyptians read and write, or was it primarily scribes that could do this?

1562. What is the name of the stone that was discovered in Egypt by a French soldier that had the same message written in both hieroglyphics and in Greek that made it easy to translate: the Rosetta Stone or the Blarney Stone?

1563. What kind of job did most ancient Egyptians have: farmers, priests, soldiers, or craftspeople?

1564. Did the Egyptians wear make-up both for Sun protection and to make a fashion statement?

1565. What accessory did many Egyptians wear around their necks made of gold, silver, or copper?

1566. What were the houses of many ancient Egyptians made from: stone or mud bricks?

1567. What was the staple food of many commoner Egyptians: bread or meat?

1568. Who is credited for inventing locks, black ink, eye makeup, parchment paper from the papyrus plant, medicine, the ox plow, and the 365 day calendar: the Egyptians or the Ethiopians?

1569. What is the name of the people that conquered Africa in 525 B.C., ruled Africa for over one hundred years, and are renowned for their handcrafted rugs: the Persians or the Babylonians?

1570. What is the name for the ancient civilization south of Egypt known for trade and for pyramids, existing between 1000 B.C. and 300 A.D: The Kingdom of Kush or the Kingdom of Axum?

1571. What is the name of the King of ancient Greece in 336 B.C, began the dynasty that ruled Africa for 300 years after he conquered Egypt and the Persian Empire, and founded the city of Alexandria: Ibn Battuta or Alexander the Great?

1572. What is the name of the dynasty of 305 B.C. when Ptolemy I became the Pharaoh and Alexandria became the first capital: Ptolemaic or Persian?

1573. What is the name of the last pharaoh of Egypt that ruled Egypt after the death of Alexander the Great, could speak seven languages, had romances with Romans Julius Caesar and Marc Antony, and supposedly allowed a poisonous cobra snake to bite her after she heard of the death of Marc Antony: Cleopatra or Queen Nefertiti?

1574. What is the name for the valley in Egypt where tombs were constructed for the Pharaohs or Kings who ruled from 1500 B.C. to 1000 B.C: the Valley of the Kings or the Tombs of the Pharaohs?

1575. What is the name of the river that flows through Egypt south to north, is the longest river in the world, is a good place for farming wheat and papyrus because of its fertile, black soil, and provides a common means for transporting goods: the Congo or the Nile?

1576. What is the geographic term for the area where the Nile River splits into several branches before emptying into the Mediterranean: a delta or a tributary?

1577. Does Egypt have deserts, mountains, oases, and wetlands?

1578. What is the name for the plant grown near the Nile River that the Egyptians used to make parchment paper in order that they could write religious texts and important documents: Eucalyptus or Papyrus?

1579. What did the ancient Egyptians use to make ropes, sandals, and baskets: Papyrus or straw?

1580. What materials did the Egyptians build their boats with: papyrus reeds or birch bark?

1581. What kind of boats did ancient Egyptians build to navigate up and down the Nile in order to conduct trade with other countries: cargo ships or reed boats?

1582. What humped animal did traders bring back from Arabia around 400 A.D. that could go several days without water, carry a big load, and had the endurance to cross the Sahara Desert?

1583. What is the word for a group of travelers on a journey through the desert: a caravan or a convoy?

1584. What did many traders from western Africa trade their ivory tusks and gold for: salt or papyrus?

1585. Did the ancient Egyptians have an organized army?

1586. What is the name for the wheeled carriage pulled by two horses that would carry two Egyptian soldiers and their bows and arrows: a caravan or a chariot?

1587. What were the Kush, Axum, Ghana, Mali, and Songhai all considered: West African Empires or Egyptian Pharaohs?

1588. Who is the Muslim leader of Mali from Morocco who wrote about his travels that included his journey to the palace in Timbuktu: Mansa Musa or Ibn Battuta?

1589. What is the term for ancient African storytellers and entertainers who would tell a story a while singing, dancing, or playing the drum: gypsies or griots?

1590. How many independent nations are located in Africa: 54 or 82?

1591. Which continent is regarded as one of the most underdeveloped continents in the world?

1592. What disease do thousands of Africans die from every year, caused by a bite from a parasite-infected mosquito: Yellow Fever or Malaria?

1593. What is the estimated population of Africa: one billion or 500 million?

1594. What is the name of the scientist that theorized that our ancestors came from Africa: Jonas Salk or Charles Darwin?

1595. What is the biggest country in Africa: Sudan or Kenya?

1596. What is the highest point in Africa located in Tanzania: Mt. McKinley or Mt. Kilimanjaro?

1597. What is the name of the cape in South Africa on the Atlantic Ocean that explorer Vasco de Gama sailed around from Portugal in order to reach the east: Cape Cod or Cape of Good Hope?

1598. What is the name of the waterway that was built in 1869 that connects the Mediterranean with the Red Sea and took over ten years to build: The Panama Canal or The Suez Canal?

1599. What is the name of the dam across the Nile River completed in 1970 that has improved irrigation and agriculture in Egypt: the Niger Dam or the Aswan Dam?

1600. What is the name of the Egyptian President that signed a peace treaty with Israel's Prime Minister Menachem Begin in 1978: Anwar Sadat or Gamal Abdel Nasser?

1601. What is the name of the area in Africa that is named this because it was the primary source of ivory at the beginning of the 19th century: Ivory Coast or Tusk Terrain?

1602. What are the two main rivers in Africa: the Nile and the Congo, or the Nile and the Niger?

1603. What are the two main deserts in Africa: the Mojave and Atacama, or the Sahara and Kalahari?

1604. Could the Sahara desert fit into the borders of the United States?

1605. Where do many African animals live: the Sahara or the savanna?

1606. What African animals can you name that live in the savannas?

1607. What is the largest living land animal in Africa?

1608. Which animals might you see at the zoo that come from Africa?

1609. What country in Africa is famous for its jungles, safaris, wildlife preserves, and national parks where you can see many elephants, giraffes, lions, zebras, and rhinoceros: Nigeria or Kenya?

1610. Which African animal is considered the fastest land animal, running up to 60 miles per hour?

1611. What would Arabic, Swahili, French, and Portuguese be categorized as?

1612. How many different languages are spoken in Africa: 200 or 2000?

1613. Do you think that many African tribes speak their own, unique language?

1614. What is the most common language spoken in Africa: Arabic or French?

1615. What is the most common religion in Africa: Islam or Christianity?

1616. What is the name of the holiday that falls in the ninth month in the Islamic calendar, is a time of praying, fasting, and self- reflection, and is celebrated throughout the world by over one billion Muslims: Kwanzaa or Ramadan?

1617. What is the biggest island off the coast of Africa: Madagascar or the Canary Islands?

1618. What craft is Africa famous for: masks or puppets?

1619. What kind of musical instrument is Africa most famous for?

1620. What is the name of the civil rights activist that was elected President of South Africa in 1994 when the first democratic elections were held: Nelson Mandela or Muammar Gaddafi?

1621. What is the term for the racist political policy in South Africa that separated people based on their skin color, forcing blacks and whites to live apart until 1993: segregation or apartheid?

1622. What is the name of the divisive Libyan leader and dictator who ruled Libya for 42 years: Nelson Mandela or Muammar Gaddafi?

1623. Do many Africans celebrate both Muslim and Christian holidays depending on their beliefs?

1624. What is the name for the weeklong reflective holiday here in the United States that honors and celebrates African heritage and history: African Week or Kwanzaa?

1625. What is the name of the Disney movie and Broadway musical, based on an imaginary animal kingdom in Africa that included Simba, Mufasa, Nala, and Scar, and the songs "Circle of Life" and "Hakuna Matata: "Animal Kingdom" or "The Lion King?"

1626. If Africa is the second largest continent in the world, which one is the largest?

1627. How many countries make up the continent of Asia: 48 or 22?

1628. What is considered to be the smallest country in the world: Vatican City near Italy, or Monaco in the south of France?

1629. What is the largest country in the world: Canada or Russia?

1630. What is the third largest country after Russia and Canada: the United States or China?

1631. What best describes the historical time periods of China: dynasties or regimes?

1632. What is the name of the first emperor of China that founded the Qin Dynasty: Qin Shi Huang or Liu Xin?

1633. While Emperor of China, was Qin Shi Huang credited with establishing several provinces within the country, a central government, a common currency, a common system of writing, and improving the infrastructure of China with new roads and canals?

1634. What large stone structure extending 5,500 miles long and now considered one of the new wonders of the world did Qin Shi Huang begin construction on with more than one million workers, in order to protect China from northern invaders?

1635. What is the name of the baked clay that was used to build the 8,000 sculptures representing the armies of the first emperor of China, Qin Shi Huang: adobe or terracotta?

1636. What is the name of the dynasty that followed the harsh rule of the Qin Dynasty when the peasants revolted and killed Emperor Qin: Ming Dynasty or Han Dynasty?

1637. Did Liu Bang change his name to Han Gaozu when he founded and became the Emperor of the Han Dynasty?

1638. Is the Han Dynasty credited with the inventions of paper, crop rotation, and iron casting?

1639. What is the name for the social code of behavior and the philosopher whose ideas were followed during the Han Dynasty: Copernicus or Confucius?

1640. What is the name for the administrative system of the Chinese government that began with the Han Dynasty, lasted for over 2,000 years, and created educated government workers who were required to pass a difficult exam: civil service or military service?

1641. Did Confucius have a philosophy of always treating others with respect, along with other rules for good behavior?

1642. What did the Han Emperors establish in order that the people would be educated and intelligent: schools or writing tablets?

1643. What is the name of the fabric originally from China that comes from the cocoons of silkworms, and was an important trade product?

1644. Did the Chinese Emperors want to keep the silk-making process a secret and were they successful for over 1,000 years?

1645. What was the most popular embroidered design on silk clothing: birds and flowers, or animals and stripes?

1646. What was a symbol of status in China: clothing or jewelry?

1647. Would a person wearing silk more likely be from the upper class or the lower class?

1648. What was the name of the trade route between China and the East and the Mediterranean that was a great source of wealth for them: The Silk Road or the Textile Trail?

1649. Was the Silk Road important for trade and commerce, or for traveling to other parts of Asia?

1650. Were many silk paintings and sculptures created during the Han Dynasty?

1651. What was the name of the religion that many Chinese people followed during the Han Dynasty that focused on a new awakening: Buddhism or Taoism?

1652. What Chinese dynasty followed the Han and then the Sui Dynasty: Tang or Ming?

1653. What industry was important during the Tang Dynasty, transporting silk, pearls, spices, and fine porcelains from one place to another in caravans: trading or road-building?

1654. What animal would the Chinese travel on in a caravan on the trade route: a horse or a camel?

1655. What was invented during the Tang Dynasty that allowed for the mass production of a book: woodblock printing or the printing press?

1656. What is the first full-length product that was produced using Chinese woodblock printing?

1657. What product was invented in its early form during the Tang Dynasty and was used for fireworks because the Chinese beleived that it scared off evil spirits: dynamite or gunpowder?

1658. What is the name of the Chinese ceramic that was developed during the Tang Dynasty: Porcelain or Bone China?

1659. What genre of literature besides the writing of short stories became very widespread and was a very important aspect of Chinese culture during the Tang Dynasty: novels or poetry?

1660. What religion emerged after Buddhism lost its place during the Tang Dynasty: Confucianism or Islam?

1661. What hot drink became popular during the Tang Dynasty: coffee or tea?

1662. What type of paper that is used in the bathroom was invented during the Tang Dynasty?

1663. What kind of money was first developed and used during the Tang Dynasty: coins or paper?

1664. What great structure in China continued to be built and re-built to keep out northern invaders during the Tang Dynasty?

1665. Did the Song Dynasty come before or after the Tang Dynasty?

1666. What two things were invented during the Song Dynasty: the magnetic compass and the iron plow, or the clock and the wheel?

1667. What was printed in great quantities through a newly-invented process called moveable type that made it possible for more people in China to read?

1668. Was the Song Dynasty one of the most advanced civilizations in the world?

1669. What product became an import crop during the Song Dynasty, yielding two harvests per year: corn or rice?

1670. What type of architecture was popular during the Song Dynasty: imperial palaces or tall pagodas?

1671. What is the name of the country to the north of China: India or Mongolia?

1672. What is the name of the desert located in Mongolia: Mojave or Gobi?

1673. Which civilization invented writing, the magnetic compass, gunpowder, the boat rudder, moveable sails, the mechanical clock, the umbrella, porcelain, the wheelbarrow, the spinning wheel, moveable type, seismographs, stirrups, matches, acupuncture, paper money, kites, tea, and ice cream: the Mongolians or the Chinese?

1674. What is the name of the calculator that was invented by the Chinese that used sliding beads to compute equations: the abacus or the compass?

1675. When Khan from Mongolia defeated the Chinese Emperor and became the new Emperor of China, what city did he establish as his home, the city that is still the capital of China today: Hong Kong or Beijing?

1676. What did the Mongol Emperors establish to promote caravan trade over long distances whereby sellers of silks, spices, porcelains and other products could travel in a single caravan with minimal risk of losing profits: merchant associations or trade associations?

1677. What is the name of the Italian explorer and trader who traveled over 24 years throughout China trading jewels and lamp oil: Marco Polo or Lawrence of Arabia?

1678. What road did Marco Polo travel along in China: the Silk Road or the Imperial Parkway?

1679. What is the name of the dynasty after the Mongols were driven out of China, was led by a self-appointed emperor named Zhu, and lasted three centuries: Ming or Zheng?

1680. What specific handiwork is the Ming Dynasty known for: porcelain pottery or woodcarvings?'

1681. What color is Ming porcelain pottery before it is glazed: brown or white?

1682. What color was the preferred colored glaze to paint on the porcelain vases: blue or red?

1683. What did Europeans call the Ming porcelain that they traded for: pottery or china?

1684. What fabric did Chinese artists paint birds, animals, and landscapes on: canvas or silk scrolls?

1685. What is the name of the art of fancy handwriting of the Chinese that uses brushes and ink to make pictures and symbols: cursive or calligraphy?

1686. What did the Chinese consider calligraphy, poetry, and painting: the Three Perfections or the Three Arts?

1687. What did the Chinese often use in their artworks: lacquer or oil paint?

1688. What is regarded as the highest form of Chinese painting: birds or landscapes?

1689. What is the name of the 5,500 mile-long wall with over 7,000 lockout towers that the Ming Dynasty peasants helped to complete with bricks?

1690. Is the Great Wall of China considered the longest or the widest man-made structure in the world?

1691. What hauling machine did the Chinese invent to help them build the Great Wall of China: the wheelbarrow or the shovel?

1692. What is the name of the Chinese canal built during the Ming Dynasty that helped the trade industry in China, and is the world's longest artificial river: Great Canal or Grand Canal?

1693. What is another name for the imperial palace built by emperors in Beijing China, considered the largest ancient palace in the world: the Taj Mahal or the Forbidden City?

1694. What Chinese building also served as a fortress complete with a moat, lookout towers, and guards: Imperial Palace or Chinese Temple?

1695. How many Chinese Emperors lived in the Imperial Palace over 500 years: 5 or 24?

1696. Did China have a fleet of explorer ships under the Chinese Admiral Zheng He before or after Columbus and his voyages in 1492?

1697. Which countries did Zheng He help to establish trade with as the commander of his treasure ship voyages: India and Africa, or America and Canada?

1698. What were Taoism, Confucianism, and Buddhism: religions or philosophies?

1699. What is the name of the country south of China, the birthplace of Buddha in 563 BC, whose teachings emphasize the rebirth of the self: Mongolia or Nepal?

1700. What is the name for the Taoism philosophy that everything in nature has two balancing forces like hot and cold or dark and light: Yin and Yang or Feng Shui?

1701. What is the name for the Chinese system for positioning a structure or the objects within a structure in such a way as to be in harmony with spiritual forces: Yin and Yang or Feng Shui?

1702. What are the two major rives in China: the Yellow and the Yangtze, or the Tigres and Euphrates?

1703. What animal is the symbol of power and good luck in China: the panda or the dragon?

1704. What is the dragon a symbol of: imperial power or the Chinese New Year?

1705. Which holiday is the biggest holiday for the Chinese: Christmas or the New Year?

1706. What utensils do the Chinese use to eat with?

1707. What is the name of a tall grass with a hollow stem that the Chinese use to make furniture, buildings, and musical instruments: bamboo or sugar cane?

1708. What animal lives near the Yangtze River in China, eats bamboo, and is considered an endangered species: the Giant Panda or the Siberian Tiger?

1709. Where are many ginseng plants and bonsai trees grown: Nepal or China?

1710. What number is considered lucky in Chinese culture: two or four?

1711. What is each year in the Chinese calendar named after: a flower or an animal?

1712. What is the name of the major mountain range in China: the Himalayas or the Pyrenees?

1713. What is the name of the tallest mountain on Earth located between China and Nepal: Mt. McKinley or Mt. Everest?

1714. What is considered to be the second tallest mountain on Earth located on the border between China and Pakistan: Mt Everest or K2?

1715. What is the most populous country on Earth: Russia or China?

1716. What is the official name for China: the People's Republic of China or the Emperor's Republic of China?

1717. What is the name for the place on the southern coast of China that is considered a special administrative region, is an important port for exporting goods, and has several attractions including Ocean Park, Victoria Bay, Victoria Peak and Disneyland: Shanghai or Hong Kong?

1718. Is China a Communist country where the Chinese government controls all economic activity and the people are given little power to elect officials, or a Republic country where the people have the power to elect government officials?

1719. What is the current capital of China: Beijing or Shanghai?

1720. What is the name of the square in the center of Beijing that is named for the gate that is located to the north of the square, separating it from the Forbidden City: Tiananmen Square or Beijing Square?

1721. What is the most populated city of China: Beijing or Shanghai?

1722. What is the name of the official language of China: Cantonese or Mandarin?

1723. How many main groups of Chinese dialects are there in China: seven or twelve?

1724. Do many Chinese people also speak English?

1725. Is the Chinese language written with letters or with symbols?

1726. What cuisine would the following foods be categorized as: wonton soup, Peking duck, rice, noodles, egg rolls, dumplings, tofu, tea, and stir-fry prepared in a large pan called a wok?

1727. What article of clothing is traditionally removed before entering a house in an Asian country?

1728. What are the two main Chinese folk dances called: the Lion Dance and the Dragon Dance, or the Tiger Dance and the Panda Dance?

1729. What is the name of the martial art that originated in ancient China and is still widely practiced today: Kung Fu or Karate?

1730. What is the name for the twelve Chinese animal signs that symbolize when a person was born that include a rat, an ox, a tiger, a rabbit, a dragon, a snake, a horse, a sheep, a monkey, a rooster, a dog, and a pig: zodiac or horoscope?

1731. In the year 1492, who "sailed the ocean blue?"

1732. What is the century of the 1500's called because it was the time of European explorers and conquerors like Hernando Cortés, Ferdinand Magellan, Francisco Pizarro, and Sir Walter Raleigh who founded the first English colony in North America: The Reformation or the Age of Discovery?

1733. Which period is known as the time of writers like Miguel Cervantes and William Shakespeare, scientists like Johannes Kepler, Galileo Galilei, and Isaac Newton, conflicts in England regarding the monarchy and religion, the establishment of Jamestown, and the arrival of the Pilgrims on the Mayflower from England to Plymouth, Massachusetts: 1600's or 1700's?

1734. Which country ruled the American colonies in the 1700's: France or Great Britain?

1735. What is the name of the war between 1754 and 1763 that arose over a dispute regarding land in the Ohio Valley, when the British defeated the French and the Native American Indians: the French and British War or the French and Indian War?

1736. What was the French and Indian War referred to as in England: the French and Indian War, or the Seven Years War?

1737. What did Britain want to collect from the American colonists in order to help pay for the costs of the French and Indian War: land treaties or taxes?

1738. What became the rally cry of the colonists who felt that the British government did not have the right to tax them given that the colonists did not have any of their own representatives in the British Parliament: "no taxation without representation" or "unfair tax act?"

1739. What is the name of the tax law that the British government passed in 1765 that required the colonists to pay a tax on all printed materials like newspapers and legal documents, and had an official British seal on it that was proof that the tax was paid: the Tax Act or the Stamp Act?

1740. Did the colonies willingly pay the taxes to the British, or did they protest and boycott British products?

1741. What is the name of the congress formed by the American colonies that gathered in 1765 with the goal of preparing a formal protest of the British taxes: the Stamp Act Congress or the Colonial Congress?

1742. What is the name of the group that was formed by some American patriots, led by Samuel Adams, opposing the taxes on them by the British Parliament, a group that wanted to protect the rights of the colonists: the Colonies for Fair Representation, or the Sons of Liberty?

1743. What is the name for the new series of tax laws, established in 1767 by Britain on American colonists that placed a tax on paper, tea, glass, and paint: the Colonial Tax Act or the Townshend Acts?

1744. Did the colonists accept the taxes as established by the Townshend Acts, or did the colonists protest and start to rebel because they felt that these tax laws violated their rights?

1745. What is the name of the event in 1770 that occurred when the tension between 50 colonists and British soldiers that were gathered outside the Custom House in Boston became so high that the soldiers fired into the crowd killing five colonists: the Boston Tea Party or the Boston Massacre?

1746. What is the name of the protest in 1773 by the American colonists against Britain's new law that only the high priced tea of the British East India Company could be sold in America, and so they proceeded to dress up like Native American Mohawk Indians, board three ships in Boston Harbor, and throw 342 crates of valuable tea into the water: the Boston Tea Protest or the Boston Tea Party?

1747. What is the name that was given by American patriots to the new set of five laws passed by Britain's Parliament in 1774 as punishment for the Boston Tea Party that included closing Boston Harbor, and further limited the rights of the colonists: the Townshend Acts or the Intolerable Acts?

1748. What is the name of the first assembly of 12 representatives from the colonies that met in Philadelphia in 1774 to write a letter to King George III of England demanding that he repeal the new taxes of the Intolerable Acts, as well as to make a plan to meet again in May of 1775 if their demands were not met: The First Colonial Congress or the First Continental Congress?

1749. Which founding father and member of the First Continental Congress made the statement in 1775, "I am not a Virginian, I am an American," and rallied his people to join Massachusetts against the British with his famous speech that ended with, "give me liberty or give me death:" John Adams or Patrick Henry?

1750. What is the name of the famous pamphlet written by Thomas Paine in 1776 that demanded complete independence from Britain, and quickly sold over 100,000 copies in a few months: The Declaration of Independence or "Common Sense?"

1751. Who is credited for saying, "lead, follow, or get out of the way:" Thomas Paine or George Washington?

1752. What is the term for the people who wanted the American colonies to gain their independence from Britain, and included Thomas Jefferson, John Adams, Benjamin Franklin, George Washington, and Samuel Adams: loyalists or patriots?

1753. What are American patriots like Washington, Jefferson, Adams, and Franklin also regarded as: Founding Fathers or Revolutionaries?

1754. What is the term for the people who lived in the American colonies who wanted to remain British citizens and remain loyal to the king: patriots or loyalists?

1755. What are the two places in Massachusetts where the colonists concealed their guns and ammunition in preparation for the war with the British: Boston and Bunker Hill or Lexington and Concord?

1756. Were the Sons of Liberty and the colonists keeping an eye on the British in case they needed to warn other colonists of an attack?

1757. What is the name of the rider whose job it was to cross the Charles River on horseback to Charleston and then to Lexington to warn John Hancock and Samuel Adams that the British were coming during his famous "midnight ride:" Paul Revere or Patrick Henry?

1758. What is the name of the other rider that set out to warn the colonists so that they would be prepared and could better fight off a British attack: Patrick Henry or William Dawes?

1759. What did the colonist Robert Newman display in the steeple of the Old North Church on the night of April 18, 1775 as a warning to the colonists how the British would attack, "one if by land, two if by sea," the "sea" being the Charles River: candles or lanterns?

1760. What was the common way to refer to the British troops because of the bright red uniforms they wore: Redcoats or Redjackets?

1761. What did Revere and Dawes yell as a warning to their fellow patriots: "the British are coming," "the Redcoats are coming," or neither, as they did not want to risk getting caught?

1762. What are the two battles that signaled the start of the Revolutionary War: Boston and Bunker Hill, or Lexington and Concord?

1763. Did Samuel Adams and John Hancock manage to escape the British in Lexington thanks to the warnings of Paul Revere?

1764. What is another name for American militiamen, so called because they could be ready to fight with just a minute's notice: Militiamen or Minutemen?

1765. Did the American side have both a militia of ordinary citizens and a Continental Army of trained soldiers?

1766. What was the main weapon during the Revolutionary War: bows or muskets?

1767. Where was the first shot fired that later became known as "the shot heard around the world," written in a poem by Ralph Waldo Emerson: Concord or Lexington?

1768. Who was the first shot fired by in Lexington: a Redcoat, a Minuteman, or is it still uncertain?

1769. Which side won battle at the North Bridge in Concord: the British or the Americans?

1770. What is the name of the city that the British forced to retreat to: Lexington or Boston?

1771. Who led the British troops: Lieutenant Colonel Francis Smith or Captain John Parker?

1772. Who led the American troops: Lieutenant Colonel Francis Smith or Captain John Parker?

1773. What are the two hills that the British wanted to control so that they would have a tactical advantage and maintain control of the sea ports: Bunker and Breeds or Concord and Lexington?

1774. Did the Battle of Bunker Hill actually take place on that hill, or did it take place on Breeds Hill, mistakenly called Bunker Hill by the British army?

1775. Which side ultimately won the Battle of Bunker Hill in part because the other side ran out of ammunition, and claimed victory even though it had more casualties and wounded: British or American?

1776. What were the American soldiers told by their commanders because they were so low on ammunition: "Do not fire until you see the whites of their eyes," or "Do not fire until you see the reds of their coats?"

1777. Which side had 30,000 professional soldiers to the other side's 15,000 colonial farmers, and 270 navy ships to the other side's eight: the British or the Americans?

1778. What were two advantages of the American side: ammunition and weapons, or knowledge of the land and determination for freedom?

1779. What is the name of the congress, led by John Hancock that met in order to discuss further strategy to form an army, fight the British, and declare their independence: the Second American Congress, or the Second Continental Congress?

1780. Who did the members of the Second Continental Congress elect in 1775 as the General of the Continental Army: George Washington or Benjamin Franklin?

1781. What bird did John Adams and Thomas Jefferson, members of the Continental Congress, choose to symbolize the United States: the hawk or the eagle?

1782. How many African Americans fought in the Continental Army: 500 or 5,000?

1783. Which representative was chosen by the Second Continental Congress and the members of the Committee of Five to write the first draft of the letter that would declare the United States independent from Britain: Benjamin Franklin or Thomas Jefferson?

1784. What is the date that the final version of the Declaration of Independence was adopted by the Second Continental Congress: July 4, 1776 or June 11, 1776?

1785. On what date does America celebrate its independence every year?

1786. How many members of the Congress signed the Declaration of Independence: 38 or 56?

1787. Who was the first congress member to write his signature, five inches long, on the Declaration of Independence: George Washington or John Hancock?

1788. Were copies of the Declaration of Independence sent to all thirteen colonies, as well as to Britain?

1789. Does the Declaration essentially declare that all states in North America be free and independent states, and that America is its own free country moving forward?

1790. Where is the original Declaration of Independence on display today: the Smithsonian Institution or the National Archives?

1791. Was the Revolutionary war still going on after the signing of the Declaration?

1792. What did George Washington offer to encourage more people to join the troops: money, land, or money and land?

1793. What is the name of the river that George Washington crossed with his army on a snowy, Christmas night in a surprise attack on the British, was a victory for the American troops, and helped to revitalize the Continental Army: Potomac or Delaware?

1794. What did the Second Continental Congress decide that the country needed to represent the united colonies that would have thirteen red and white stripes and a blue area with thirteen stars, and passed a Resolution to accomplish this on June 14, 1777?

1795. When do we celebrate Flag Day, originally observed in Waubeka, Wisconsin at Stoney Hill School in 1885, officially approved as a day national observance by Congress, and signed into law by President John Truman: June 14th or July 4th?

1796. Has the American flag gone through many transformations since the original version of 1777?

1797. How many stars are on the American flag currently?

1798. What are "Old Glory," "The Star-Spangled Banner," and "Stars and Stripes" nicknames for?

1799. What is the name of the battle that was won by the American troops in New York in 1777 after the surrender of the British General and over 6,000 British soldiers, and was a turning point in the Revolutionary War for the American side: Yorktown or Saratoga?

1800. Which European country did Ben Franklin convince to support the American effort after the Battle of Saratoga, resulting in this country sending military aid to America: France or Spain?

1801. Which European country sent several ships to America in 1778 providing them with weapons and setting up blockades so that the British could not receive supplies?

1802. Did many women help out the Revolutionary War effort?

1803. What is the name of the war General that helped the Americans win several battles including Saratoga, but was and is regarded as a traitor after he changed sides, acted as a spy, and sold American military secrets to the British: Benedict Arnold or Samuel Adams?

1804. What is the name of the place near Philadelphia where the Continental Army made their camp during the harsh winter of 1777-1778, and the place where the military leaders of George Washington of the American Continental Army, General von Steuben of Prussia, and General Marquis de Lafayette of France all helped to train the army: Yorktown or Valley Forge?

1805. What is the name of the last battle of the American Revolutionary War that took place in Virginia, lasted 20 days, and ended when British General Cornwallis and the out-numbered British army surrendered to Washington and the American troops with the showing of a white flag: Valley Forge or Yorktown?

1806. What is the name of the official peace treaty between Britain and the United States that was signed on September 3rd, 1783 in France that officially ended the American Revolutionary War, and was finally ratified by King George III of England in 1784: The Treaty of Trent or the Treaty of Paris?

1807. What is the name of the war in America between the British and the American Colonists that lasted from 1775-1783?

1808. Did each of the thirteen states in the United States have to create and adopt their own state constitution after the Revolutionary War?

1809. What document did the members develop that helped to establish a central government, was finally ratified by the thirteen states in 1781, and is regarded as our first constitution: the Articles of Confederation or the Bill of Rights?

1810. What is the name for the uprising that took place in Massachusetts in 1786 by farmers protesting high taxes, tax collectors, and foreclosures on farms that further emphasized the need for a strong central government: Farmers' Revolt or Shays' Rebellion?

1811. What is the name of the first plan that James Madison of Virginia and other delegates drafted in 1787 in Philadelphia proposing a strong central government while maintaining citizens' basic rights, and contained specific ideas that would become part of the U.S. Constitution: the Virginia Plan or the Constitution?

1812. What is the name for the series of 85 newspaper articles written by James Madison, Alexander Hamilton, and John Jay in 1787 that were published anonymously promoting the ratification of the U.S. Constitution: the Constitution Papers or the Federalist Papers?

1813. What is the name of the first ten amendments to the Constitution written by George Mason and James Madison, reflect the American ideals of liberty, a limited government, and the rule of law: The Preamble or the Bill of Rights?

1814. What is the name of the meeting of the delegates of colonial America in 1787 to discuss Madison's Virginia Plan and the structure of the central government, and outlined the roles of the executive branch, the legislative branch, and the judicial branch: The Constitutional Convention or the Philadelphia Convention?

1815. Which branch of government carries out the laws of the country, and is led by the President: legislative, executive, or judicial?

1816. Which branch of government includes the justices and the courts, and interprets the laws and the constitution: executive, legislative, or judicial?

1817. Which branch of government makes the laws, and includes the Senate and the House of Representatives, collectively called the Congress: legislative, executive, or judicial?

1818. What is the name of the solution to the issue of fair representation in the legislative branch of the government that would give each state equal representation in the Senate and representation in the House of Representatives based on its population: the Connecticut Compromise or the Virginia Compromise?

1819. What two bodies make up the United States Congress?

1820. How many senators does each state have in the Senate: two or four?

1821. How many total senators are in the United States Senate?

1822. How many House Representatives does each state have: the number proportional to the population of that state, or four representatives?

1823. How many total representatives are there in the U.S. House of Representatives: 400 or 435?

1824. What is the name of the compromise that was reached by the delegates in 1787 at the Constitutional Convention regarding representation based on state population and whether or not that would include slaves, agreeing that "free persons" would count as one, and slaves or "non-free persons" would count as three-fifths of a person: The Slavery Compromise or the Three-Fifths Compromise?

1825. How many years was proposed by the delegates to wait before passing any new laws that would regulate the slave trade: 10 or 20?

1826. What is considered the supreme law of the United States and the binding agreement among all people: The Bill of Rights or The U.S. Constitution?

1827. What is the name for the introduction to the U.S. Constitution that states: "We the People of the United States, in order to form a more perfect Union, establish justice, insure domestic tranquility, provide for the common defense, promote the general welfare, and secure the blessings of liberty to ourselves and our posterity, do ordain and establish this Constitution for the United States of America:" the Bill of Rights or the Preamble?

1828. What is the name for the system that the writers of the Constitution devised so that each of the three branches of the government limits the power of the others, ensuring that no one branch becomes too powerful: checks and balances, or branch monitoring?

1829. Does the President have the power to oppose or "veto" a law that is passed?

1830. In what year was the U.S. Constitution approved by all states: 1776 or 1790?

1831. What is the word for a change or an alteration: an amendment or a bill?

1832. What is the name for the first 10 amendments to the U.S. Constitution: the Preamble or the Bill of Rights?

1833. Which amendment in the Bill of Rights guarantees the freedom of religion, freedom of speech, freedom of the press, the freedom to assemble, and the freedom to petition: the First Amendment or the Second Amendment?

1834. Does each state have a government with the three different branches and a constitution?

1835. Who is the executive leader of the United States government: the President or the Congress?

1836. Who is leader of the state government: the senator or the governor?

1837. What is the name of the current governor of the state you live in?

1838. Who is the leader of the city government: the mayor or the alderman?

1839. What is the name of the current mayor of the city you live in?

1840. What do we pay to the local, state, and federal governments to run them and pay for schools, roads, and the salaries of public workers: duties or taxes?

1841. Is it important for American citizens to participate in some way in the government?

1842. Which president stated in 1863 that government should be "of the people, by the people, and for the people:" President Lincoln or President Johnson?

1843. Who became the first President of the United States in 1789 and is considered to be "the Father of the Country?"

1844. Who was the first "First Lady" of the United States, the wife of George Washington: Martha Washington or Abigail Washington?

1845. Who was the first Vice-President of the United States: John Adams or Thomas Jefferson?

1846. What is the term for the group of advisors to the President of the United States: Secretaries or Cabinet?

1847. Is the Vice-President of the United States considered a member of the President's Cabinet?

1848. What is the term for each cabinet member in the United States each of whom is in charge of a specific area of government: Secretary or Ambassador?

1849. How many executive departments make up the President's cabinet: 10 or 15?

1850. What is the name for the Secretary that handles international relations: Secretary of State or Secretary of Defense?

1851. Are there executive departments led by Secretaries for Agriculture, Education, Defense, Energy, Health, Homeland Security, Labor, State, Transportation, and the Treasury?

1852. Is the Attorney General considered part of the President's Cabinet?

1853. Who was the Secretary of State to George Washington: Thomas Jefferson or Alexander Hamilton?

1854. Who was the Secretary of the Treasury to George Washington: Thomas Jefferson or Alexander Hamilton?

1855. How many years are considered one term for a U.S. President: two or four?

1856. How many terms is a U.S. President limited to, according to the Constitution: two or four?

1857. Do candidates that run for a government typically represent a specific political party?

1858. What was the political party of Thomas Jefferson and his followers: Democratic-Republican or Federalist?

1859. What was the political party of Alexander Hamilton and his followers: Republican or Federalist?

1860. What were the country's first two political parties: Democratic-Republican and Libertarian, or Democratic-Republican and Federalist?

1861. What are the two main political parties in the United States currently: Republican and Democrat, or Federalist and Libertarian?

1862. What was the first capital of the United States: Boston or New York City?

1863. What is the present day capital of the United States of America?

1864. What is the name of the official residence of the President of the United States, located in Washington, D.C. that started with President John Adams?

1865. What is the name of Washington's home in Virginia that he retired to after his presidency: Mount Vernon or Monticello?

1866. What is the name of the office building in Washington, D.C. that houses the United States Congress: the U.S. Capitol or the White House?

1867. Who was the second President of the United States: Thomas Jefferson or John Adams?

1868. Who was the Vice-President to second President John Adams: Madison or Jefferson?

1869. What is the name of the wife of John Adams and the mother of our 6th President John Quincy Adams, who believed in equal rights for all people, including women and blacks: Martha Adams or Abigail Adams?

1870. Who was the third President of the United States and the principle author of the Declaration of Independence: Thomas Jefferson or Alexander Hamilton?

1871. Who owned the land west of the Mississippi from Canada to Mexico during the early years of Jefferson's Presidency: France or Spain?

1872. What is the name of the French territory that was named for the King of France, King Louis the Fourteenth: St. Louis or Louisiana?

1873. Whom did Jefferson ask Secretary James Monroe to talk with in France about the sale of the French territory collectively known as Louisiana: Napoleon Bonaparte or King Louis XIV?

1874. What is the name of the land deal of 1803 when President Jefferson bought Iowa, Missouri, Arkansas, Nebraska, Kansas, Oklahoma, South Dakota and parts of other states for $15 million dollars from France, nearly doubling the size of the United States: the American Acquisition or the Louisiana Purchase?

1875. What two explorers did President Jefferson ask in 1804 to explore the west, the newly purchased Louisiana Territory, and along the way met several Native American Tribes including a Shoshone Indian, Sacajawea, who helped them as an interpreter: Lewis and Clark, or Henry Hudson and Marco Polo?

1876. How many years was the expedition of Lewis and Clark, a journey that included navigating the Great Falls in Montana as well as the rugged Rocky Mountains while on foot, on horseback, and in canoes: one year or two years?

1877. How did Lewis and Clark document their findings on their expedition regarding geographical features, the Missouri River, weather, over 180 plant species, and over 120 mammals, reptiles, birds, and fish including grizzly bear, buffalo, woodpeckers, sheep, deer, prairie dogs and trout: kept detailed written journals, or shared their observations with the Indians?

1878. Who was the fourth President of the United States: James Monroe or James Madison?

1879. What is the name of the two-year war in the early 1800's between the United States and Britain that arose over trade, shipping, and naval law disagreements: the Seven Years War or the War of 1812?

1880. What is the name of U.S. naval ship nicknamed "Old Ironsides," that managed to capture 24 enemy ships during the War of 1812: USS Constitution or the USS Enterprise?

1881. What symbolic building was burned in the Battle of Washington that was re-built and painted white to duplicate the lime-based whitewash that was applied to this building in 1798: The Capitol or The White House?

1882. What is the name of the treaty that was signed in 1814 to end the War of 1812 giving the United States a victory: the Treaty of Paris or the Treaty of Ghent?

1883. What is the name for the final battle of 1812 won convincingly by the Americans, led by General Andrew Jackson, occurring 15 days after the Treaty of Ghent was signed because neither side was aware of the existing peace treaty: the Battle of New Orleans or the Battle of Louisiana?

1884. Who was the fifth President of the United States, elected in 1816, re-elected in 1820, and has a foreign policy doctrine named for him that opposed further European colonization and interference with nations in the western hemisphere: James Monroe or James Madison?

1885. Was slavery an issue in the colonial America in 1820?

1886. Which part of the country owned slaves and depended on them to work on their large plantations and farms: the North or the South?

1887. Which part of the country did not own slaves and earned a living by working in factories or managing a small farm: the North or the South?

1888. What is the term used to refer to people that wanted to abolish or do away with slavery: revolutionists or abolitionists?

1889. What is the name of the compromise that served to maintain the balance of slavery between the anti-slavery North and the pro-slavery South that allowed Missouri to enter the Union as a slave state, and Maine to enter the Union as a free state: the Missouri Compromise or the Maine Compromise?

1890. What is the name of the proclamation by President James Monroe in his address to Congress in 1823 that stated that the United States would not tolerate any European presence, intervention, or colonization in the Western Hemisphere, and that the United States would assume a neutral role in European affairs: the Monroe Plan or the Monroe Doctrine?

1891. Who was the sixth President of the United States who opposed slavery, supported freedom of speech, and only served one term: Andrew Jackson or John Quincy Adams?

1892. Who was the seventh President of the United States elected in 1828, was a commander in the war of 1812, was known as the "people's president," removed Native American Cherokees from their land, is pictured on the U.S. twenty dollar bill, and the capital of Mississippi is named for him: Andrew Jackson or Andrew Johnson?

1893. What was President's Jackson goal regarding Indian land: transfer Indian land into U.S. territory, or allow all Native American Indians to keep their land?

1894. What is the name of the bill that President Jackson convinced Congress to pass in 1830 that would allow the government to force the Native Americans to Indian Territory, more than 1,000 miles away: the Indian Removal Act or the Indian Reservation Act?

1895. What is the name given for the forced relocation of Native American Cherokee Indians from their homeland of Georgia to the Indian Territory of Oklahoma, and was so named because of the brutal journey that it was: the March of Pain or the Trail of Tears?

1896. What is the term for a person that takes action to improve social or economic conditions: reformer or revolutionary?

1897. What is the name of the lady that believed in the rights of the mentally ill, and their treatment in institutions in the early 1800's: Dorothea Dix or Clara Barton?

1898. What is the name of the reformer of American education who worked to improve public schools and the number of children attending those schools: Horace Mann or Dorothea Dix?

1899. Who are the two women who believed in equality and women's rights, and organized a convention in Seneca Falls, New York in 1848: Lucretia Mott and Elizabeth Stanton, or Elizabeth Stanton and Amelia Bloomer?

1900. What is the name of the editor of a magazine who attended a convention in Seneca, New York promoting the right of women to wear comfortable clothing, and had bloomers, the short pants worn under a skirt, named for her: Amelia Bloom or Amelia Bloomer?

1901. Who is the African American woman, abolitionist, and women's rights activist who was born into slavery, gained her freedom in 1827, and developed a great following after her 1851 speech, "Ain't I a Woman," at the Ohio Women's Rights Convention: Sojourner Truth or Harriet Tubman?

Social Studies – 5th Grade

1902. What is the name of the study of the Earth's surface that includes the climate, vegetation, and soil: geology or geography?

1903. What is the meaning of "geo:" Earth or planet?

1904. What is the name for the sphere that is made up of all the Earth's gases: lithosphere or atmosphere?

1905. What is the name for the sphere that is the solid, rigid outer layer of the Earth, and includes physical materials like soil and rocks: lithosphere or hydrosphere?

1906. What is the name for the sphere that is made up of all the Earth's water, and includes the water on the surface, the water underground, and the water in the air: atmosphere or hydrosphere?

1907. What are two geographical reference points in the Earth to describe a location: equator and prime meridian, or the Tropics of Cancer and Capricorn?

1908. What is the name of the imaginary line that circles around the Earth midway between the North Pole and the South Pole, dividing it into the Northern and Southern Hemispheres?

1909. What do you think the South American country of **Ecuador** translates to in English?

1910. What is the reference point that refers to everything north of the equator: Northern Hemisphere or Southern Hemisphere?

1911. What is the reference point that refers to everything south of the equator?

1912. What is the climate like as you move farther away from the equator: warmer or colder?

1913. What is the name of the imaginary line that runs between the North Pole and the South Pole, passes through Greenwich, England, measures zero degrees longitude, becomes the 180 degree meridian on the other side of the Earth, and divides the Earth into the Eastern and Western Hemispheres: the equator or the prime meridian?

1914. What is another name for the prime meridian, named for the place in England that it passes through, separating east from west: London Meridian or Greenwich Meridian?

1915. What is another name for 180 degrees longitude on the other side of the earth that is designated as the place where each calendar day begins: International Date Line or prime meridian?

1916. What would change either forward or backward if you crossed the International Date Line: the clock or the date?

1917. Are the regions to the east one calendar earlier than the regions to the west?

1918. If you cross the International Date Line going west would Saturday become Sunday or Friday?

1919. If you cross the International Date Line going east would Saturday become Sunday or Friday?

1920. Could there be two different calendar days at the same time on the Earth?

1921. What is the name for the lines that run around the Earth horizontally or parallel to the equator, and measure how far north or south an object or place is on the Earth: latitude or longitude

1922. What is the name for the lines that run vertically around the Earth, are referred to as meridians, and measure how far east or west a place is from the prime meridian: latitude or longitude?

1923. Which are the lines that connect the North Pole with the South Pole: latitude or longitude?

1924. Is the prime meridian located at 0 degrees latitude or 0 degrees longitude?

1925. What is the name for the latitude and longitude numbers that indicate a specific location on the Earth: reference points or coordinates?

1926. What is the term for the line running at a north latitude that specified the boundary between Pennsylvania and Maryland, was originally surveyed by astronomers Charles Mason and Jeremiah Dixon between 1763 and 1767 who were called on to define the boundary between the free and the slave states, and later came to be known as the dividing line between the North and the South: North-South Line or Mason-Dixon Line?

1927. What is the name for the line of latitude and imaginary circle closest to the North Pole located 67 degrees north of the equator: the Arctic Circle or the Antarctic Circle?

1928. What is the name for the frozen sections of ice located at the North and South Poles: polar ice cap or frozen tundra?

1929. What is the name for the line of latitude and imaginary circle closest to the South Pole located at 67 degrees south of the equator: the Arctic Circle or the Antarctic Circle?

1930. What is the name for the line of latitude and imaginary circle located 23 ½ degrees north of the equator: Tropic of Cancer or Tropic of Capricorn?

1931. What is the name for the line of latitude and imaginary circle located 23 ½ degrees south of the equator: Tropic of Cancer or Tropic of Capricorn?

1932. What is the area within the Tropic of Cancer and Tropic of Capricorn: the tropics or the desert?

1933. What do the terms tropical, temperate, and frigid refer to: latitude zones or climate zones?

1934. Would the weather in the tropics be very hot or very cold?

1935. Would the weather in the Frigid Zone be very hot or very cold?

1936. What would the weather be like in the Temperate Zone: hot or moderate?

1937. What climate zone would the Arctic and Antarctic be in: temperate or frigid?

1938. What determines whether it is day or night: the rotation of the Earth, or the Earth's revolution around the Sun?

1939. What determines the seasons: the rotation of the Earth only, or the rotation and revolution of Earth because it creates changes in lightness, darkness, and temperature?

1940. Does latitude have a connection with the seasons?

1941. What season are the countries in the Northern Hemisphere in during the months of June, July, and August when the Earth is tilted on its axis, and the North Pole is pointed more *towards* the Sun: summer or winter?

1942. What season are the countries in the Southern Hemisphere in during the months of June, July, and August when the Earth is tilted on its axis, and the South Pole is pointed *away* from the Sun: summer or winter?

1943. What season are the countries in the Northern Hemisphere in during the months of December, January, and February when the Earth is tilted on its axis, and the North Pole is pointed *away* from the Sun: summer or winter?

1944. What season are the countries in the Southern Hemisphere in during the months of December, January, and February when the Earth is tilted on its axis and the South Pole is pointed *towards* the Sun: summer or winter?

1945. Are the seasons the same or the opposite in the Northern and Southern Hemispheres?

1946. Are the months the same or the opposite in the Northern and Southern Hemispheres?

1947. What is the term given for the two times a year, June 21st and December 21st, when the tilt of the Earth's axis reaches its maximum angle with respect to the Sun, and the rays of the Sun directly shine on one of the two tropics: solstice or equinox?

1948. What day is the longest day of the year in terms of hours of sunlight in the Northern Hemisphere: June 21st or December 21st?

1949. What day is the shortest day of the year in terms of hours of sunlight in the Northern Hemisphere: June 21st or December 21st?

1950. What is the term given for the two times a year, March 21st and September 21st, when the tilt of the Earth's axis is straight with respect to the Sun, and the rays of the Sun directly shine on the equator: solstice or equinox?

1951. What would the passage of day and night, the phases of the moon, and the revolution of the Earth in its orbit all determine: the seasons or the passage of time?

1952. How many years are there in one millennium: 100 or 1000?

1953. How many years are there in one century: 100 or 1000?

1954. How many years are there in one decade: 100 or 10?

1955. How many days are there in one year: 365 or 365 ¼?

1956. What extra day do we have every four years to match the calendar with the solar year and allow for the extra ¼ day in the year: February 29th or September 31st?

1957. What is the term we use when we have February 29th on the calendar: leap day or extra day?

1958. Who were the first people to add a leap day every four years: the Maya or the Egyptians?

1959. What Roman leader reorganized the 12 Roman months into a 365 day calendar with a leap year day added every four years, and so named the ***Julian*** calendar: Ptolemy or Julius Caesar?

1960. What calendar replaced the Julian calendar because it resulted in throwing the solar calendar off by one day every 128 years, was named for Pope Gregory XIII who first introduced it in 1582, and is the calendar system currently in use in most of the world today: the Mayan calendar or the Gregorian calendar?

1961. How many days are there on average in one month?

1962. How many days are there in one week?

1963. What are the two days of the weekend?

1964. How many hours are there in one day?

1965. How many minutes are there in one hour?

1966. How many seconds are there in one minute?

1967. What kind of timing device was used my many ancient civilizations before clocks: windmills or sundials?

1968. Do many towns and cities have a large clock tower?

1969. What is the reference point for measuring time: the equator or the prime meridian?

1970. How many general time zones is the Earth divided into, that are designed to match the hours it takes for the Earth to rotate once on its axis: 24 or 12?

1971. Which country would have Central Time, Mountain Time, Pacific Time, and Eastern Time?

1972. Which time zone would you be in if you lived in Wisconsin: Central or Eastern?

1973. Which time zone would you be in if you lived in Colorado: Pacific or Mountain?

1974. Which time zone would you be in if you lived in California: Eastern or Pacific?

1975. Which time zone would you be in if you lived in New York: Eastern or Pacific?

1976. What time zone are you located in?

1977. Do Alaska and Hawaii have their own time zones?

1978. What time is it when the Sun is directly overhead, and shadows are at their shortest: noon or 3:00?

1979. What is time referred to as: basic or standard?

1980. What is the term for something that many countries do to gain one more hour of sunlight, and to save energy by setting back their clocks one hour, and lasts between April and October?

1981. What do we say to refer to the time before noon: A.M. or P.M?

1982. What do we say to refer to the time after noon until midnight: A.M. or P.M?

1983. What is the English translation of the Latin term ***meridiem***: medium or midday?

1984. Which abbreviation stands for the Latin words *ante meridiem*, or the hours before the Sun shines right on the meridian: A.M. or P.M?

1985. Which abbreviation stands for the Latin words *post meridiem*, or the hours after the Sun shines right on the meridian: A.M. or P.M?

1986. Are there many different maps that are used to represent the Earth?

1987. Is there a difference in how the size of a country may appear on a flat map versus a globe?

1988. What is the term for people who make maps: calligraphers or cartographers?

1989. What is the term that is used to refer to different kinds of maps: spheres or projections?

1990. What is the name of the person that is credited with creating the best-known map projection in the world in the 1500's by projecting the Earth's surface on a flat map: Gerardus Mercator or Christopher Columbus?

1991. Should the type of projection or map a person uses like globe, flat, conic, physical, or relief relate to what type of geography that person wants to learn?

1992. What are the two largest bodies of water that are easily identified on a projection or map?

1993. What is the term for bodies of water that collect in basins, or large depressions in the land: rivers or lakes?

1994. Were some lakes on the Earth formed from glaciers?

1995. Can lakes be salty?

1996. What kind of lake would the Great Salt Lake in Utah be considered: salty or freshwater?

1997. On which continent would you locate Lake Chad and Lake Victoria: Africa or Asia?

1998. On which continent would you locate Lake Maracaibo and Lake Titicaca, the world's highest navigable lake: South America or North America?

1999. On which continent would you locate the Aral Sea and the Caspian Sea: Asia or Africa?

2000. Are the Caspian Sea and the Aral Sea considered oceans or salty lakes?

2001. What lakes can you name in the United States and Canada?

2002. What are the names of the five Great Lakes located in the United States and Canada?

2003. What type of map indicates governmental boundaries of cities, counties, states, and countries: political or relief?

2004. What type of map indicates landforms like plains, deserts, and mountains often with contour lines: political or relief?

2005. Are major rivers indicated on a political map or a relief map?

2006. What major rivers in the world can you name?

2007. What major rivers can you name in the United States?

2008. Are mountain ranges indicated on a relief map or a political map?

2009. What mountain ranges in the world can you name?

2010. Are deserts often included on a political map or a relief map?

2011. What deserts in the world can you name?

2012. How many continents or landmasses can be located on a world map: five or seven?

2013. What are the three countries that make up North America?

2014. How many states make up the United States and can be located on a political map?

2015. How many geographic regions is the United States divided into: five or eight?

2016. What is the name for the region of the United States that includes the states of Maine, Massachusetts, New Hampshire, Connecticut, Rhode Island, New Jersey, New York, Pennsylvania, and Vermont: New England or the Northeast?

2017. What is the name for the division in the Northeast that includes the states of Maine, Massachusetts, New Hampshire, Connecticut, Rhode Island, and Vermont, and is known for Pilgrims, the first Thanksgiving, lobsters, and beautiful fall colors: Mid-Atlantic or New England?

2018. What is the name for the region of the United States that includes Washington D.C., New York, West Virginia, Delaware, Maryland, and Pennsylvania, is very densely populated: Northeast or Northwest?

2019. What is the name for the region of the United States that includes the states of Alabama, Georgia, Kentucky, Louisiana, Mississippi North Carolina, South Carolina, Virginia, Tennessee and Florida and is known for cotton plantations, peaches, oranges, beaches, and music: Mid-Atlantic or Southeast?

2020. What is the name for the region of the United States that includes the states of Illinois, Indiana, Iowa, Kansas, Michigan, Minnesota, North Dakota, South Dakota, Missouri, Ohio, and Wisconsin, and is known for Great Lakes and the Mississippi River: Great Plains or Midwest?

2021. What is the name for the region of the United States that includes the states of Montana, Wyoming, Colorado, Utah, Nevada, and California: West or Pacific Northwest?

2022. What is the name for the region of the United States that includes the states of Arizona, New Mexico, Nevada, Utah, and Colorado, is dry with many deserts, and borders Mexico: Southwest or Northwest?

2023. What are geographical regions further divided into: sections or divisions?

2024. What is the name for the physical region of the United States that includes the states of Alaska, Washington, Idaho, and Oregon, and borders Canada: Northeast or Pacific Alaska Region?

2025. What is the name for the physical region of the United States located in the Midwest that includes the states of Kansas, Nebraska, Iowa, and Missouri, and is rather sparsely populated with vast fields of land: Great Plains or Southwest?

2026. What is the name for the physical region of the United States located in the Midwest that includes the states or Minnesota, Wisconsin, Illinois, Indiana, and Ohio, and so named because this area includes Lakes Superior, Michigan, Huron, and Erie: North Central or Great Lakes?

2027. What is the name for the physical region of the United States that includes the states of Montana, Wyoming, Utah, Colorado, New Mexico, North Dakota, and South Dakota, and named for the mountain range that passes through these states: Appalachian Mountain or Rocky Mountain?

2028. What is the name for the physical region of the United States that includes the states of California, Nevada, and Arizona, and named for the ocean nearest to them: Pacific or Atlantic?

2029. What is the name for the physical region of the United States that includes the states of Pennsylvania, West Virginia, Virginia, Maryland, Delaware, and New Jersey, so named because these states are half way down the coast on this ocean: Mid-Atlantic or Mid-Pacific?

2030. What is the name for the physical region of the United States that includes the states of Kentucky, Tennessee, North Carolina, South Carolina, Georgia, Alabama, Mississippi, and Florida: Southeast or Lower-Atlantic?

2031. What is the name for the physical region of the United States that includes the states of Texas, Oklahoma, Arkansas, and Louisiana: Southwest or Southeast?

2032. What is the name for the physical region of the United States that includes the states of New York, Vermont, New Hampshire, Maine, Massachusetts, Maryland, Rhode Island, and Connecticut: Northeast or Northwest?

2033. What is the name of the state outside the continental United States, is a group of islands in the Pacific, and has a warm climate?

2034. What is the name of the state outside the continental United States, has a sparse population, and has a cold climate?

2035. What state do you live in?

2036. What states border the state you live in?

2037. What is the term for the sections that a state is divided into: regions or counties?

2038. What is the term for the center of population, business, and culture: a town or a city?

2039. What city in the United States is known as the "Windy City:" Chicago or Milwaukee?

2040. What city in the United States is known as the "Motor City:" Philadelphia or Detroit?

2041. What city in the United States is known as the "Big Apple," or, "The City That Never Sleeps:" New York or Las Vegas?

2042. What city in the United States is known as the "City of Angels:" Las Vegas or Los Angeles?

2043. What city in the United States is known as the "Mile High City:" Denver or Salt Lake City?

2044. What city in the United States is known as "Bean town:" Baltimore or Boston?

2045. What city in the United States is known as "The Big Easy:" New Orleans or New York?

2046. What city in the United States is known as the "City by the Bay:" San Francisco or San Diego?

2047. What city in the United States is known "Philly," or, "The City of Brotherly Love?"

2048. What city in the United States is known as the "Gateway to the West," and is famous for its arch: St. Louis or Indianapolis?

2049. What city in the United States is known as the "Steel City:" Pittsburgh or Detroit?

2050. What city in Europe is known as "The City of Love:" Venice or Paris?

2051. What city in the world is known as the "Holy City:" Jerusalem or Fatima?

2052. What fictitious city known as the "Emerald City?"

2053. What is the term for a human settlement that is smaller than a city but larger than a village: town or municipality?

2054. What type of community or city typically has a high-density population, tall buildings called skyscrapers, public transportation, and large schools: urban or rural?

2055. What type of community typically has a low-density population, is located in the countryside, and has buildings, farms, and open spaces: suburban or rural?

2056. What type of community is often located close to cities, has residents who live in houses with yards, and has residents who drive or take a train in to the city: urban or suburban?

2057. What type of community best describes where you live: rural, urban, or suburban?

2058. What is the term for the people who live in a community and are familiar with local businesses, parks and landmarks: residents or patrons?

2059. What is the name for the central part of town or city that many cities and communities have that are often surrounded by shops, restaurants, and a city hall: the plaza or the town square?

2060. Do many city or town squares have a statue, monument, or fountain in the center?

2061. What is the name of one of the largest squares in the world that is located in the historic center of Mexico City, includes the National Palace, and has the Mexican flag in the center: the Zócalo or the Plaza Mayor?

2062. What is the name of one of the most famous city squares in England that was named for the battle that Britain won over Napoleon and the French in 1805, has a large column and statue of Lord Nelson in the middle, and is surrounded by four lions and several fountains: Plaza San Marco or Trafalgar Square?

2063. What is the name for the main square in Venice, Italy that includes a basilica and a large space in the middle: Piazza San Marco or Old Town Square?

2064. What is the name of the largest city square in the world located in Beijing, China, that is surrounded by several monuments and governments, has a flag in the center, has four marble lions guarding the gate, and was the site of a famous massacre in 1989: Trafalgar Square or Tiananmen Square?

2065. What is the name of the square in Krakow, Poland that is the largest medieval town square in Europe, is surrounded by historic palaces and churches, and has a small palace called Cloth Hall at its center: Main Market Square or Old Town Square?

2066. What is the name of the famous square in New York City near Broadway and West 42nd street, has video screens, LED signs and flashing lights, and is famous for the ball drop on New Year's Eve: Rockefeller Center of Times Square?

2067. What is the name of the square located in front of the Basilica in Vatican City, Rome, and has an Egyptian obelisk at the center of the ellipse: Plaza San Marco or St. Peter's Square?

2068. What is the name of the city square in Madrid that is surrounded by government buildings, shops, and cafes, at one time hosted bullfights, markets, and soccer games, and has a statue of Phillip III in its center: the Zócalo or the Plaza Mayor?

2069. What is the name of the square in Moscow, Russia that is surrounded by Saint Basil's Cathedral, Lenin's Mausoleum, and the State History Museum: Red Square or Main Market Square?

2070. What is the name of the statue located in Copenhagen, Denmark of a lady sitting on a rock that was built in honor of a play: the Little Mermaid or the Little Lady?

2071. What is the name of the statue in Russia that was built to symbolize the Battle of Stalingrad and was the tallest structure in the world in 1967 measuring 280 feet high: Motherland Calls or Russian Lady?

2072. What is the name of the marble statue in Florence, Italy from the renaissance that is considered the masterpiece of Michelangelo, and represents a Biblical king: David or Goliath?

2073. What is the name of the Pre-Columbian Mexican civilization that sculpted large, helmeted stone heads from basalt stone with large facial features in the lowlands of Mexico: the Olmecs or the Zapotecs?

2074. What is the name of the limestone sculpture at Giza in Egypt on the west bank of the Nile River with the head of a pharaoh wearing a headdress and the body of a lion, and is considered to be one of the oldest statues in the world: Pharaoh Khafre or Great Sphinx?

2075. What is the name of the statue of Jesus Christ on top of a mountain in Rio de Janeiro, Brazil that is a symbol of Christianity: Christ the Redeemer or Statue of Christ?

2076. What is the name of the 50 stone statues, each weighing several tons, located on Easter Island off the coast of Chile, South America that were built by Polynesians: Stonehenge or Moai?

2077. What is the name of the prehistoric group of standing stones located in England that were constructed thousands of years ago by an unknown civilization, and is believed to have been built as an astronomic observatory and religious center: Machu Picchu or Stonehenge?

2078. What is the name of the monument located in New York Harbor that was a gift from France, is a lady wearing a crown and holding a torch, and is a symbol of American freedom: the Liberty Bell or the Statue of Liberty?

2079. What is the name of the tower in Toronto, Canada built as a communication tower in 1973: the CN Tower or the Space Needle?

2080. What is the name of the observation tower over 605 feet high in Seattle, Washington that was built for the 1962 World's Fair: the Space Needle or the CN Tower?

2081. What would the Burj Khalifa in Dubai, the Makkah Royal Clock Tower in Mecca, One World Trade Center in New York City, and the Willis Tower in Chicago all be categorized as: the tallest buildings in the world, or the largest structures in the world?

2082. What is the name for the famous clock tower in London, England that has a bell weighing 13 tons, is now called Elizabeth Tower, and is the one of the largest clock tower in the world: Big Ben or Wrigley Clock Tower?

2083. What is the name for the world famous tower in Italy that began to sink after it was built in 1173 due to being constructed on an uneven foundation, and is famous for its tilt and 296 steps: the Leaning Tower of Pisa or the Tower of Italy?

2084. What is the name of the tower that is the iconic symbol of France, was constructed as an entrance for the International Exhibition of Paris in 1889, and is one of the most famous and most visited monuments in the world: the Paris Tower or the Eiffel Tower?

2085. What is the name of the famous domed building located in Washington, D.C. that is the meeting place for the Congress of the United States: the White House or the United States Capitol?

2086. What is the name of the famous cathedral in London with a large dome: St. Paul's Cathedral or Notre Dame Cathedral?

2087. What is the name of the famous domed gothic basilica in Florence, Italy called the Florence Duomo, is the symbol of the city, and is considered to be the largest brick dome ever built in the world: Santa Maria del Fiore or the Uffizi?

2088. What is the name of the largest concrete dome in the world located in Rome, Italy that was built as a temple for the Roman gods in 126 A.D: the Acropolis or the Pantheon?

2089. What is the name of the tallest dome in the world that was built on Vatican hill in Rome, Italy by several architects including Michelangelo, is considered the center for Christianity, and is the world's largest church: St. Peter's Cathedral or St. John's Cathedral?

2090. What is the name of the white marble mausoleum with a dome located in India, was built by a Muslim emperor in memory of his third wife, and is regarded as one of the eight wonders of the world: the Mausoleum of India or the Taj Mahal?

2091. What is the name of the colorful cathedral in Red Square in Moscow, Russia, was built by Ivan the Terrible in 1534, and is distinctive because of its nine colorful onion domes on top of the cathedral: the Moscow Cathedral or St. Basil's Cathedral?

2092. What is the name of the famous bridge in New York that connects Brooklyn and Manhattan over the East River, and at one time was the longest suspension bridge in the world: the Brooklyn Bridge or Manhattan Bridge?

2093. What is the name of one of the world's largest steel arch bridges located in Australia: the Sydney Harbour Bridge or the Sydney Opera House?

2094. What is the name of the bridge in London, England near Big Ben Clock Tower that has two towers connected at the top with two walkways, and is a suspension bridge over the Thames River: Tower Bridge or London Bridge?

2095. What is the name of the reddish-orange suspension bridge in San Francisco, California that was painted a bright color so it would be visible in the thick fog: the Golden Gate Bridge or the San Francisco Bridge?

2096. What is the name of the medieval stone arch bridge over the Arno River in Florence, Italy, translates as "old bridge" in Italian, and has shops, gold jewelry stores, and art galleries all along it: Ponte Vecchio or Puente Viejo?

2097. What is the name of the wall that is a national war memorial located in Washington, D.C., is dedicated to those who served and died in the Vietnam War, is made of black granite, and is engraved with the names of over 58,000 soldiers: Veterans Wall or Vietnam Veterans Memorial?

2098. What is the name of the famous wall that was built by the East Germans to divide East Germany from West Germany when each side had opposing political parties, and was finally torn down in 1989: the Iron Curtain or the Berlin Wall?

2099. What is the name of the wall in the old city of Jerusalem, Israel that is also regarded as the Wailing Wall, and is a religious center and place of pilgrimage for Jews: the Western Wall or the Holy Temple Wall?

2100. What is the name of the massive, protective walls that were built in the city-state Mesopotamia, includes the Ishtar Gate, and is one of the ancient wonders of the world: the Walls of Mesopotamia or the Walls of Babylon?

2101. What is the name of the wall in China that was initially started to protect China from the countries to the north, was built primarily during the Ming Dynasty, and is over 13,000 miles long: the Great Wall of China or the Great Border?

2102. What is the name of the rock in Massachusetts that marks the place where the Pilgrims arrived on the Mayflower, and is stamped with the date 1620: Pilgrim Rock or Plymouth Rock?

2103. What is the name of the stone in a castle in Ireland that is said to bring good luck if it is kissed: the Irish Stone or the Blarney Stone?

2104. What is the name of the limestone rock that is located in a strait south of Spain, is almost 1,400 feet high, and is under the jurisdiction of Great Britain: the Rock of Gibraltar or British Rock?

2105. What is the name of the piece of an Egyptian stone that weighs 1,700 pounds, became useful for translating Egyptian hieroglyphics into Greek because both were found on the stone, and is the most visited display in the British Museum: the Rashid Stone or the Rosetta Stone?

2106. Are many monuments and landmarks throughout the world made of stone?

2107. Which country in the world is known as the "Gift of the Nile:" Egypt or Morocco?'

2108. Which country in the world is known as the "Land of the Rising Sun:" Japan or China?

2109. Which country in the world is known as "The Boot:" Italy or Spain?

2110. Which country in the world is known as "The Land Down Under:" Australia or New Zealand?

2111. Which country has a vast, remote area called the "Outback:" New Zealand or Australia?

2112. Which country in the world is known as "The Red Dragon:" China or Japan?

2113. Which country in the world is known as the "Land of Milk and Honey:" Switzerland or Austria?

2114. Which country in the world is known as "The Emerald Isle:" Scotland or Ireland?

2115. Which country in the world is known as "The Holy Land:" Israel or India?

2116. Which country in the world is known as "The Great White North:" Canada or Greenland?

2117. Which country in the world is known as "The Melting Pot:" Canada or the United States?

2118. Which country in the world is known as "The Land of Fire and Ice:" Finland or Iceland?

2119. Which country in the world is known as "The Land of the Incas:" Bolivia or Peru?

2120. Which country in the world is known as "The Land of Hope and Glory:" England or Scotland?

2121. What is the nickname that references the American Government: "Uncle Sam" or "Melting Pot?"

2122. On which continent are China, India, Japan, Iran, Korea, and Russia: Asia or Africa?

2123. What general name is used to refer to an area of the world that includes Jordan, Iraq, Iran, Saudi Arabia, Pakistan, Afghanistan, and Israel: the Far East or the Middle East?

2124. What general name is used to refer to an area of the world that includes Indonesia, Singapore, Thailand, Korea, and Hong Kong: the Middle East or the Far East?

2125. What general name is used to refer to an area of the world that includes Russia, Poland, the Czech Republic, Hungary, Croatia, and Slovakia: Eastern Europe or Western Europe?

2126. What general name is used to refer to an area of the world that includes Spain, France, Germany, Italy, Austria, Switzerland, England, and Ireland: Eastern Europe or Western Europe?

2127. What general name is used to refer to an area of the world that includes Great Britain, Ireland, and over 6,000 smaller islands: the United Kingdom or the British Isles?

2128. What general name is used to refer to an area of the world that includes the countries of Great Britain, Scotland, Wales, and Northern Ireland: the British Isles or the United Kingdom?

2129. What general name is used to refer to an area of the world that include the countries of Denmark, Norway, and Sweden: The Netherlands or Scandinavia?

2130. What name is used to refer to the European country that is a sovereign state with twelve provinces in Western Europe, and three islands in the Caribbean: Belgium or The Netherlands?

2131. What is another term that is commonly used to refer to the seat of government in the Netherlands, with Amsterdam as its capital: Holland or The Hague?

2132. What country is famous for windmills, wooden shoes, and tulips: England or Holland?

2133. What is the nationality and language of a person living in the United Kingdom: English or Scottish?

2134. What is the nationality and language of a person living in Holland or the Netherlands: Swedish or Dutch?

2135. What is the language of a person living in Denmark, also the name for a type of donut: Kringle or Danish?

2136. What is the nationality of a person living in Denmark: Danish or Dutch?

2137. What is the nationality and language of a person living in Sweden: Swiss or Swedish?

2138. What is the nationality and language of a person living in Norway: Norse or Norwegian?

2139. What is the nationality of a person living in Belgium, also the name for a type of waffle: Swedish or Belgian?

2140. What language might a Belgian speak besides French and German: Dutch or Belgian?

2141. What is the nationality and language of a person living in Ireland?

2142. What is the nationality and language of a person living in France?

2143. What is the nationality and language of a person living in Spain?

2144. What is the nationality and language of a person living in Portugal: Spanish or Portuguese?

2145. What is the nationality of a person living in Brazil: Spanish or Portuguese?

2146. What is the nationality and language of a person living in Germany?

2147. What is the nationality and language of a person living in Italy?

2148. What is the nationality of a person living in Switzerland?

2149. What three languages are spoken in Switzerland: French, German, and Italian, or French, Spanish, and Dutch?

2150. What is the language of a person living in Austria: Austrian or German?

2151. What is the nationality and language of a person living in Poland?

2152. What is the nationality and language of a person living in Greece?

2153. What two languages are spoken in Vatican City: Latin and Italian, or Greek and Italian?

2154. What are two languages spoken in Israel: Latin and Hebrew, or Hebrew and Arabic?

2155. What is the number one language in the world that is spoken in China, Taiwan, Singapore, and Malaysia: Mandarin Chinese or Indonesian?

2156. What language is second in the world, spoken in Spain, Latin America, Mexico, and the United States?

2157. What language is third in the world, spoken in Australia, the United Kingdom, and the United States?

2158. What language is fourth in the world, spoken in India, Fiji, and Nepal: Hindi or Arabic?

2159. What language is fifth in the world, spoken in North Africa, East Africa, and the Middle East: Arabic or Hindi?

2160. What are the two official languages of Canada: French and English, or Canadian and French?

2161. What is the official language of Mexico?

2162. What is the official language of the United States: English or none?

2163. What language or languages do you speak?

2164. What is your nationality or your ethnic background?

2165. Do many people of the United States have more than one nationality?

2166. What civilizations can you name?

2167. What were three major civilizations of the Americas that existed before the arrival of the Europeans: Olmec, Zapotec, and Inca, or Maya, Aztec, and Inca?

2168. What two countries are primarily associated with the Maya civilization: Mexico and Guatemala, or Mexico and the United States?

2169. Which country is primarily associated with the Aztec civilization: Mexico or Guatemala?

2170. Which country is primarily associated with the Inca civilization: Peru or Argentina?

2171. What did the Maya develop throughout southern Mexico and Guatemala: towns or city-states?

2172. Did each Mayan city-state have its own government?

2173. Who was each Mayan city-state ruled by: a king or a priest?

2174. Did the Maya follow strict laws and have a court system?

2175. What is the name of the Maya city-state in the jungle of Guatemala with six large pyramids, and a great plaza: Tikal or Teotihuacan?

2176. What is the name of the city-state in the valley of Mexico that existed at the time of the Maya but was mysteriously abandoned by an earlier civilization, and includes the pyramids of the Sun and the Moon: Tenochtitlan or Teotihuacan?

2177. Who did the Maya build large temples in their city-states in honor of: gods or priests?

2178. What would the Mayan priests often do on the flat temples on top of the pyramids: perform sacrifices, or eat their meals?

2179. What is the name of the Mexican peninsula where the Maya established part of their civilization and built several pyramids: the Yucatan or the Iberian?

2180. What is the name of the most powerful Mayan city-state located in Mexico's Yucatan Peninsula that is dominated by the pyramid El Castillo in honor of the Mayan God Kukulkan or "Feathered Serpent," has a temple, several ball courts, and is one of the most visited tourist sites in Mexico: El Caracol or Chichen Itza?

2181. How many steps did the Maya include on the El Castillo pyramid that relate to the calendar year: 365 or 12?

2182. Which civilization built the pyramids located in the Petén in Guatemala that include El Tigre and La Danta, and were only recently discovered because they were covered by dense jungle: the Maya or the Aztecs?

2183. What did the Maya build to purposely align with movements of the Sun and the Moon: pyramids or temples?

2184. What animal appears every spring and fall equinox on the Maya pyramid El Castillo, when the Sun falls on the main stairway creating a shadow 120 feet long that joins with its serpent stone head at the bottom of the stairway?

2185. What was the name of the serpent god of the Maya: Itzamna or Kukulkan?

2186. Who was the main god of the Maya, the god of fire who created Earth: Itzamna or Kukulkan?

2187. Was religion important to the Maya civilization?

2188. Did the Maya believe that their rulers were related to their gods?

2189. Which ancient civilization had city-states that included Palenque, Uxmal, and Tulum: the Aztecs or the Maya?

2190. What was the name of the rain god of the Maya: Chac or Kukulkan?

2191. What did the Maya use to track time and religious rituals: clocks or calendars?

2192. How many calendars did the Maya have: one or three?

2193. How did the Maya use their religious calendar, the Tzolkin, their solar calendar, the Haab, and their Long Count calendar to track specific times and events: separately or simultaneously?

2194. Which Maya calendar predicted that the current cycle of life after 5126 years would end on December 21, 2012: The Long Count or the Haab?

2195. What is the name for Mayan books: codices or glyphs?

2196. Which Pre-Columbian civilization developed one of the most advanced number systems in the Americas: the Inca or the Maya?

2197. What kind of writing system did the Maya have: cave paintings or hieroglyphics?

2198. What number concept are the Maya credited for: zero or infinity?

2199. What number is the Maya math system based on: twenty or ten?

2200. What symbols did the Maya use to represent their numbers: ones and zeroes, or dots and bars?

2201. Did the Maya have a social class system?

2202. What is the correct order of the Maya hierarchy from most to least powerful: king, noble, commoner or noble, priest, and peasant?

2203. Did many of the Maya commoners work as farmers and hunters?

2204. What type of agriculture did the Maya peasant farmers practice: slash-and-burn or subsistence cultivation?

2205. What was the staple food of the Maya: wheat or maize, a type of corn?

2206. What did the Maya eat that comes from the Cacao tree: coconut or chocolate?

2207. What did the Maya often use for money: cacao beans or corn kernels?

2208. What is the name for the sinkhole that served as a source of water for the Maya, and may have been used for performing sacrifices: a cenote or a well?

2209. Which Mayan social class lived in palaces: the nobles or the commoners?

2210. Which Mayan class lived in huts made of mud with thatched roofs: the nobles or the commoners?

2211. What did the Maya use to play ball games as part of their religious ceremonies: a round stone or a rubber ball?

2212. What part of the body could not be used in the Mayan ball game: the hands or the feet?

2213. Which side might be sacrificed to the Gods as a result of the ball game: the losing side or the winning side?

2214. Did the Maya perform many dances like the "Monkey Dance" and the "Snake Dance?"

2215. What kind of art sculptures were the Maya famous for: clay or stone?

2216. Did the Maya use drums, wind instruments, and rattles to make music?

2217. What is the name of the pages that were folded like an accordion to form a book: a codex or a stela?

2218. What is the name for the large slab of stone in the shape of a pillar that is covered with carvings and hieroglyphics by the Maya: a codex or a stela?

2219. What is the name for the book or codex that contained information about Maya mythology and religion: Popol Vuh or Stela?

2220. Were wood and jade carvings also Mayan art forms?

2221. Did the Maya use a potter's wheel to make their pottery?

2222. What medium was used by the Maya to make masks: plaster or clay?

2223. What is the name of the rock that the Maya used to make tools: obsidian, a type of volcanic rock, or basalt stone?

2224. Who wore the more elaborate clothing and feathered headdresses: the Mayan nobles or the Mayan peasants?

2225. What is the name for the feathered jungle bird that the Maya used to make their headdresses: the Quetzal or the Tikal?

2226. What is the term for the peak time period or "golden age" of the Maya civilization between 250 and 900 A.D: pre-classic or classic?

2227. Is there some mystery attached to why the Maya abandoned their cities and what ultimately led to their disappearance?

2228. Did war, drought, or disease possibly contribute to the collapse of the Maya civilization?

2229. When did the Maya civilization end, also marking the arrival of the Spanish conquistadors: the 1400's or the 1500's?

2230. What is the name of another advanced civilization of Mexico: the Inca or the Aztec?

2231. What did the Aztecs observe, that they took as a sign from their god to build their city there: an eagle on a cactus holding a snake, or a hawk in a nest with a fish in its mouth?

2232. What was the name for the ancient capital city of the Aztecs that was built on a swampy island in a lake that is now modern Mexico City: Teotihuacan or Tenochtitlan?

2233. What was the Aztec Empire divided into: city-states or communities?

2234. What is the term for the raised roads that the Aztecs built in Tenochtitlan to connect with the mainland, along with the canals that served as water roads: overpasses or causeways?

2235. When might the Aztecs remove the causeways and bridges: when they wanted to navigate a boat, or when they were under attack by an enemy tribe?

2236. What is the Aztec name for the temple that was built in the center of the city: the Templo Mayor or the Temple of the Sun?

2237. Where were the palaces of the Aztec Emperors located: near the Temple, or on hill overlooking the city?

2238. Where was the Aztec government located: at Tenochtitlan or at the Emperor's palace?

2239. Who was the supreme ruler of the land in Aztec times: the Sun god or the Emperor?

2240. What were Montezuma I and Montezuma II famous for: serving as powerful Aztec Emperors, or serving as enemy warriors to the Aztecs?

2241. Did the Aztecs have a social class system of an emperor, nobles, and peasants?

2242. Were priests, judges, and military leaders considered high level or low level Aztec officials?

2243. Did the Aztecs believe that their Emperor was appointed by their gods?

2244. What did the Aztecs consider to be the most important part of their religion: honoring the Moon or honoring the Sun?

2245. What rituals did the Aztecs practice to please their gods: fasting or sacrifices?

2246. What did the Aztecs believe they needed to sacrifice to the Sun so that the Sun would rise on that day: human blood or human teeth?

2247. What kinds of animals were the Aztec gods represented with: lions and bears, or serpents and jaguars?

2248. What is the name of the most powerful Aztec god, the god of war, Sun and sacrifice: Tlaloc or Huitzilopochtli?

2249. What is the name of the Aztec god of rain and water: Tlaloc or Huitzilopochtli?

2250. What is the name of the Aztec god whose name means "feathered serpent," the god of life and wind: Huitzilopochtli or Quetzalcoatl?

2251. What was the basic unit of Aztec culture: the family or the government?

2252. What is the name of the language that was spoken by the Aztecs: Spanish or Nahuatl?

2253. What language are the words chocolate, coyote, avocado and chili: Spanish or Nahuatl?

2254. Did the Aztec men work as farmers and warriors?

2255. What is a term for the Aztec method of farming whereby the Aztecs created artificial floating islands in shallow lake beds in order to grow crops: terracing or chinampas?

2256. What was the Aztec's main crop that could be stored for a long time and ground up into flour to make tortillas and other foods: wheat or maize?

2257. What food did the Aztecs succeed in introducing the world to, made from heated corn kernels: tortillas or popcorn?

2258. What was the role of Aztec women: to cook and sew in the home, or to help on the farm and create handicrafts?

2259. Did Aztec women weave all the clothes?

2260. Was the clothing worn by the Aztec nobility the same or different as the clothing worn by the commoners?

2261. Which social class of Aztec society would wear the feathers and the jewelry: the nobles or the peasants?

2262. What did the Aztecs use to make chocolate: cocoa beans or cocoa bark?

2263. What Aztec word does chocolate come from: chocolatl or choco?

2264. What is the term for the structure that was built and used by many Pre-Columbian civilizations that brought fresh water into the city: a cenote or an aqueduct?

2265. Did the Aztecs have marketplaces to buy and sell food and crafts?

2266. How did the Aztecs use pottery, sculptures, feather-work, and jewelry: for honoring their gods, or for decorating their houses?

2267. What is one of the most famous sculptures of the Aztecs, weighs over 24 tons, and measures 12 feet in diameter: the Aztec Calendar or the Aztec Sundial?

2268. What was an important form of art for the Aztecs, passed down orally from one generation to the next: poetry or drama?

2269. Were Aztec children required by law to attend school?

2270. What is the name for the Aztec writing system of symbols: code or glyphs?

2271. What is the name of the Aztec book that was the same for the Maya: codex or slate?

2272. Did the Aztecs play a ball game on a ball court with a rubber ball as a way of preparing for war?

2273. What time measurement device did the Aztecs use to measure the passing of time according to the Sun, and as a guide for having their festivals and religious ceremonies: the Aztec Calendar or the Sundial?

2274. How many calendars did the Aztecs follow: one or two?

2275. If the Aztecs used one solar calendar to mark time, what did their other calendar calculate: weather and seasons, or festivals and ceremonies?

2276. What did the Aztecs use to cure sicknesses besides steam baths: herbs or cornhusks?

2277. Were the Spanish at an advantage or disadvantage over the Aztec warriors and Montezuma with their horses and their guns?

2278. Which country did Hernán Cortés, governor of Cuba, want to take the Aztec treasures to after hearing of the Aztec riches and gold: Cuba or Spain?

2279. What disease did the Spanish bring with them to the New World: smallpox or chicken pox?

2280. Who was the Spanish conquistador who ended the rule of the powerful Aztec empire in 1521, after 200 years in the Valley of Mexico: Francisco Pizarro or Hernán Cortés?

2281. Which Aztec city did Hernán Cortés finally succeed in capturing and conquering in 1521: Teotihuacan or Tenochtitlan?

2282. What is the new name for the capital of New Spain after Tenochtitlan was taken over by the Spanish: Madrid or Mexico City?

2283. What is the name of the Indian civilization that ruled Peru at the time that the Aztecs ruled the Valley of Mexico: the Inca or the Toltec?

2284. What is the name of the Indian group before the Incas, famous for their long lines that include images of monkeys, spiders, and fish that can be observed when flying over the plateaus along the southern coast of Peru: Moche or Nazca?

2285. What is the name for the mountains in Peru where the Incas established their cities?

2286. Did the Incas have a social class system of rulers, nobles, and peasants?

2287. Did the Inca believe that their rulers were descendants of their gods?

2288. Was the Inca ruler considered a king and the most powerful leader in the land?

2289. What is the name of the Inca ruler translated as "sole ruler:" Sapa Inca or Sola Inca?

2290. What is the name of the Sun god of the Inca: Sol or Inti?

2291. What is the name of the capital city of the Inca Empire that was established as a city-state where the Sapa Inca lived and ruled the surrounding lands: Lima or Cuzco?

2292. What is the altitude of the Inca city of Cuzco: 11,000 feet above sea level, or 4,000 feet above sea level?

2293. Did the Inca Empire extend to the countries of Ecuador, Chile, Argentina, and Bolivia at the height of its power?

2294. What is the name of the language of the Inca people: Nahuatl or Quechua?

2295. What was the job of most Inca peasants: farming the land, or weaving textiles?

2296. Did some Inca commoners work as artisans and make colorful crafts and pottery?

2297. What is the trade name for many Incas who built massive walls out of large stones that fitted together so perfectly that no mortar was necessary: bricklayers or stonemasons?

2298. Did the Incas have extensive stone roads that connected their cities?

2299. What kind of bridges did the Inca build: rope suspension bridges or stone-paved bridges?

2300. What animals did the Inca raise to make wool and colorful textiles from wool dyed with plants: sheep or llamas?

2301. What animal similar to the llama was raised by the Incas and shaved for its wool: alpaca or camel?

2302. How did the Incas turn steep hills into usable farmland: they created terraces on the steep slope, or they simply plowed and tilled the hillside?

2303. Did the Inca develop water and irrigation systems to help grow their crops?

2304. What was the most important crop of the Incas: corn or potatoes?

2305. Were corn, potatoes, beans, squash, ducks, and fish all part of the Inca diet?

2306. What did the Inca men and women wear: colorful tunics and dresses, or white linen pants and dresses?

2307. What kind of houses did the Inca families live in: adobe huts or stone longhouses?

2308. What were the Inca peasants required to pay to the government: taxes or farming dues?

2309. Which social class of the Inca attended school: the children of nobles, the children of the peasants, or all children?

2310. What were the two purposes of the Inca calendar: to mark religious occasions and the seasons for planting crops, or to monitor the movement of the Sun and to predict the solstices?

2311. What did the Inca use for medicine: herbal tea leaves or coca leaves?

2312. What is the name for the large stone city of the Inca Empire that was built as a royal estate for an Inca Emperor and other nobles, and located 8,000 feet above sea level in the Andes Mountains: Chichen Itza or Machu Picchu?

2313. What is the name of the explorer who re-discovered the lost city of Machu Picchu high in the Andes in 1911 in the deep jungle: Francisco Pizarro or Hiram Bingham?

2314. What is the name of the explorer and Spanish conquistador who joined Vasco Nuñez de Balboa and crossed the Isthmus of Panama to get to the Pacific Ocean: Hernan Cortés or Francisco Pizarro?

2315. What was Francisco Pizarro's motivation to lead his own expedition and explore South America: gold or jade?

2316. What was Francisco Pizarro's goal on his third expedition to South America: to conquer the Inca and claim all the gold, or to establish new settlements and colonize South America?

2317. Who had the advantage of guns, horses, cannons, and better weapons: the Inca or the Spanish?

2318. Who is considered the conqueror of the Inca Empire in 1533: Cortés or Pizarro?

2319. Where did many explorers come from to explore the "New World," and to increase trade opportunities: Europe or Asia?

2320. Which European country on the Iberian Peninsula explored the oceans and Africa in the 1400's under Prince Henry the Navigator and Bartolomeu Dias, in search of new trade routes: Spain or Portugal?

2321. What is the name of the famous Italian explorer who "sailed the ocean blue in 1492" on behalf of the Spanish King and Queen?

2322. What are the names of the King and Queen of Spain who agreed to fund the voyage of Columbus to the New World with the hope of spreading Christianity, opening new trade routes, and obtaining spices from the Indies to flavor up their food: Ferdinando and Isabella, or Felipe and Sofia?

2323. What land is between Europe and Asia, land that Columbus did not know existed: Australia or the Americas?

2324. Which country did Columbus believe he could sail to by traveling west: China in the East Indies, or America?

2325. What were the names of Columbus's three ships?

2326. What was the flagship or principle ship of Christopher Columbus: the Niña, the Pinta, or the Santa María?

2327. What was the name that Columbus gave to the island in the Bahamas where he and his men landed on October 12, 1492: San Salvador or India?

2328. What was the name that Columbus gave to the natives because he believed he had landed somewhere in the East Indies: Natives or Indians?

2329. What animal did Columbus bring over on his second voyage to the New World: the chicken or the horse?

2330. How many total voyages did Columbus make to the Americas: three or four?

2331. When Columbus died in 1506, did he still believe that he had successfully sailed to Asia?

2332. What is the date of Columbus Day that is celebrated in Spain and the Americas: October 10th or October 12th?

2333. What places can you name in the United States that are named for Columbus?

2334. Who is the Italian explorer, navigator, and cartographer (mapmaker) after whom the continents of North and South America are named: Amerigo Vespucci or Americus Vasco?

2335. Are there many plazas, statues, parks, subway stops, and monuments named for Columbus in Mexico, the Bahamas, Spain and Portugal?

2336. What is the name of the Portuguese explorer who wanted to find a trade route around Africa to India: Vasco de Gama or Pedro Cabral?

2337. What is the name of the Portuguese explorer who set out for India, landed in South America, and claimed the country of Brazil for Portugal: Vasco de Gama or Pedro Cabral?

2338. What is the language spoken in Brazil: Spanish or Portuguese?

2339. What tactical advantage did the Portuguese have when they landed in India that they used to help them establish a trading post, and to control trade routes that had originally been controlled by Muslims: cannons or muskets?

2340. What is the name of the Portuguese explorer that is known for leading the first expedition to sail around the world in 1519 with the support of King Charles of Spain: Vasco de Gama or Ferdinand Magellan?

2341. What was the primary goal of Magellan: to discover another route to Eastern Asia, or to bring home spices from the "Spice Islands?"

2342. What is the name for the strait located in the southern tip of South America that allows the passage of ships from the Atlantic to the Pacific, and is named for a Portuguese explorer: the Strait of Magellan or the Strait of Gibraltar?

2343. What were the Trinidad, the Santiago, the Victoria, the San Antonio, and the Concepción: the five ships of Magellan, or the names that Magellan gave to five islands he discovered?

2344. What is the name of the cape on the southern tip of Africa that the Magellan expedition sailed around on the return voyage to Spain: the Cape of Magellan or the Cape of Good Hope?

2345. Which ocean, meaning "peaceful," is Magellan credited for naming: the Atlantic or the Pacific?

2346. How long did it take Magellan to cross the Pacific once he sailed through the Strait of Magellan on the way to the east: four days or four months?

2347. Was Magellan able to see his expedition through until the end, or was he killed in a battle with natives of the Philippines?

2348. How many of the 260 sailors successfully completed the 42,000-mile voyage around the world in 1522 on the Victoria, the only surviving ship: 28 or 18?

2349. What is the name of the sailors from the Netherlands who also started to explore the sea and find new trade routes after breaking away from Spain: the Dutch or the French?

2350. What did the English have in the East Indies with the East India Company: a trade monopoly or a trade partnership?

2351. When Pizarro, Columbus, De Gama, Magellan, and other Europeans came to the Americas, where do we say they came from: the Old World or the New World?

2352. What is the name for the lands that Europeans wanted to establish in the New World while governing those lands from their own country: colonies or settlements?

2353. How many colonies did the British have in the United States that later became known as our original first states: ten or thirteen?

2354. Did the Europeans set up colonies in the New World to farm and to mine for gold and silver?

2355. What people living in the colonies were forced to work on the farms and plantations in the New World: the English or the natives?

2356. What was a principal crop grown on larger plantations that was a big industry in Portuguese colonies: corn or sugarcane?

2357. What is the term for the transportation of slaves from across the ocean from the Old World to the New World: international trade zone or transatlantic slave trade?

2358. What types of crops were grown on the large plantations in the 1600's: sugar, coffee, and cotton, or corn, wheat, and potatoes?

2359. Which continent did the European colonists import slaves from after many of the natives of the colonized lands died from European diseases: Asia or Africa?

2360. What are the names of the two coasts of Africa where many slaves were sold from: the Gold and Angolan Coasts or the Northern and Eastern Coasts?

2361. What is the term for the three-way system that took finished goods like guns and molasses from Europe to Africa, slaves from Africa to the colonies in the Americas, and raw materials like sugar, cotton and tobacco from the New World back to Europe: the Slave Passage or Triangular Trade?

2362. What is the term for the second part of the triangle trade route between the 1500's and 1800's that carried hundreds of slaves on a cramped ship from Africa to the New World on a voyage that often took over three months: the Second Leg or the Middle Passage?

2363. What is the name of the colonial city where a Dutch ship, the White Lion, released 20 slaves in 1619 that it captured, and marked the beginning of slavery in America: Jamestown or Boston?

2364. What is the estimate of the number of slaves that came from Africa to the New World to work as slaves: two million or twelve million?

2365. Did places in Europe like Italy and Greece have a renewed focus on books and learning during the time of European exploration to the New World?

2366. What languages were many Greek language books translated into by Islamic scholars: Arabic or Latin?

2367. What language were many books written in Arabic translated into: Greek or Latin?

2368. What is the name for the revival of Greek and Roman architecture, art, literature, and learning that began in the 14th century in Italy, quickly spread throughout Europe, and was regarded as a "rebirth:" Renaissance or Medieval?

2369. What was the time frame of the Renaissance: 1400-1700 or 1300-1600?

2370. What is another name for the Age of Exploration in Europe that took place at the same time as the Renaissance between the 1400's and 1600's: Age of Enlightenment or Age of Discovery?

2371. During the Age of Discovery, did the Europeans succeed in discovering new routes to Asia and the Americas?

2372. What is the name of the most powerful empire of the time that ruled the Middle East for close to 600 years from 1299 until 1923, captured the Turkish capital Constantinople and renamed it Istanbul in 1453, and forced many artists and scholars to leave the Middle East for Italy: the Ottoman Empire or the Turkish Empire?

2373. Did the start of the Renaissance mark the beginning or the end of the Dark Ages?

2374. What is the term for the way of thinking that was characterized by a renewed interest in science, art, and music: liberal arts or humanism?

2375. Are history, poetry, and philosophy considered liberal arts or humanities?

2376. What is the name of the city in Italy that the Renaissance is said to have started, around 1350: Rome or Florence?

2377. What was the inspiration for the humanists of Florence, Italy to think about life in a new way: the ancient writings of the Greeks and Romans, or the teachings of ancient philosophers?

2378. What is the name of the rich and powerful family in Florence, Italy who promoted the humanist movement by supporting and sponsoring many artists, building churches to display artworks, building a library to provide books, and making Florence the center of learning and art: Plato or Medici?

2379. Who were Michelangelo, Raphael, Botticelli, Donatello, and Leonardo da Vinci, all supported by the Medici family: Renaissance architects or Renaissance artists?

2380. Who painted the *Sistine Chapel* in Rome and sculpted the *David*: Michelangelo or Leonardo da Vinci?

2381. Who painted the *Mona Lisa* and *The Last Supper*: Michelangelo or Leonardo da Vinci?

2382. Who is Galileo Galilei, whose scientific research was supported by the Medici family: an Italian scientist or an Italian artist?

2383. What did Galileo develop during the Renaissance: the Scientific Method or the telephone?

2384. Who invented the telescope, discovered the moons of Jupiter, the phases of Venus, sunspots, and observed that the Moon is covered with craters: Galileo or Johannes Kepler?

2385. What part of the first mechanical clock did Galileo design and develop during the Renaissance: the pendulum or the second hand?

2386. What is the name of the study of stars and celestial bodies that developed during the Renaissance: Astrology or Astronomy?

2387. Did Nicolaus Copernicus theorize that the Earth and planets orbit the Sun, or that the Sun orbits the Earth and the planets?

2388. What Renaissance scientist developed the three laws of planetary motion: Johannes Kepler or Johannes Gutenberg?

2389. What is the name of the Italian author who wrote "The Divine Comedy" at the beginning of the Renaissance in Florence in the early 1300's, considered the greatest work of Italian literature: Dante or Ficino?

2390. Who is Filippo Brunelleschi: a Renaissance artist or a Renaissance archiitect?

2391. What is the name of the Italian artist who painted a mural in a convent in Milan, Italy during the high renaissance in 1495 entitled *The Last Supper*: Leonardo da Vinci or Michelangelo?

2392. What is the name of Leonardo da Vinci's portrait of a lady that hangs in the Louvre museum in Paris, and is regarded as the most famous and most visited artwork in the world?

2393. What is the name of the Italian artist and sculptor that sculpted one of the most visited sculptures in the world, the *David* in Florence in 1501, as well as the ceiling of the *Sistine Chapel* in 1508 in Vatican City?

2394. What is the name of the Italian artist famous for his fresco painting on a library wall in the Pope's palace at the Vatican entitled *The School of Athens*, a painting that includes ancient Greek philosophers like Aristotle, Plato, Socrates, Euclid, and Pythagoras, was painted in 1511, and is considered this artist's masterpiece: Raphael or Michelangelo?

2395. What was the profession of Donatello, Jan Van Eyck, Masaccio, Botticelli, Leonardo da Vinci, Michelangelo, Raphael, and Caravaggio: Renaissance architects or Renaissance artists?

2396. Which artist is known as the "father of Renaissance painting:" Donatello or Masaccio?

2397. Did the art and architecture of Florence also spread to other Italian cities like Rome, Milan, Bologna, and Venice?

2398. Did Renaissance architecture include domes, columns, and arches?

2399. What kind of architecture does the Sistine Chapel in Vatican City and St. Peter's Basilica in Rome reflect: Modern or Renaissance?

2400. Did the Renaissance spread to other parts of Europe as well?

2401. Were the courts of princes important during the time of the Renaissance?

2402. What is the name of the famous Italian author who wrote "The Prince," a story about how a prince should lead and act during times of conflict and war: Castiglione or Machiavelli?

2403. What was the main church during the Renaissance: Catholic or Protestant?

2404. What was a popular form of entertainment during the Renaissance: music and dance, or reading and cooking?

2405. Were checkers, chess, masquerade balls, and festivals all Renaissance forms of entertainment?

2406. Did the type of food, clothing, and education depend on the social status of a person during the Renaissance?

2407. What specific dance was first introduced during the Renaissance: folk dance or ballet?

2408. What is the term for the form of vocal music that became popular during the Renaissance, with singers singing in distinct voices: choir or madrigal?

2409. What musical instrument was first made in Italy in the 1500's: the flute or the violin?

2410. What was the most important invention made during the Renaissance in 1440 that made it possible for information to be communicated to many people in a timely manner: the radio or the printing press?

2411. Who invented the printing press in 1440 with moveable metal pieces that paved the way for many books to be printed in Latin, English, Italian, German, and French: Johannes Gutenberg or Johannes Kepler?

2412. What was the first book that was mass produced by Gutenberg: The Gutenberg Poems or The Gutenberg Bible?

2413. What is the name for the spreading of Renaissance ideas to France, Germany, and England: The Northern Renaissance or The Southern Renaissance?

2414. What is the name of the German priest who opposed many Catholic Church practices and thought that the Bible was the only religious authority: Martin Luther or Luther Martin?

2415. What was the name given to the German Priest Martin Luther and others who publicly objected to the teachings of the church: Reformists or Protestants?

2416. What was the name given to the followers of Martin Luther: Lutherans or Protestants?

2417. What did Martin Luther's call for a new type of Christianity become known as: the Reformation or the Inquisition?

2418. What is John Calvin known as, a French man who aligned his beliefs with his interpretation of the Bible, and developed a system known as Calvinism: a Protestant or a Lutheran?

2419. What was the result of the Reformation: Christianity sub-divided into groups that included Catholics, Lutherans, Baptists, and Mennonites, or Christianity only reflected the teachings of the Catholic Church?

2420. What is the name of the Spanish Catholic Priest who founded the Society of Priests that became known as Jesuits, and established many schools in America: Ignatius of Loyola or Martin Luther?

2421. What is the name of the English king that is most famous for separating the churches in England, and having eight wives: King Henry VIII or King Edward VI?

2422. What is the name of the church created in England by King Henry VIII after he wanted to break ties with the Catholic Church when it refused to allow him to divorce his wife because she did not produce a male heir for him: The Puritan Church or the Church of England?

2423. What era was considered the golden age, the age of peace and prosperity when art, music, theatre, literature, and exploration all flourished in the 1600's: Elizabethan or Shakespearean?

2424. Who wore, silk, velvet, and ruffled collars: the monarch, or the monarch and the nobility?

2425. What did Queen Elizabeth I, who never married claiming she was married to her country, try to convert the Church of England into: a Catholic Church or a Protestant Church?

2426. What is the term given for people that wanted to *purify* the church by doing away with some Catholic traditions: Protestants or Puritans?

2427. Was England united or divided, having both devoted Catholics and devoted Puritans?

2428. What was the Elizabethan Era most famous for: its music or its theatre?

2429. What are the "Red Lion," the "Curtain," and the "Globe:" famous theatres in England or famous plays in England?

2430. Who is considered the greatest writer in the English Language, famous for his plays, dramas, and 14-line sonnet poems?

2431. What genre were Shakespeare's works, "Romeo and Juliet," and "A Midsummer Night's Dream: poems or plays?

2432. Were Shakespeare's works, "Hamlet," "Macbeth," "King Lear," and "Othello" sonnets or plays?

2433. How many lines does a sonnet poem have: 12 or 14?

2434. Who were Shakespeare's plays often performed for: Elizabeth I and King James I, thousands of spectators, or both nobles and spectators?

2435. What did Elizabeth I do to share in the riches of the Spanish ships on their trade routes: pirate them and claim the riches for England, or send out her own ships to claim the riches?

2436. Was there tension between the King Phillip II of Spain and the Elizabeth I, the monarch of England?

2437. What is the name of the fleet of 130 Spanish ships that King Phillip II of Spain put together to take over England: The Spanish Galleons or The Spanish Armada?

2438. Whom did Elizabeth I dub a knight, and appoint as the naval captain of the British fleet: Sir Francis Drake or Sir Duke?

2439. Which side won the naval battle in 1588 due to a surprise attack and a storm, and became the most powerful naval force in the world: the English or the Spanish?

2440. Was the Spanish Armada thought to have been invincible?

2441. Did Sir Francis Drake and the British continue to dominate the seas, as well as take over other treasure ships?

2442. What is Sir Francis Drake credited for besides defeating the mighty Spanish Armada: he was the first Englishman to sail around the world, or he was the second Englishman to sail around the world?

2443. How long was the reign of Queen Elizabeth I: 44 years or 14 years?

2444. What is the name of the state that Sir Walter Raleigh named for Queen Elizabeth I because she was celebrated as England's "virgin queen:" Virginia or West Virginia?

2445. Who was Queen Elizabeth I succeeded by: James I of Scotland or Charles I of Denmark?

2446. What book did King James I develop a new translation of that had a great impact on religious life and Protestant practices: the King James Bible or the Holy Bible?

2447. What is the name of the first permanent English colony in 1607 named for King James I in Virginia: Kingston or Jamestown?

2448. Did King James I believe that he was an agent of God here on Earth and should never be disobeyed?

2449. Did King James I and his son Charles I rule England with or without an English Parliament?

2450. Did tensions escalate between Puritans and Protestants when Charles I, a Protestant, married a Catholic?

2451. Which New England state did many Puritans emigrate to: Massachusetts or Virginia?

2452. What kind of war resulted in 1642 because of the religious tension between the Parliament and Royalists, or those who supported the King: the English Civil War or the English War of Succession?

2453. Which side won the English Civil War in 1649: the Parliament or the Royalists?

2454. Who is the General who lead the Parliament known as the Roundheads, and became England's new leader: Oliver Cromwell or Charles II?

2455. Did Oliver Cromwell enforce strict Puritan rules in England, or were religious expectations loosened up?

2456. Did the English people accept the strict Puritan laws or did they want to bring back the monarchy?

2457. What is the name of the new king in 1660 that brought back the Church of England: Charles II or Charles III?

2458. Was King James II, the brother of Charles II, a Catholic King or a Protestant King?

2459. Who became the new monarchs after King James II left for France, running away from Dutch troops that wanted to restore the Protestant faith: William and Mary, or Edward and Victoria?

2460. What was the name given to the English Revolution in 1688-1689 that resulted in the peaceful overthrow of the unpopular King James II: the Protestant Revolution or the Glorious Revolution?

2461. What did the English Parliament pass in 1689 that established the powers of the Parliament, and placed limits on the powers of the monarch as proclaimed basic liberties: the Bill of Rights, or the Magna Carta?

2462. Did many Renaissance ideas spread to Western Europe during the 1400's?

2463. Did Renaissance art and architecture also influence Russian culture?

2464. What is the name of the Russian prince who was regarded as the Grand Prince of Moscow between 1462 and 1505, is credited with uniting many Russian provinces, freeing Russia from the Mongols, and even went so far as to call himself "czar:" Ivan the Great or Ivan the Terrible?

2465. What is the name of the grandson of Ivan the Great who reigned between 1533-1547, was the first crowned czar of Russian with the title Grand Prince of Moscow, had St. Basil's Cathedral built for him at the Kremlin in Moscow, and is named for his strict rule and control: Ivan the Horrible or Ivan the Terrible?

2466. What is the name of the Russian czar in the late 17th century who is best known for his reforms, helping to establish Russia as a powerful nation extending the border to the Baltic Sea, and building a new capital city, St. Petersburg that is named for him: Peter the Great or Peter the Terrible?

2467. What is the name of the longest ruling empress of Russia who increased the territory of the empire, and modernized Russia under her reign: Empress Catherine or Catherine the Great?

2468. Did emperors and empresses lead other Asian nations during the 1400's and 1500's?

2469. What is the name for the Asian country made up of four islands with Tokyo as its capital?

2470. What types of storms are common in Japan: monsoons, typhoons, and tsunamis, or tornados, blizzards, and hurricanes?

2471. What is Japan also known as: "Land of Storms," or "Land of the Rising Sun?"

2472. Did many landowners in Japan often fight each other for more power?

2473. What is the name for the four-tiered class system in Japan that included the emperor seat at the top, followed by the daimyo or landholder, the samurai warrior, and the peasants: Feudalism or socialism?

2474. In the Japanese Feudal system, were the emperor and shogun or general at the top or the bottom of the pyramid?

2475. Was the daimyo, the Japanese landowner, above or below the emperor?

2476. What is the name for the military warriors in feudal Japan that carried two swords: samurai or swordsmen?

2477. What is the correct order of importance of the Japanese feudal structure among the peasants: farmers, artisans, and merchants, or merchants, artisans, and farmers?

2478. What is the name of the religion or way of life practiced in Japan that began in India and spread throughout Asia, and is a belief system based on enlightenment: Buddhism or Shintoism?

2479. What is the name of the prince from India in the 6th century who chose to help the poor rather than keep his riches, whose name means "enlightened one," and is the person that the Japanese belief system is based on: Buddha or Shinto?

2480. What do many Buddhists practice to help them focus and become "enlightened:" Yoga or Meditation?

2481. Are their many statues, temples, and shrines throughout Asia in honor of Buddha?

2482. What works of art did the Japanese create with bridges, plants, and flowers that help the Japanese to meditate and further serve to quiet the mind: parks or gardens?

2483. Who is the French artist who painted an artwork called "Japanese Footbridge" in the impressionist style because he was greatly inspired by the beauty of Japanese gardens: Claude Monet or Edgar Degas?

2484. What is the term for the Japanese belief system that incorporates the worship of nature spirits and Japanese ancestors: Shintoism or Buddhism?

2485. What is the general term for the period of re-birth that lasted between the 1300's and the 1600's and impacted many regions of the world: Medieval Ages or Renaissance?

2486. What is the name for the American time period between 1607 and 1763: the Colonial Period or British Expansion Period?

2487. In which direction did many early settlers move: east or west?

2488. What natural barrier prevented the early settlers from moving farther west: the Rocky Mountains or the Appalachian Mountains?

2489. Did many early settlers desire more land than was available for hunting and farming in 1775?

2490. What is the name of one of the first territories settled that includes the states of Ohio, Illinois, Indiana, Wisconsin, and Michigan: Northwest Territory or Northeast Territory?

2491. What is the name of the frontiersman that led settlers through the Cumberland Gap, a narrow passage through the Appalachian Mountains and into the state of Kentucky: Daniel Boone or Davy Crocket?

2492. What is the name of the trail or road that was paved on Boone's second expedition into Kentucky: the Western Road or the Wilderness Trail?

2493. Did Daniel Boone meet up with some resistance from the Indians who did not welcome new settlers?

2494. What is the name of the transaction made by President Thomas Jefferson when he made in a deal with France to acquire land west of the Mississippi River to the Rocky Mountains, in exchange for $15 million dollars, nearly doubling the size of the country: the Treaty of Paris or the Louisiana Purchase?

2495. What are the names of the two explorers that Jefferson sent out to explore and map the Louisiana Territory and the Wild West: Lewis and Clark or Boone and Crocket?

2496. How did the Native American woman Sacagawea help them on their journey: as a cook or as an interpreter?

2497. What trade industry became popular in the early 1800's, and the Great Lakes provided passageways that helped the transport of this trade, further attracting frontiersmen and mountain men to the West: the fur trade or the gold trade?

2498. Did many American traders continue to settle lands in the Eastern States like New Mexico, California, and Oregon?

2499. What is the term that is often used to describe the early settlers who travelled from place to place throughout the west: explorers or pioneers?

2500. What is the name of the people that settled in Great Salt Lake in Utah, led by Brigham Young, where they could avoid persecution and peacefully observe the teachings of the Church of Jesus Christ of Latter Day Saints: Mormons or Christians?

2501. What attracted thousands of people to California in 1848 after a man noticed shiny flakes of this metal in the water running through his sawmill?

2502. What is the term for the influx of people to California in 1848 and 1849: the Gold Rush or the Fur Trade?

2503. What is the name that was given to the more than 90,000 gold prospectors who arrived from Mexico, China, Europe, and Australia in 1849 with the dream of striking it rich: forty-niners or prospectors?

2504. What is the name of the process of separating the dirt and gravel from the gold: sifting or panning?

2505. What is the name that referred to the camps that would grow into towns during the gold rush because of the arrival of all the miners: ghost towns or boom towns?

2506. What is the name given to the boom towns after they were abandoned, like the Californian city of Bodie: ghost towns or deserted towns?

2507. In which state are the ghost towns "Virginia City" and "Nevada City: California or Montana?

2508. What is the name that was given to the caravans of pioneers who would travel thousands of miles in covered wagons pulled by oxen or mules through rugged terrain on their journey to California, often invading Indian land and angering Native Americans in the process: wagon trains or prairie schooners?

2509. What was the greater danger to the westbound wagon trains: conflicts with Native Americans, or weather, crossing rivers, and the risk of disease?

2510. What is the name for the primary route that the pioneers took in covered wagon trains between 1841 and 1849 when migrating to the west, a journey that began in Missouri and crossed Kansas, Nebraska, Wyoming, Idaho, and Oregon: the Westward Trail or the Oregon Trail?

2511. When were "Westward Ho," and "There's Gold in Them Thar Hills" popular refrains: during the Gold Rush, or during the Lewis and Clark Expedition?

2512. What kinds of homes did many early pioneers build: log homes or longhouses?

2513. Whose role was it to cook, clean, make soap, spin wool, make clothing, wash, iron, and tend to the garden: the frontiersman, the frontier woman, or the frontier children?

2514. Whose role was it to build a cabin, build a barn, and farm the field with a plow and oxen: the frontiersman, the frontier woman, or the frontier children?

2515. Whose role was it to milk the cows, feed the chickens, chop the wood, and help out with other pioneer chores: the frontiersman, the frontier woman, or the frontier children?

2516. Which two seasons of the year would the children attend school, all grade levels in a one-room schoolhouse with one teacher, learning basic reading, writing, spelling, and history: summer and winter, or spring and autumn?

2517. Which two seasons of the year would the children stay home to help with the planting and the harvesting: summer and winter, or spring and autumn?

2518. Who would sing, dance, play fiddles, and play with simple toys for entertainment during colonial America: farmers or pioneers?

2519. Why were droughts, tornados, wildfires, and locusts a big concern to the pioneers?

2520. Who invented the plow in 1837 that made farming easier for the pioneers: John Deere or Allis Chalmers?

2521. What group of people would often help the pioneers with the planting of crops and using certain herbs for medicine: the English colonists or the Native Americans?

2522. What were the bathrooms of the pioneers called: outhouses or longhouses?

2523. What were many pioneer houses made from: log and adobe, or wood and brick?

2524. How did the pioneers put together their log cabins with the trees on their land: with nails, or with notches they would cut on the ends of the logs?

2525. What would pioneers use to seal the cracks between the logs: mortar or mud?

2526. Did many pioneer homes have a stone fireplace and a few pieces of furniture?

2527. What is the term for the belief of many people in the United States that it was their right and the country's destiny to expand west all the way to the Pacific Ocean: Westward Manifesto or Manifest Destiny?

2528. Which southern state did many Americans immigrate to in 1821 even though it was governed by Mexico: Arizona or Texas?

2529. Who won the battle between Mexico and the Texans in 1836 when Mexican General Santa Anna and his soldiers surrounded a Spanish Mission called the Alamo in San Antonio, Texas that was the fortress for 180 Texans: the Mexicans or the Texans?

2530. What two famous frontiersmen were defeated at the battle of the Alamo: Davy Crockett and Jim Bowie, or Daniel Boone and Wild Bill?

2531. What did the Texans yell six weeks later during the fight with the Mexicans: "Remember the Alamo," or "Texas belongs to America?"

2532. What did Texas become after General Santa Anna was captured and the Mexicans were defeated at the Battle of San Jacinto in 1836: the State of Texas or the Republic of Texas?

2533. When did Texas officially become a state: 1845 or 1855?

2534. What is the name of the war that was fought between the United States and Mexico over the State of Texas and the border: the Spanish-American War, or the Mexican-American War?

2535. Who is the American President that declared war on Mexico and sent troops to defend the border in 1846: James K. Polk or Abraham Lincoln?

2536. What capital city did the American army claim victory after defeating General Santa Anna and his Mexican troops in 1847: Monterrey or Mexico City?

2537. What is the name of the Peace Treaty that gave the United States the states of California, Nevada, Utah, Oklahoma, Wyoming, Colorado, Arizona and New Mexico in exchange for 15 million dollars, extending the U.S. border to the Rio Grande: the Treaty of Guadalupe Hidalgo or the Treaty of Paris?

2538. How much of its territory was Mexico forced to give up after losing the Mexican-American War: thirty percent or fifty percent?

2539. What is the name for the monument in Mexico City at Chapultepec Castle that honors the six Mexican students who defended the Castle against American troops, translates "the boy heroes," and is now a Mexican National Holiday: Los Niños Heroes or "Los Heroes Muchachos?"

2540. Did the United States now extend its territory from the Atlantic to the Pacific?

2541. Did the states in the 1800's rely on both industry and agriculture?

2542. What part of the United States relied on steel, machinery, and industry in the 1800's: North or South?

2543. What part of the United States relied on agricultural crops like tobacco and cotton and had many farms and plantations: North or South?

2544. What did the South depend on to work the farms and plantations in the 1800's: Slavery or Machinery?

2545. Did many people living in the Northern states support or oppose slavery in the 1800's?

2546. What part of the United States wanted all the new states admitted into the Union to be Free states: the North or the South?

2547. What part of the United States wanted all the new states admitted into the Union to be Slave states: the North or the South?

2548. What is the name for the boundary between Maryland and Pennsylvania that separated the Free states from the Slave states, or the North from the South in 1763, by British surveyors Charles Mason and Jeremiah Dixon: the Mason-Dixon Line or the Division Border?

2549. What is the name of the agreement that was reached in 1820 that maintained the balance of Free states and Slave states when Maine was admitted as a Free State, and Missouri was admitted as a Slave State: the Maine Compromise or the Missouri Compromise?

2550. What is the name given to many people from the Northern States like Frederick Douglass, William Lloyd Garrison, and Harriet Beecher Stowe that wanted to end slavery: revolutionists or abolitionists?

2551. What is the name of the abolitionist author who wrote a novel in 1852 entitled, "Uncle Tom's Cabin" depicting the brutality of slavery, and fueled the human rights debate before the Civil War: Frederick Douglass or Harriet Beecher Stowe?

2552. What is the name of the ruling made by the Supreme Court in 1857 that did not award a slave and his family their freedom when their owner moved back to the slave state of Missouri after living in the free state of Wisconsin, taking the family with him to work as slaves, and ruled that slavery was legal in all U.S. Territories: the Dred Scott Decision or the Frederick Douglass Decision?

2553. What is the name given for the series of seven debates between the Republican candidate Abraham Lincoln for the Illinois Senate in 1858, and Senator Stephen A. Douglas on slavery that helped Lincoln receive national attention, and paved the road for his future presidency: the Slavery Debates, or the Lincoln-Douglas Debates?

2554. Which states believed that they had the right to stay in the Union or to leave the Union if slavery was no longer allowed based on their Constitutional rights: the Northern states or the Southern states?

2555. Which candidate opposed slavery, but stated that he did not want to interfere with the slavery practices of the Southern states, and was elected president in 1860: Stephen A. Douglass or Abraham Lincoln?

2556. What action did many Southern states take in 1861 because of their position in support of slavery: remain in the Union or secede (leave) the Union?

2557. What did the Southern states call themselves after they decided to secede from the Union in 1861 and form their own country: the Union States or the Confederate States?

2558. Was President Lincoln for or against slavery and a strong federal government?

2559. Who was the President of the Confederate States or the Confederation, as it was known: Robert E. Lee or Jefferson Davis?

2560. What is the name for the war in the United States starting in 1861 between Abraham Lincoln and the Union States of the North who opposed slavery, and Jefferson Davis and the Confederate States of the South who supported slavery: the American War of Independence or the American Civil War?

2561. What is the name of the battle near South Carolina that signaled the start of the American Civil War on April 12, 1861 where the Southern or Confederate States first started firing: the Battle of Fort Sumter or the Battle of Shiloh?

2562. What is the name of the first major land battle of the Civil War in July of 1861 when the Union army attacked the Confederate army along a creek in Virginia: the Battle of Bull Run, or the Battle of Shiloh?

2563. What is the nickname that was given to the Confederate General Thomas Jackson after he and his troops arrived at the Battle of Bull Run and held their ground similar to a "stone wall:" General Jackson Wall or "Stonewall" Jackson?

2564. What is the formal name given to the states that seceded from the Union, and had their own constitution that supported the rights of states and slavery: The Separate States or The Confederate States?

2565. Who was the President of the Confederacy: Thomas Jefferson or Jefferson Davis?

2566. Who is the leader that is credited for stopping abolitionist John Brown's raid on Harpers Ferry in 1859 to take possession of the arsenal of weapons: Robert E. Lee or Ulysses S. Grant?

2567. What is the name of the Commander and General of the Confederate Army of Virginia and the military advisor to President Jefferson Davis during the American Civil War: Robert E .Lee or Ulysses S. Grant?

2568. What is the name of the city where the Confederates established their capital: Richmond or Williamsburg?

2569. What is the name of the military leader who had his first victory in Tennessee when he captured Fort Donelson in 1863, and was appointed the Chief General of the entire Union army by President Lincoln: Robert E. Lee or Ulysses S. Grant?

2570. What was Ulysses S. Grant's nickname after he told the commanders of the Confederate army, "No terms except an unconditional and immediate surrender can be accepted:" "Unconditional Surrender" Grant, or "Immediate Surrender" Grant?

2571. What was the age range of most Civil War soldiers: 15-25 or 12-22?

2572. Did weather, fatigue, infection, disease, and lack of food and medical supplies pose challenges for many Civil War soldiers?

2573. What was the nickname that the Southerners gave to the Northerners: "Yankees" or "Rebels?"

2574. What was the nickname that the Northerners gave to the Southerners: "Yankees" or "Rebels?"

2575. What finally became the standard uniform color of the Union North: blue or gray?

2576. What finally became the standard uniform color of the Confederate South: blue or grey?

2577. What were the typical weapons of the American Civil War: muskets and rifles, or bows and swords?

2578. What did the Civil War soldiers carry their gear in: a knapsack or a duffle bag?

2579. What is the name for what the Union established to guard the eastern coastline and the ports with their ships after the start of the Civil War that was designed to prevent supplies, weapons, and the export of cotton into the Confederate States: the Union Blockade or the Anaconda Blockade?

2580. What was unique about the 1862 Confederate ship known as the "Merrimack" and the Union ship known as the "Monitor" that makes them different from their wooden ship counterparts, and would forever change the future of naval warfare: they were the first underwater ships, or they were the first ironclad ships with cannons to engage in battle?

2581. What is the meaning of emancipate: to keep someone captive against his or her will, or to set someone free?

2582. What is the name given for the order given by President Lincoln in 1862 that declared "that all persons held as slaves" within the Confederate States "are, and henceforward shall be free," and later paved the way for the Thirteenth Amendment to the Constitution: the Freedom of Slaves Act or the Emancipation Proclamation?"

2583. When did President Lincoln announce the Emancipation Proclamation that promised freedom to the slaves in the South starting on January 1, 1863: five days before or five days after the Union victory at the Battle of Antietam?

2584. Did many African Americans join the Union forces after the Union government passed a law, and as a result of the Emancipation Proclamation?

2585. What is the term used during the Civil War that referred to a network of people and hideouts that slaves used to escape the South and seek freedom in the North: the Underground Tunnel or the Underground Railroad?

2586. Where would slaves have to escape to in order to be completely safe from being returned to their owners: Canada or Mexico?

2587. What is the term given for the person that led slaves along the Underground Railroad during the Civil War: engineers or conductors?

2588. What is the term used for the hideouts for the slaves along the Underground Railroad: stations or tracks?

2589. What is the name of the African American woman and former slave that acted as a conductor in the Underground Railroad, leading many slaves to freedom, and also served as a spy for the North? Sojourner Truth or Harriet Tubman?

2590. What is the name of the battle led by Confederate General George Pickett when General Lee called on him to make a direct attack of the Union Army killing over half of the Confederate soldiers: Pickett's Charge or Pickett's Battle?

2591. What is the name of the three-day battle in Pennsylvania that is regarded as one of the most important and deadliest battles of the Civil War in July of 1863, and was a turning point after the Union was able to stop General Lee's invasion of the North: the Battle of Gettysburg or the Battle of Shiloh?

2592. What is the name of the two-minute speech given on November 1, 1863 by President Lincoln at a dedication ceremony at a cemetery in Pennsylvania, and is regarded as one of the most famous speeches in history: Lincoln's Inauguration Address, or Lincoln's Gettysburg Address?

2593. What are the words of the first line of President Lincoln's Gettysburg Address: "It was the best of times, it was the worst of times" or "Four score and seven years ago…?"

2594. What is "score" another word for: twenty or ten?

2595. Does "four score and seven years ago" equal the year 1776, when the signers of the Declaration of Independence declared "all men are created equal?"

2596. What is the name of the Union General's march in the spring of 1864 from Tennessee to Georgia, when he and his Union forces took control of Atlanta, proceeded to Savannah, and took control of the sea port, destroying everything along their way: Sherman's March to the Sea, or the March to Savannah?

2597. Was President Lincoln elected to a second term?

2598. What side was winning during the time of Lincoln's re-election after the capture of Richmond, Virginia: the Union or the Confederacy?

2599. Which side was nearly twice the size as the other: the Union or the Confederacy?

2600. Which General surrendered to the other on April 9, 1865 in Appomattox, Virginia: General Lee surrendered to the Union General Ulysses S. Grant, or General Grant surrendered to the Confederate General Robert E. Lee?

2601. Was the surrender and the terms for the surrender discussed respectfully between Lee and Grant on April 9, 1865 at Appomattox Courthouse in Virginia?

2602. Which war is still regarded as the deadliest war in American History, with a death toll of over 600,000: the American War of Independence or the American Civil War?

2603. What happened to President Lincoln five days later on April 14th while he and his wife Mary Todd Lincoln were seated in the President's box watching a play at a theatre near the White House?

2604. What is the name of the theatre where President Lincoln was shot in the back of the head: Washington's Theatre or Ford's Theatre?

2605. What is the name of the actor who silently crept up behind President Lincoln and shot him behind the head, motivated because the Confederates had all but lost the Civil War: John Wilkes Booth or General Lee?

2606. What did John Wilkes Booth break after jumping onto the stage after shooting President Lincoln: his arm or his leg?

2607. How long before John Wilkes Booth was caught and shot by soldiers after trapping him in a barn in Virginia: one day or twelve days?

2608. How is the Ford Theatre used today: as a warehouse or as a Museum?

2609. What is the name of the President who became the 17th President of the United States after the assassination of President Lincoln: Jefferson Davis or Andrew Jackson?

2610. What is the period of time called after the Civil War ended between 1865 and 1877: Expansion or Reconstruction?

2611. What had been Lincoln's vision as part of the Reconstruction process after the Civil War: to bring the Confederate states back into the Union, or to allow the Southern states to have their own government?

2612. What was the condition of many of the Southern states after the Civil War: they were in good condition, or they were largely destroyed?

2613. Was the Reconstruction period a time of rebuilding the North or rebuilding the South?

2614. What troops occupied many Southern states during Reconstruction to make sure that the laws were being followed: Federal troops or Union troops?

2615. Could people in the Southern states receive a pardon simply by pledging loyalty to the Union under President Lincoln's Reconstruction plan?

2616. What became President Johnson's nickname because he vetoed many Reconstruction laws that were passed by Congress: "The Opposition President," or "The Veto President?"

2617. What did the U.S. House of Representatives want to do to President Johnson because he had vetoed many bills and because he wanted to stop the Republican's plans regarding Reconstruction: re-elect him to office or impeach (remove) him from office?

2618. Was President Johnson found guilty or not-guilty by the Senate by one vote?

2619. What is the name given for the laws that were passed by Southern states that did not allow blacks the right to vote, own land, attend school, or other basic rights: Black Rules or Black Codes?

2620. What three amendments were added to the Constitution to protect the rights of people and to help with the Reconstruction process in that the newly passed laws would outlaw slavery, declare every

U.S. citizen equal under the law, and give all people the right to vote: the 1st, 2nd, and 3rd amendments, or the 13th, 14th, and 15th amendments?

2621. Did the Southern states have to ratify or accept the new amendments to the Constitution in order to be readmitted to the Union?

2622. Which side helped the Reconstruction process by building roads, building schools, and promoting farming: the Union or the Confederacy?

2623. What is the name for Northerners who moved to the South because they wanted to help with Reconstruction, so named for what they used for travel bags: scalawags or carpetbaggers?

2624. What is the name of the agency that was set up by the federal government to fight against the Black Codes and help to distribute land and build schools: The Freedmen's Bureau or The Freedom Bureau?

2625. Was there still conflict in the South between blacks and whites during Reconstruction?

2626. What is the name for the Post Civil War society organized in the South, wore hooded garments, and aimed to suppress the newly acquired rights of blacks by means of terrorism: the Ku Klux Klan or the White Supremes?

2627. Was there still conflict between the rights of people in 1877 when Reconstruction ended?

2628. In which century were many African Americans finally able to benefit from the Thirteenth, Fourteenth, and Fifteenth Amendments guaranteeing all citizens their rights: the 19th Century or the 20th Century?

2629. Where did many people migrate to after the American Civil War: West or East?

2630. What is the name given to the West because of its reputation as being less civilized: the "Wild West" or the "Crazy West?"

2631. What is the name of the act that Congress pass in 1862 that made public lands in the West available for a low fee where a home could be built: the Homestead Act or the Farm Act?

2632. What kind of home did many pioneers build on the prairie that was cool in the summer and warm in the winter: an adobe house or a sod house?

2633. Who often worked as ranchers with cattle and cattle drives in the old west: Cowboys or Indians?

2634. What is the term for when the cowboy would work to gather all the cattle together: a round up or a cattle drive?

2635. What is the term for the process of moving a herd of cattle from one place to another: a round up or a cattle drive?

2636. Were there a lot of cattle ranches in the West after the Civil War?

2637. What did cowboys wear on their heads to protect their heads from the Sun: a ten-gallon hat or a scarf?

2638. Who would wear chaps, boots, and bandanas: Cowboys or Indians?

2639. What is the name of the sporting event that includes bull-riding, calf roping, and bareback bronco riding?

2640. What is the name of the musical instrument that a cowboy would often play: a guitar or a harmonica?

2641. Who were "Wild Bill Hickok" "Billy the Kid," "Jesse James," "Wyatt Earp," "Butch Cassidy," and "Sundance" famous for in the Old West: gunfighters, bandits, and outlaws, or cowboys, sheriffs, and ranchers?

2642. What is buffalo hunter William F. Cody who organized Wild West shows better known as: "Buffalo Bill" or "Wild Bill Hickok?

2643. Who was the star attraction and famous lady sharpshooter that performed in Buffalo Bill's Wild West Shows: Annie Oakley or Calamity Jane?

2644. What was the mail delivery service between Missouri and California that followed the Oregon Trail in 1861 and 1862, and included Buffalo Bill: the Pony Express or the Postal Trail?

2645. What means of communication replaced the Pony Express in 1861: the telephone or the telegraph?

2646. What means of transportation was built between 1863 and 1869 that replaced the wagon trains, and covered over 1,700 miles: the Transcontinental Railroad or the Continental Railway?

2647. Were there conflicts between cowboys, pioneers, and Native Americans during the time of Westward Expansion?

2648. What is another name given for the West: the American Frontier or the American Wilderness?

2649. Which state did Secretary of State William Seward purchase from Russia for seven million dollars in 1867: Hawaii or Alaska?

2650. What was discovered in Juneau, Alaska in 1868: gold or silver?

2651. Did the United States have several treaties in place with the Native Americans to settle land disputes?

2652. Did many great Native American Indian Tribes live on the American Frontier in the late 1800's and early 1900's?

2653. Were many Indian Tribes forced to live on Reservations assigned by the government?

2654. Were the Indian leaders Buffalo Bill and Crazy Horse for or against Westward expansion?

2655. What was the main cause of tension between some Native American Indians and White settlers: land rights or fishing rights?

2656. What is the name of the teacher and nurse during the American Civil War who founded the American Red Cross in 1881: Florence Nightingale or Clara Barton?

2657. What is the name of the man who married Martha, lived at Mount Vernon, led his troops across the Delaware River in 1776 on Christmas Day, supposedly cut down a cherry tree on his father's property, and helped select the site for the capital on the Potomac River that is named for him?

2658. Who is the current President of the United States?

2659. Who is the current First Lady of the United States?

2660. Who are Thomas Jefferson, J.F. Kennedy, Abraham Lincoln, Franklin D. Roosevelt, Dwight D. Eisenhower, Harry S. Truman, Richard Nixon, Ronald Reagan, Betty Ford, and George W. Bush?

2661. Who are Martha Washington, Abigail Adams, Mary Todd Lincoln, Dolly Madison, Eleanor Roosevelt, Claudia "Lady Bird" Johnson, Jaqueline Kennedy, Nancy Reagan, and Laura Bush?

2662. Who are Amelia Earhart and Charles Lindbergh: famous aviators or famous inventors?

2663. Who are Clara Barton, Elizabeth Blackwell, and Florence Nightingale: famous nurses or famous reformers?

2664. Who are Alexander Graham Bell, Thomas Edison, Samuel F.B. Morse, Eli Whitney, Benjamin Franklin, and the Wright Brothers: famous authors or famous inventors?

2665. Who are Dorothea Dix, Helen Keller, Frederick Douglass, and Lucretia Mott: famous reformers or famous military heroes?

2666. Who are P.T. Barnum, Annie Oakley, and the Ringling Brothers: famous cowboys or famous entertainers?

2667. Who are Buffalo Bill, Daniel Boone, Davy Crockett, and Kit Carson: famous frontiersmen or famous Native Americans?

2668. What famous American can you name and what is that person best known for?

2669. What country of the world is known for being a "melting pot" because of its diverse population; its colorful history; being regarded as the land of opportunity; freedom and liberty; many national parks and monuments; and for baseball, football, and hot dogs?

2670. What country of the world is known for its long river the Rio Grande; speaking Spanish; Pre-Columbian ruins and artifacts; Pre-Columbian Indian groups that include the Olmecs, the Toltecs, Maya, and the Aztecs; the pyramids of the Sun and the Moon at Teotihuacan; the Maya ruins of Chichén Itza, Palenque and Tulum; the resort cities of Cancun, Riviera Maya, and Puerto Vallarta; the cliff divers of Acapulco; Chapultepec Park; Alameda Park; The Palace of Fine Arts; The Zócalo main square; La Avenida Juarez; The National Museum of Anthropology; The Basilica of Our Lady of Guadalupe, the patron saint; The Aztec Stadium seating over 100,000 spectators; silver and copper; black pottery; serape blankets and woven textiles; food markets; chocolate; the holidays Cinco de Mayo and Dia de los Muertos; Mariachi music; colorful folk dancing; monarch butterflies; the Chihuahua; the volcano Popocatepetl; the poinsettia; bullfighting; the agave cactus; the Spanish conquistador Hernan Cortes; the Aztec God Quetzalcoatl; the priest Miguel Hidalgo; war hero

Pancho Villa; the Zapotec Indian president Benito Juarez; artists Diego Rivera and Frida Kahlo; guitarist Carlos Santana; and foods that include tamales, tortillas, enchiladas, guacamole, jalepeños, enchiladas, and chicken with mole sauce?

2671. What country of the world is known for a fortress built by the Spanish to keep out invaders and pirates called Castillo de San Felipe del Morro; the Taino Indians; the tropical rainforest called El Yunque; the native tree frog called the Coquí, named for the sound that it makes; tropical birds; exotic flowers and orchids; the Cathedral of San Juan Bautista; the colonial Spanish architecture, narrow streets, and colorful buildings of Old San Juan; the largest radio telescope located in Arecibo; baseball; beaches; scuba diving; rum; salsa music; lace; hammocks; coconuts; bananas; musical instruments that include bongos, congas, guiros, and the cuatro guitar; foods that include banana turnovers called mufongo, suckling pig called lechón, and rice and beans called arroz con habichuelas; gold and silver; the Spanish explorer and first governor of this country, Juan Ponce de Leon; many baseball players including the Pittsburgh Pirate hall of famer Roberto Clemente; the Broadway actress who played the role of Anita in West Side Story, Rita Moreno; the blind singer of "Feliz Navidad," José Feliciano; and translates into English as "rich port?"

2672. What country of the world is known for being settled by the native Tainos Indians; as the first colony founded by Christopher Columbus; for sharing the island of Hispañiola with Haiti; being named for the Spanish Saint Dominic; the province of Duarte, named for one of this country's founding fathers, Juan Pablo Duarte; the tropical island of Catalina; the Punta Cana Resort and many scenic beaches; baseball and several Major League baseball players; the merengue dance and bachata music; Pico Duarte, the highest peak in the Caribbean; the Cathedral of Santa Maria in the Colonial zone of Santo Domingo, the oldest cathedral in the Americas; products like rum, stone jewelry, gold, textiles, paintings, dolls, sugar, and coffee; fashion designer Oscar de la Renta; a seven meat stew called sancocho; mashed plantains called mangú; fried bananas called tostones; and a cake called bizcocho dominicano?

2673. What country of the world is known for being the largest island in the Caribbean; the Plaza de Armas and the Spanish Morro Castle located in Havana; Fidel Castro, a polarizing socialist military leader for several decades; rum; the mojito rum cocktail; habanero hot sauce; cigars; being the birthplace of the Salsa dance; the Cha-cha-cha dance; Rumba song and dance; singers Desi Arnaz, Jon Secada, and Celia Cruz; José Martí, a revolutionary writer and leader who fought for this country's independence, and author of the poem that inspired the song, "Guantanamera;" baseball and several baseball players; the U.S. naval base of Guantanamo; the 1961 failed military invasion, supported by President John F. Kennedy at The Bay of Pigs; and beautiful beaches?

2674. What country of the world is known for Tortuguero National Park; the Monteverde Cloud Forest Reserve; the National Theatre in San Jose; rain forests; volcanoes; sea turtles; tropical birds and flowers; the Scarlet Macaw; the Quetzal bird; exports that include coffee, bananas, and sugar; soccer; a rice and black bean dish called gallo pinto; fried bananas called tostones; colorful oxcarts, canopy zip-lining; surfing; water rafting; and is a country that translates as "Rich Coast" in English?

2675. What country of the world is known for the native Maya Indians; the ruins of the Maya city El Mirador located in a tropical jungle; the island of Flores that is connected to the mainland by a causeway; the Chichicastenango Market; the Santa Catalina Arch in the colonial city of Antigua; Lake Atitlán located in the highlands; the ancient Mayan ruins of Tikal located in the lowland rainforest; the Mayan ruins of Quiriga featuring 22 carved stelae, tall sculpted stones covered with figures and glyphs; coffee; bananas; active volcanoes; women carrying giant baskets on their heads; colorful woven textiles; leather; jewelry; fruit juice drinks called licuados; tamales; the colorful chicken buses called camionetas; traditional music called marimba; fiestas; cathedrals; tropical birds; tropical animals; and exotic flowers?

2676. What country of the world is known as "the land of the volcanoes" having over 20 volcanoes; the San Salvador Volcano; world surfing competitions; the Gothic cathedral of Saint Anne; soccer; the national dish, a stuffed tortilla called pupusa; earthquakes; Mayan ruins; coffee; and translates from Spanish as, "the savior?"

2677. What country of the world is known for its mestizo population; the freshwater lake Managua where sharks live; animals like toucans, boa constrictors, wild boars, and sea turtles; exports of coffee, bananas, and sugarcane; the old Cathedral of Managua; the colorful houses, horse-drawn carriages, and Victorian architecture of Granada; the fishing village of San Juan del Sur; the Masaya volcano;; the San Sebastian Festival in January; the diving and snorkeling of the Corn Islands; the Metropolitan Cathedral in Leon; the poet Ruben Dario; and its civil wars?

2678. What country of the world is known for its location on an isthmus, and having coastlines on both the Caribbean Sea and the Pacific Ocean; the explorers Christopher Columbus and Vasco Nuñez de Balboa; indigenous native people called Kuna; exports that include bananas, coffee, rice, and beans; having over 1,400 tree species including the square tree; golden frogs; sea turtles; Miraflores Lock; and for having a 51-mile long canal that was built as an international maritime trade path connecting the Atlantic Ocean and the Pacific Ocean?

2679. What country of the world is known for the highest waterfall called Angel Falls at 3,212 feet; Miraflores Palace; Caracas Cathedral; La Isla Margarita; Pico Bolivar, also called Mirror Peak; cornflower bread sandwiches called arepas; the Orinoco River; the giant otter called a river-wolf; large oil reserves; several Major League baseball players; politician Hugo Chavez; war hero Simón Bolivar; and is a country so named because the Italian explorer Amerigo Vespucci thought that the area around Lake Maracaibo resembled the waterways of the Italian city of Venice?

2680. What country of the world is known for having the largest Gothic basilica in the Americas located in the historic center of Quito called The Basilica del Voto Nacional; St. Francisco Church; Cotopaxi Volcano; the city of Baños at the foot of an active volcano and called the "Gateway to the Amazon;" the wood, jewelry, woven textiles, and stone carvings located in the markets of Otavalos; soccer; foods that include the yucca tortilla, potatoes, llapingacho potato pancakes, concha corn, guinea pig called cuy, locro potato soup, the aji chile pepper, shrimp ceviche and melcocha taffy; volcanic islands called The Galapagos where giant tortoises, sea lions, penguins, and iguanas are found, and served as the inspiration for Charles Darwin's Theory of Natural Selection; and is a country named for its location given that the equator runs through it?

2681. What country of the world is known for the Gold Museum of Bogotá; the beach resort city of Cartagena; the small towns called pueblos; jungles; wine; soccer; is named for the famous maritime explorer; the painter Fernando Botero, famous for his exaggerated depictions of people and animals; the Botero Musuem; author of "One Hundred Years of Solitude," Gabriel Garcia Marquez; singers Shakira and Juanes; designer Carolina Herrera; cornmeal bread called arepa; tamales; white cheese buñuelos; and world-renowned coffee?

2682. What country of the world is known for having the highest capital city La Paz; Yungas Road, considered to be one of the most dangerous in the world; Lake Titicaca; the jaguar, the titi monkey, and the 9.000 species of birds found in Madidi National Park; the llama; the historical buildings of Sucre where the liberator Simón Bolivar wrote this country's constitution; the annual Oruro Carnival, a folk festival held before Ash Wednesday involving thousands of dancers and musicians; having the largest salt flats, Salar de Uyuni; pottery; colorful woven textiles; soccer; and is the place where the American bank robbers Butch Cassidy and the Sundance Kid were killed in a shootout in 1908?

2683. What country of the world is known for Iguazu Falls; Perito Moreno Glacier; "La Boca" district of Buenos Aires with its colorful houses; Baroliche City at the foot of the Andes Mountains; the sea lions, penguins, and elephant seals in the Valdes Peninsula; the Mendoza Wine Fields; its historical buildings, outdoor cafes, and wide boulevards; the tango dance; gaucho cowboys; vast plains of grass called the pampas; foods that include grilled gaucho steak, empanadas, mate tea, roast beef called carne asado, chorizo sausage; shrimp ceviche, chipas cheese bread, and dulce de leche dessert; religious leader Pope John Francis; world leader Juan Perón; and political wife and activist Evita Perón?

2684. What country of the world is known as a landlocked country; for the colonial district of the capital city Asunción; the waterfalls in Ciudad de Este; spindle lace; having a view of Iguazu Falls; the San Blas Festival in February; as having one of the largest hydraulic complexes in the world and recognized as one of the seven modern wonders of the world, the Itaipú Dam; and the Paraguay river cruises?

2685. What country of the world is known for its beautiful beaches along the golden coast or the Costa de Oro; the fishing village of Aguas Dulces; the old city quarters of Montevideo; the popular summer destination, the beaches of Punta del Este; high consumption of beef; soccer; leather goods; mate tea; wines; gaucho cowboys; author Horacio Quiroga; and the home of the rugby team survivors of "Uruguayan Air Force Flight 571" who survived for three months after crashing into the Andes Mountains?

2686. What country of the world is known for Los Pinguinos National Monument that is home to more than 120,000 penguins; the Santiago residence of the President, La Moneda Palace; the brightly colored houses and bohemian culture of Valparaiso; the Valle de la Luna or Valley of the Moon named for its extensive sand dunes located in the Atacama Desert; the three granite peaks at Torres del Paine; the volcanoes and Lake Chungará located at Lauca National Park; foods that include corn tamales called humitas, sea bass, empañadas, and wines; soccer; poet Pablo Neruda; writer Gabriela Mistral; and the 887 statues called Moai located thousands of miles off the coast of this long, narrow country, a Polynesian island known as Easter Island?

2687. What country of the world is known for the images of monkeys, spiders, and lizards called the Nazca Lines; the group of reed islands in Lake Titicaca called Uros Islands; the Plaza de Armas in Cuzco;

The Sacred Valley of the Inca located in the Andes; The Inca Trail; the walled complex of the Inca called Saksayhuaman; foods that include beef tenderloin called lomo saltado, potato croquets called papas rellenas, quinoa, fried guinea pig called cuy, and pumpkin fritters called picarones; llamas and alpacas; llama fur blankets, scarves, hats, sweaters, and mittens; brightly colored hand-woven textiles; chullo hats with ear flaps; silver jewelry; soccer; the serpent, puma cougar, and condor; pan pipes; flute music; and the ancient Inca fortress of Machu Picchu located in the Andes over 7,000 feet above sea level, and re-discovered by explorer and archeologist Hiram Bingham in 1911?

2688. What country of the world is known for the largest rainforest, the Amazon; the 4,000 mile long Amazon River; piranhas; the annual Rio Samba Parade and Carnival in Rio de Janeiro; samba music and dance; drums and percussion instruments; champion soccer teams; the majestic Iguazu Falls; Copacabana Beach; speaking Portuguese; exporting sugarcane and coffee; clay pottery and ceramics; lace; hammocks; leather sandals; Indian woodworks; cangas beachware; havaianas flip-flops; feather art; black beads; juice bars; foods that include the acai berry, bananas; shrimp stew, fried yucca sticks, black bean stew called feijoada, and candy treats called bridgardeiros; the soccer players Ronaldo and Pele; politician Jimmy Hoffa; and the statue of Jesus Christ towering over 130 feet called Christ the Redeemer?

2689. What country of the world is known for its glaciers and volcanoes, and nicknamed "the land of fire and ice;" being founded by the Vikings of Scandinavia; its location on two tectonic plates; being a land of geysers, waterfalls, and hot springs; sheep; black and white birds called Puffins; Reykjavik, the capital city where most of this country's inhabitants live; whale watching; a geothermal spa called The Blue Lagoon; the Gullfoss waterfall; believing in the existence of elves; midnight golf; handball; the soft cheese yogurt snack called Skyr; visits by the Yule Lads during Christmastime; the fishing industry; cod; the Aurora Borealis or Northern Lights; hand knit wool sweaters, blankets, and knit goods; and the birthplace of the first European to reach the New World, Leif Ericson?

2690. What country of the world is known for its long history; royalty; Stonehenge; Big Ben; London Bridge; Buckingham Palace; Windsor Castle; the River Thames, Westminster Abbey; double decker red buses; Trafalgar Square; St. Paul' Cathedral; Hyde Park; a wax museum called Madame Tussauds; William Shakespeare; Robin Hood; Isaac Newton; Charles Darwin; the Beatles; Wimbledon tennis; cricket; rugby; tea time; pubs; Oxford University; and Cambridge University?

2691. What country of the world is known as the "Emerald Isle" for its green countryside; the cliffs of Moher; sheep; Aran sweaters; foods that include potatoes, stew, soda bread, and whiskey; pubs; Guiness Beer; the Blarney Stone; Saint Patrick's Cathedral; dance and jigs; Celtic folk music; red hair; shamrocks; leprechauns; Waterford crystal; the harp; Limericks; writer Oscar Wilde; its capital city of Dublin; and the song "Molly Malone?"

2692. What country of the world is known for its medieval castles; royalty including Mary, Queen of Scots; green countryside; a 3,000 year old tree; freshwater lochs; golf courses; the Edinburgh Theatre Festival; the Glasgow Cathedral; the Loch Ness monster; the unicorn; scotch whiskey; bagpipes; kilts; having the largest population of redheads; the author of "Ivanhoe," Sir Walter Scott; Mary; Queen of Scots; the scientist and inventor, Alexander Graham Bell; the author of "Don Juan," Lord Byron; and the actor of several "James Bond" movies, Sean Connery?

2693. What country of the world is known for King Ludwig's Castle; Lichtenstein Castle; Neuschwanstein Castle; the Berlin Wall; military leader Adolf Hitler; the Holocaust; Anne Frank, The Black Forest; Cuckoo clocks; Hummel figurines; the Glockenspiel clock in Munich; the Bavarian Alps; beer; Oktoberfest; gesundheit; the waltz; the first printed book; the Edelweiss flower; gingerbread houses; composers Beethoven and Bach; Fahrenheit; the Mercedes and Volkswagen cars; ethnic clothing called Lederhosen and the Bavarian dress called Dirdnl; kindergarten; foods that include liverwurst, bratwurst, knackwurst, frankfurter, sauerkraut, sauerbraten, wiener schnitzel, pretzel, stollen fruit cake, apple streusel, and the food named for the city of Hamburg, the hamburger?

2694. What country of the world is known for the Old Market Place in Warsaw; Main Market Square in Krakow; Malbork Castle; Gdansk Old Town; Auschwitz, the Nazi concentration camp during World War II; The Wieliczka Salt Mine; the bison of the Bialowieza primal forest; the kobza bagpipe; Pope John Paul II; the composer Frederic Chopin; scientist and astronomer Nicolas Copernicus; the Russian Tsar Catherine the Great; radioactivity scientist and physicist Marie Curie; world leader Lech Walesa; the author of "Heart of Darkness," "Lord Jim," and "The Secret Sharer," Joseph Conrad; foods that include sausages, kielbasa, pierogi dumplings, and Paczki doughnuts; sharing the Oplatek Christmas wafer at Christmastime; glassware; wood carvings; Babushka scarves and shawls; paper art; stoneware; embroidery; paper art; and dolls?

2695. What country of the world is known for its rich history; the renaissance; ancient theatres; the opera; Pompeii; the Colosseum; the Pantheon; St. Peter's Basilica; the Trevi Fountain; Vatican City; the Pope; the Sistine Chapel; St. Peter's Cathedral; the Leaning Tower of Pisa; the Spanish Steps in the Piazza di Spagna in Rome; the Uffizi Gallery; the Ponte Vecchio bridge; the Piazza del Duomo; Michelangelo's "David" statue in Florence; painter and inventor Leonardo da Vinci; the gondola boats of Venice; the countryside of Tuscany; the Roman general Julius Caesar; the philosopher of nursing and social reformer Florence Nightingale; the explorer Christopher Columbus; the map maker Amerigo Vespucci; the traveler Marco Polo; the scientist Galileo Galilee; the author of "Dante's Inferno," Dante Alighieri, the political leader Benito Mussolini; Fontanini Nativity sets; the Shroud of Turin cloth with the face of Jesus; gold; leather; the Ferarri car; the Milan fashion district; Gucci bags; designers Giorgio Armani and Yves Saint Laurent; foods that include parmesan cheese, mozzarella cheese, provolone cheese, pasta, pizza, spaghetti, fettecini, linguini, lasagna, panini, tortellini, pepperoni sausage, pistachios, olive oil, wine, risotto rice, spumoni, cannoli, bologna, antipasto, gelato, tiramisu, cappuccino, and latte; and the islands of Sardinia, Capri, and Siciily?

2696. What country in the world is known for the Lisbon Oceanarium; the Vasco de Gama Bridge; the Shrine to Our Lady of Fatima; the stone maritime fortress Belem Tower; port wine; pottery; tile paintings; the lynx; beaches; the Douro River; the first explorer to sail around the world, Ferdinand Magellan; the first explorer to discover a sea route to India, Vasco de Gama; soccer player Cristiano Ronaldo; actress Carmen Miranda; cuisine that includes cod, sardines; squid, roast suckling pig, and caldo verde soup; and has the distinction of being the world's largest producer of cork?

2697. What country of the world is known for the Eiffel Tower; Notre Dame Cathedral with its rose windows and Gothic architecture; the Seine River, the Champs-Elysees Parisian street; the Arc de Triomphe; the Louvre art museum; the Mona Lisa portrait by Leonardo da Vinci; the Palace of

Versailles; the Basilica of Sacre-Coeur; the Normandy island of Mont St. Michel; the Pompidou Center, a modern art museum; D-Day and the beaches of Normandy; the island of Corsica; the castles and wine fields of the Loire Valley; the Mediterranean coastline oasis known as the Riviera; the Pere-Lachaise Cemetery with the tomb of The Doors singer Jim Morrison; the Revolution; countryside chateaus; the author of "Les Miserable" and "The Hunchback of Notre Dame," Victor Hugo; an annual 2,100 mile bike race; fashion design; perfume; wine; cuisine that includes cheese, crepes, escargot snails, onion soup, and truffles; author Alexandre Dumas; philosopher Albert Camus; military heroine Joan of Arc; the long-reigning monarch King Louis XIV; military and political leader Napoleon Bonaparte; scientists Louis Pasteur and Marie Curie; World War II general Charles De Gaulle; impressionist artists Claude Monet, Edgar Degas, Paul Cezanne, Mary Cassatt, Henri Matisse, Camille Pissarro, and August Renoir; designers Coco-Chanel, Christian Dior, Louis Vuitton, and Givenchy; and words and phrases that include a la carte, a la mode, au gratin, bon appetit, au jus, ballet, bouquet, bon voyage, boutique, café, chef, cliché, clique, cordon bleu, cul-de-sac, debut, décor, déjà vu, encore, en route, entrée, entrepreneur, façade, faux pas, fiancée, garage, genre, hors-d'oeuvres, Mardi Gras, matinee, menu, petite, potpourri, renaissance, restaurant, resume, RSVP, sauté, turquoise, and vinaigrette?

2698. What country of the world is known as an independent principality; the Monte Carlo Casino and Opera House; the Grimaldi family; the former Prince Rainer and Princess Grace; the reigning Prince Albert II; the Prince's Palace; grand prix car racing; and is considered a resort area for the rich and famous?

2699. What country of the world is known for its diverse provinces; The French and Indian War; ice hockey; freshwater lakes; Lake Ontario; the St. Lawrence River; the province of Nova Scotia; The Toronto Zoo; Niagara Falls; Glacier National Park; Banff National Park; the CN Tower; the Rockies; The Quebec Winter Carnival; Ojibwa Indians; the Inuit people of the Northwest Territories; the lumber industry; maple syrup; the maple leaf; geese; moose; beaver; caribou; lynx; fish; furs; bacon; petroleum; the Viking explorer Leif Erikson's arrival in Newfoundland in 1000 AD; free health care; and majestic scenery?

2700. What country of the world is known for The Great Barrier Reef coral system; The Sydney Opera House; The Sydney Harbour Bridge; Ayers Rock; a grand slam tennis tournament; the kangaroo, koala bear, platypus, dingo, and emus; the Tasmanian Devil marsupial; the original people of the area called the aborigines; the large sandstone structure called Ayers Rock; the crop circles of Melbourne; the collection of limestone rocks off the ocean shore called The Twelve Apostles; the beaches of Queensland; the remote inland area known as "The Outback;" the former wildlife explorer and crocodile hunter Steve Irwin; the 1986 film "Crocodile Dundee;" and is often referred to as the "land down under?"

2701. What country of the world is known for its indigenous people called the Maori; its pristine lakes, jagged mountains, volcanoes, and beaches; the southernmost capital city of Wellington; the sky tower of Auckland; Franz Josef Glacier; the geysers and hot springs of Rotorua; the penguins, whales, dolphins, and marlins at The Bay of Islands; the waterfalls and mountain scenery at Milford Sound in Queenstown; the native flightless bird called the kiwi; sheep; rugby; golf; the volcano at

Lake Taupo; foods that include mussels, oysters, lamb, cheese, and fish and chips; greenstone jewelry; wood; glass; jade; the father of nuclear physics for his orbital theory of the atom, Ernest Rutherford; and the first man to reach the peak at Mount Everest in the Himalayas, Sir Edmund Hillary?

2702. What country of the world is known for royalty; King Juan Carlos and Queen Sofia; King Ferdinand and Isabella; the sponsorship of the voyages of Christopher Columbus; the Royal Palace; Madrid's Plaza Mayor; the Prado Museum; Retiro Park; La Tomatina tomato fight; bullfighting; the running of the bulls in Pamplona; the April Fair in Sevilla; the Alcazar and Aqueduct in Segovia; the "hanging houses" of Cuenca; the Sagrada Familia church in Barcelona by the architect Antonio Gaudi; El Escorial monastery; the Mezquita of Cordoba; the Alhambra Moorish palace in Granada; the prehistoric cave paintings in Altamira; the novel "Don Quixote de la Mancha" by Miguel de Cervantes; the Jai Alai court game; the Real Madrid soccer team; the FC Barcelona soccer team; flamenco music and dancing; the guitar; beaches; swords; LLadró porcelain figurines; ceramics; the hand fan; wine; the spice saffron; olives; sangria; tapas snacks; the national rice dish Paella; Iberico ham; manchego cheese; squid and churros with hot chocolate; art masters Pablo Picasso, Diego Velázquez, Francisco de Goya, El Greco, Joan Miró, and Salvador Dalí; singers Julio and Enrique Iglesias; tennis player Rafael Nadal; Barcelona soccer player Xavi; and words that include adobe, albino, alfalfa, alligator, armada, avocado, banana, barbecue, bronco, burro, burrito, cafeteria, canoe, canyon, cargo, chile, chocolate, cilantro, embargo, enchilada, fajita, fiesta, galleon, guacamole, hammock, habanero, hacienda, huarache, hurricane, iguana, jaguar, jalepeño, lasso, llama, machete, macho, maize, mariachi, matador, mesa, mestizo, mole, mosquito, mustang, nacho, nopal, ocelet, oregano, paella, papaya, patio, peso, pimento, pinto, piñata, plaintain, plaza, poncho, potato, pronto, pueblo, quesadilla, ranch, rodeo, rumba, salsa, savannah, serape, serrano, siesta, silo, sombrero, stampede, stockade, taxi, tobacco, taco, tamale, tango, tomato, tornado, tuna, vaquero, vanilla, vigilante, wrangler, and yucca?

2703. What country of the world is known for the Berbers and Arabs; the Atlas Mountains; the Sahara Desert; camels; the cities of Tangier and Casablanca; the markets of Marrakesh; the Islam religion; compacted towns called medinas; the medieval medina of Fes; fez hats; hijab headscarves; foods that include couscous rice, olives, grilled kebobs, coffee, and mint tea; the Kasbah market of Tangier; handicrafts that include textiles, jewelry, leatherwork, and ceramics?

2704. What country of the world is known for The Egyptian Museum in Cairo; the twin rock temples of Abu Simbel; the Valley of the Kings near Luxor that includes the tomb of the boy-king Tutankhamen; the Nile River; the Red Sea Reef; the ancient religious site of Karnak with its 134 massive pillars; The Pyramids of Giza; The Great Sphinx of Giza; The Underground Library of Alexandria; world leaders Anwar Sadat and Yasser Arafat; ancient pharaohs Cleopatra, Khufu, Tutankhamen, Ramses II, and Snefu; military commander Muhammad Ali; General Ptolemy; Queen Nefertiti; papyrus paper; belly dancing; the national pasta dish called koshari; couscous; beef kebobs; Anise and Hibiscus teas; alabaster ceramics; gold jewelry; cartouche personalized hieroglyphic pendants; long gowns worn by men called jallabiyas; dresses worn by women called kaftans; headscarves worn by women called hijabs; souvenir wood carvings; scarves; Stella beer; spices; and mother of pearl boxes?

2705. What country of the world is known for being regarded as the holy land for Christians, Muslims, and Jews; The Western Wall, a Jewish religious site, located in the old city of Jerusalem; the largest freshwater lake called the Sea of Galilee; the city of Nazareth where Jesus was believed to have lived; speaking both Hebrew and Arabic; the religious site known as Temple Mount; The Shrine of the Bab and its garden Terraces; the Islamic building known as The Dome of the Rock; The Mount of Olives; the Masada, an ancient fortress built by the Roman ruler Herod the great overlooking the Dead Sea; the Jewish symbol on the flag known as The Star of David; the religious leader David; Prime Minister Menachem Begin; Saint Joseph; Saint John the Baptist; Prime Minister Golda Meir; world leaders Benjamin Netanyahu, Ariel Sharon, and Yitzhak Rabin; and first books of Hebrew scripture called the Torah?

2706. What country of the world is known for being the largest Arab state; for the coral reefs of the Red Sea; as the birthplace of Islam; the Islamic holy sites of Mecca and Medina; having the largest oil reserves in the world along the Persian Gulf; the large capital city of Riyadh; having the largest continuous sand desert; camels; Persian rugs, terrorist Osama Bin Laden; and being one of the settings for the collection of Arabic folk tales as told in "One Thousand and One Nights?

2707. What is the name of the emirate located in the Persian Gulf, part of the United Arab Emirates Federation, known for having the world's tallest skyscraper called Burj Khalifa standing at 2,717 feet high with 163 stories: Dibba or Dubai?

2708. What country of the world is known as a war-torn nation; for the cave complex at Tora Bora; the Gardens of Babur; The Kabul Zoo; The Friday Mosque; The Statues of Buddha; hand-made carpets; having one of the oldest dog breeds, the Afghan Hound; and having a native of this country, a twelve-year-old girl named Sharbat Gula, as the subject of a famous photograph on the 1985 Time Magazine cover that was taken by journalist Steve McCurry while she was living as a refugee in Pakistan during the Soviet Union's occupation of this country?

2709. What country of the world is known for its long history and ancient civilizations; the number of monkeys in its capital city of New Delhi; The Kanha National Park, a wildlife reserve that served as the inspiration to Rudyard Kipling in writing his novel, "The Jungle Book;" the city of Varanasi on the River Ganges; the populous city of Calcutta; the Taj Mahal, a white domed marble mausoleum now regarded as one of the "new" wonders of the world; many ancient temples; poverty and diversity; the predominant Hindu religion; the Hindu belief that cows are sacred; camel races; the high regard for the endangered Bengal Tiger; the Himalaya mountain range; the snow-clad peaks of Kashmir; the film industry in Bombay; heavy monsoon rains; a garment worn by women called a sari; a garment worn by men called a dhoti; the game of cricket; exotic spices; fried banana chips; elaborate wedding ceremonies; henna tattoos; dances and festivals; using a social structure called the caste system; Mahatma Gandhi, the man regarded as the father of the nation; Prime Minister Indira Gandhi; nun and saint Mother Teresa; and products that include tea, incense, bangle bracelets, marble work, pottery, ceramics, shawls, silk saris, carpets, henna dye, drums, wooden flutes, leather shoes, Benkura terracotta horses, and dancing dolls?

2710. What country of the world is known for containing ten of the world's highest peaks, is landlocked between China to the north, and India to the south; the medieval and modern flair of the capital city of Kathmandu; and Mount Everest, the highest summit on earth in the Himalayas towering 29,029 feet high: Nepal or Mongolia?

2711. What country of the world is known for The Grand Palace and giant Buddha statues in the capital city of Bangkok; temples, museums, and pagodas; the Buddhist religion; the Chiang Mai Night Bazaar; the island of Ko Phi Phi; tsunami storms; lotus flowers; tigers, leopards, elephants, cobras, crocodiles, rhinoceros, exotic birds, and the black and white tapir; this country was originally known as Siam; the Siamese cat originated here; kickboxing is the national sport; golf courses; a leading manufacturer of electronics; being the largest producer of pineapples; resorts, beaches, and many islands; the three-wheeled motorbike with a cab in the back called a tuk-tuk; being the largest exporter of rice' and for the national dish of stir-fried rice noodles called Pad Thai?

2712. What country of the world is known for its long war against the North; the five royal palaces in the capital city of Seoul; the historical center of the city of Hanoi; the Cu Chi Tunnels that served as hiding places during the war; Independence Palace in Saigon, a name that was changed to Ho Chi Minh City in 1975 when it was taken over by the North, effectively marking the end of the war; the bay of dragons called Ha Long Bay; honoring the dragon, the turtle, and the horse; being the largest exporter of black pepper and cashew nuts; the Sa Pa rice terraces; having over 10,000 motor bikes on the road every day; for wearing cone-shaped hat called a non la; and engaging in the martial art of Tae Kwon Do?

2713. What country of the world is known as a collection of over 7,100 islands located off the coast of Asia; Saint Agustin Church in the capital city of Manila; mountains, volcanoes, and earthquakes;; the explorer Ferdinand Magellan who claimed the land for Spain in 1521 and named the area after the Spanish King Phillip II; The Chocolate Hills on the island of Bohol; the 2,000-year-old Banaue Rice Terraces carved into the mountains; abundant wildlife including hundreds of species of birds; the beaches and resorts on the island of Boracay; the abundance of coral species and seashells; inventing karaoke and the yo-yo; world leaders Ferdinand Marcos and Corazon Aquino; exports that include electronics, clothing; mangoes, bananas, coconuts, and pineapples; and as having several elaborate festivals?

2714. What country of the world is known as an island nation consisting of more than 6,800 islands often referred to as "the land of the rising son;" bowing as a way of greeting; many volcanoes, earthquakes, and tsunamis; for The Hiroshima Peace Memorial, a tribute to the lives that were lost when the atomic bomb was dropped by the U.S. in 1945; launching a surprise air attack on the U.S. Naval Base at Pearl Harbor in Hawaii on December 7, 1941; The Temple of the Golden Pavilion; the active volcano with its symmetrical cone, Mount Fuji; being the only country in the world with a reining emperor; the main residence of the Emperor, the Tokyo Imperial Palace; the Great Buddha statue; being a world leader in robotics and electronics; the headquarters for companies like Sony, Toyota, Nintendo, Panasonic, Honda, Sharp, and Toshiba; not wearing their shoes inside their homes; traditional silk dresses tied with a wide belt called kimonos; a traditional coat called a happi; traditional shoes; a near 100% literacy rate; the art of shodo, a style of calligraphy; the national sport of sumo; practicing martial arts that include karate, judo, sumo, and Aikido; chopsticks; hand fans; bamboo umbrellas called wagasas; hand-painted prints; paper lanterns made of traditional wasi paper and glued onto a bamboo frame; traditional dolls; kitchen knives; pottery and porcelain; Samurai sword replicas; short, three line poems called haikus; elaborate ornamental gardens; Seiko, Citizen, and Casio watches; the art of paper folding called origami; ornamental trees grown in a pot called bonsai; foods that include rice, sushi, tofu, tempura, teriyaki, and chicken cooked on a grill called a hibachi; green tea and tea ceremonies; a rice wine drink called sake; the human-powered vehicle called a rickshaw; and words that include futon, tycoon, typhoon, gingko, honcho, ramen, soy, sushi, teriyaki, Sudoku, tsunami, yen, and wasabi, a spicy green sauce?

2715. What country of the world is known for its savannah wildlife safaris; acacia trees; forests, deserts, and plains; the Swahili language; the black rhino, leopard, hyena, cheetah, zebra, wildebeest, giraffes, and birds of Nairobi National Park; the coral reefs of Malindi; the lion, cheetah, leopard, elephant, crocodile, buffalo, and hippo of the Samburu National Reserve; the volcanic landscape of Tsavo National Park; the flamingos of Lake Nakuru; Amboseli National Park with its abundance of the elephants, giraffes, and views of Mount Kilamanjaro, Africa's tallest mountain, in Tanzania; the dense lion population and the migration of zebra and wildebeest at the Masai Mara National Reserve; foods that include ugali cornmeal, mashed peas and potatoes called irio, grilled maize, chapati flatbread, samosa pastries, coffee, and chai tea; beadwork, jewelry, bags, mango wood carvings, ebony carvings, soapstone, sisal baskets, kitengela glassware, and painted cloths called batiks?

2716. What country of the world is known for wildlife safaris; white sandy beaches; savanna animals like elephants, giraffes, and zebras at the Selous Game Reserve; the elephants, hippos, giraffes, wildebeest, flamingos, and migratory birds at Lake Mnyara National Park; Stone Town located on the Spice Island of Zanzibar; Lake Victoria; the tallest free-standing mountain and inactive volcano, Mount Kilimanjaro; and the zebra and wildebeest migration and big game safari at Serengeti National Park: Tanzania or Angola?

2717. What country of the world is known for the scenic beauty of Cape Town and the Cape Peninsula; The Cape of Good Hope, where the Atlantic Ocean meets the Indian Ocean, discovered in 1486 by the Portuguese navigator Bartholomeu Dias while searching for a sea route from Europe to India; the Victoria and Alfred Waterfront at Cape Town; the forests, mountains, lagoons, rivers, lakes, and beaches along the Garden Route; the "city of gold," Johannesburg; Blyde River Canyon Nature Preserve; the Drakensberg mountain range; the vineyards at Cape Winelands; and the largest game reserve at Kruger National Park?

2718. What country of the world is known for the scenic Alps; the Vienna State Opera; Mirabell Palace; the Hohensalzburg Castle; the Melk Abbey; the golden roof of Innsbruck; the Danube River; Vienna coffee; the Landler folk dance; the Porsche car; the composers Wolfgang Amadeus Mozart and Franz Schubert; the political leader Adolf Hitler; the psychologist Sigmund Freud; the scientist Cristian Doppler;; the chef Wolfgang Puck; Swarovski crystal; the Christmas carol "Silent Night" by author Josef Mohr and composer Franz Gruber; and the filming of the movie "The Sound of Music" with Julie Andrews and Christopher Plummer in the city of Salzburg?

2719. What country of the world is known for speaking French, German, and Italian: the Matterhorn in the Alps: villas and chateaus; clocks and watches; cows; the long alphorn; army knives; the Bank, the United Nations office in Geneva; the Red Cross; the folk hero William Tell, Johanna Spyri's book

"Heidi;" billionaire Ernesto Bertarelli;, the cities of Basel, Bern, Zurich, Lucerne, and Geneva; cheese, fondue, and chocolate; tennis players Roger Federer and Martina Hingis; figure skater Denise Biellmann; and downhill skier Pirmin Zurbriggen?

2720. What country of the world is known for its ancient history; the city-states of Athens and Sparta; the Acropolis citadel and the Parthenon temple in Athens; Olympia, the home of the first Olympic games; the alphabet; the island of Crete; the philosophers Socrates, Plato, and Aristotle; the playwrights Aeschylus, Sophocles, and Euripides; the leaders Alexander the Great and Pericles; the Titan God Zeus; the Olympian Gods Zeus, Poseidon, Apollo, Athena, and Aphrodite; the heroes Hercules, Odysseus, and Achilles; the Peloponnesian War; the poet Homer, author of the epics the "Iliad" and the "Odyssey;" the author of fables, Aesop; the "father of geometry;" Euclid; the scientist and mathematician Archimedes; and foods that include Baklava, olives, wine, Spanakopita spinach pie, pita bread, hummus, baked feta, and gyros?

2721. What country of the world is known for being the home and headquarters of the European Union and NATO in Brussels; speaking Flemish and French; the Antwerp diamond center; The Museum of Cocoa and Chocolate; lace; tennis players Justin Henin and Kim Clijsters; fashion designers Diane von Furstenberg and Liz Claiborne; bicycle racing champion Eddy Merckx; and foods that include waffles, chocolate, beer, French fries, and Brussels sprouts?

2722. What country of the world is known for the Copenhagen Zoo; the Copenhagen Open Air Museum; the Tivoli Gardens; the bronze Little Mermaid Statue; as the inventor of Lego plastic bricks; the Round Tower Observatory; wind power; the Kronborg Castle, the setting for Shakespeare's "Hamlet;" the Fairy Tales of Hans Christian Anderson; the scientist Niels Bohr; Danish pastries; and for being the oldest existing kingdom in the world?

2723. What country of the world is known for having two capitals, Amsterdam and The Hague; speaking Dutch; tulips; windmills; wooden clog shoes; cheese markets; hollandaise sauce; herring; apple pie; the Anne Frank House; the Keukenhof Gardens; having the largest seaport in Europe in the city of Rotterdam; bicycling everywhere; the painter of "Starry Night," "Sunflowers," and "The Bedroom," Vincent Van Gogh; the painter of "The Night Watch" and "Self-Portrait with Beret and Turned Up Collar;" Rembrandt; and having part of this country called Holland?

2724. What country of the world is known for royalty; the Vikings; the Royal Palace of Stockholm; the Stockholm Globe Arena; the St. Lucia candle festival during Christmastime; IKEA furniture; H & M clothing; Electrolux appliances; the Volvo and Saab cars; ice hockey; Nobel prizes; the scientists Alfred Nobel and Anders Celsius; the "Pippi Longstocking" books by author Astrid Lindgren; glassworks; Absolut Vodka; meatballs; pickled herring; the musical group ABBA; tennis player Bjorn Borg; and golfer Annika Sorenstam?

2725. What country of the world is known for the Sebelius Monument in Helsinki; Helsinki Cathedral; the Santa Claus Village amusement park; the Northern Lights; saunas; Nokia phones; glass ornaments and birds; jewelry; bread cheese; lingonberry porridge; apple donuts; textile art; festivals, speaking Finnish, and having an excellent education system?

2726. What country of the world is known for Vikings and longships; the Viking Ship Museum in Oslo; fjords; the Geiranger Fjord; glaciers; the medieval wooden stave churches; having the world's longest road tunnel; telemark skiing; collecting more medals at the Winter Olympics than any other nation; soccer; reindeer, elk, and the Arctic fox; eating whale meat; consuming more coffee than any other country; waffles; trolls; the fishing industry; salmon; oil; the explorer that led the first Antarctic expedition, Roald Amundsen; the Norse explorer who was the first European to land in North America, Leif Ericson; the author of "Matilda," "The Gremlins," and "Charlie and the Chocolate Factory," Roald Dahl; the playwright and author of "A Doll's House," Henrik Ibsen; the expressionist painter of "The Scream" Edvard Munch; the figure skater Sonja Henie; the actress Marilyn Monroe; hand-knit sweaters, hats and scarves; and for hosting the annual presentation of the Nobel Peace Prize in Oslo?

2727. What country of the world is known as the largest country; for its massive export of oil; nine time zones; the ruble currency; the fortified fortress in Moscow called The Kremlin; the period of hostile relations that developed after World War II with the United States referred to as the Cold War; the distinctive architecture of the colorful Saint Basil's Cathedral located in Moscow's Red Square; the 4,000 mile Trans-Siberian Railway; The Valley of Geysers; The Hermitage Museum in St. Petersburg founded by Catherine the Great in 1764; the first artificial Earth satellite called Sputnik; the classic ballet company based at the Bolshoi Theatre in Moscow; ballet dancer Mikhail Baryshnikov; founder of the Bolsheviks and leader of a revolution Vladimir Lenin; political leader Joseph Stalin; world leaders Vladimir Putin, Boris Yeltsin and Mikhail Gorbachev; scientist Ivan Pavlov; author of "War and Peace," "The Death of Ivan Ilych," and "Anna Karenina," Leo Tolstoy; author of "Crime and Punishment," Fyodor Dostoyevsky; short story author and playwright Anton Chekhov; symphony composer of "Swan Lake," Pyotr Tchaikovsky; songwriter of "Puttin' on the Ritz" and "White Christmas," Irving Berlin; tennis players Maria Sharapova, Anna Kournikova, and Victoria Azarenka; figure skaters Oksana Baiul and Evgeni Plushenko; Faberge jeweled eggs that were created for the Imperial Family; wooden nesting dolls; foods that include black caviar; cabbage soup; meat kebobs; smetana sour cream; Blini pancakes, and vodka; as the host country for the 2014 winter Olympics held in Sochi; and the fur cap with ear flaps called a Ushanka?

2728. What country of the world is known for its massive size and as having the largest population; a one child policy; Mandarin and Cantonese languages; over 3,500 written symbols or characters; a walled enclosure in Beijing called The Forbidden City containing the palaces of 24 emperors of the Ming and Qing Dynasties; the famous portrait of the former Communist leader Mao Zedong Tiananmen Square in Beijing; the Jade Buddha Temple and the People's Square in the populous city of Shanghai; The Great Wall that is 5,500 miles long and visible from the moon; thousands of life-size figures called The Terracotta Warriors; pottery; the Giant Panda; the international trade route called The Silk Road; the dragon; a separate administrative region called Hong Kong; the martial art kung fu; chopsticks; foods that include fried rice, white rice, chow mein noodles, potstickers, Peking duck, Kung Pau chicken, Wonton soup, tea, and soy sauce; a special calendar and New Year; a Spring Festival, a Fall Festival, a Lantern Festival, a Winter Solstice Festival, and a Dragon Boat Festival; having the highest production of electronics; over one billion dollars in exports; Feng Shui, the art of creating harmonious surroundings; silk products; calligraphy; jade and pearl jewelry; kites; paper cuttings; lanterns; silk textiles; pottery and porcelain; the teacher and philosopher Confucius; President Xi Jinping; writer Mo Yan; basketball player Yao Ming; tennis player Li Na; and the words and phrases that include chop chop, chop suey, chow, chow mein, Feng Shui, gung-ho, hoisin, ketchup, kowtow, lo mein, no can do, shih tzu, tangram, wok, and won ton?

2729. What country are Puerto Rico, Guam, the Virgin Islands, Samoa, and the Northern Mariana Islands territories of?

2730. Which countries would you like to travel to someday?

Chapter 2 – Civics

Civics – Pre-School

1. Do we have rules and laws?
2. Do rules and laws help keep us safe?
3. What are some rules of a school?
4. What are some rules at home?
5. What is the name of the President of the United States?
6. What are the jobs of some community helpers?
7. Do we live in a neighborhood?
8. Do we live in a community?
9. What are the names of some businesses in our community?
10. What is the purpose of having a post office?
11. What is the purpose of having banks?
12. What is the purpose of having a fire department?
13. What is the purpose of having a police station and policemen?
14. Is it our duty as a citizen to obey the laws?
15. Who enforces the laws: the police or the fire department?
16. Is it important for citizens to obey traffic signs and traffic lights?
17. What is the purpose of having schools?
18. Are some children schooled at home?
19. Is the classroom part of a school community?
20. Are churches, temples, mosques, and synagogues also part of a community?
21. What are schools, restaurants, parks, stores, movie theatres, pools, and playgrounds all a part of: a community or a village?
22. May people of the same community have different beliefs?

23. What is the name of our town or city?

24. What is the name of our state?

25. What is the name of the country we live in?

26. Do people of different cultures live here in America?

27. It is good behavior to be civic and friendly with others?

Civics – Kindergarten

28. What are the names of some people that help us in our community?

29. What are the names of some people that help us in our school?

30. Is it important to obey the rules of the school?

31. Is it good to cooperate with others?

32. It is important to respect others who may be different than us?

33. How do you show responsibility in school and at home?

34. Where in the community do we go to buy groceries?

35. Where do we go to mail a letter or package?

36. Where do we go to check out a book or look for information?

37. Where do we go to deposit or take out money?

38. What are some jobs that people have?

39. What kinds of vehicles do police officers use in their job?

40. What kinds of vehicles do firemen and firewomen use in their job?

41. What are some other ways of transportation we can use to travel from one place to another?

42. Why do we follow rules at home and in school?

43. What is the name of the rule that states, "Treat others as you would want to be treated?"

44. Do rules and laws help to keep a community organized and safe?

45. Is there a consequence or something that happens to you if you break a rule?

46. Is it good citizenship to follow the rules of a game or a sport?

47. Why do we need to follow laws?

48. What does the community and state have that makes the laws: police officers or a government?

49. Who in our local community has the job of enforcing the laws?

50. What happens to someone who breaks a law?

51. Do all citizens have rights?

52. Do all citizens have responsibilities?

53. Do you think honesty and respect are important traits in being a good citizen?

54. What does our country flag look like?

55. What is the American flag of the United States of America: a symbol or a landmark?

56. Do we have a state flag?

57. What may we say if we choose to show our allegiance to our American flag?

58. Can you name a song that may show patriotism to America?

59. Do all countries have a flag that symbolizes their country?

60. What is the name of a song that represents the United States?

61. Do citizens observe national holidays?

62. What might be something you could do for a community service project?

Civics – 1st Grade

63. What is the term that describes the study of the rights and duties of citizens: laws or civics?

64. What are two examples of school rules?

65. Is there a consequence if a student breaks a rule?

66. Are rules and laws in place to keep us safe?

67. Whose job is it to establish laws: the citizens or the government?

68. What is a consequence if a citizen breaks a law?

69. Are there workers in your school like a playground supervisor or a crossing guard that help keep you safe?

70. What is the name of the person whose job it is to keep you safe, and enforce the rules at swimming pools or lakes: coast guard or lifeguard?

71. Who are some people in your school who enforce the rules to help maintain safety and order?

72. Do we have a local government with elected leaders?

73. Do we have a state government with elected leaders?

74. Do we have a national government with elected leaders?

75. What do all citizens have a right to do to elect leaders into office?

76. What is the name of the process of electing a candidate: an assembly or an election?

77. Do all citizens have civic duties in their community, state, and country?

Civics – 2nd Grade

78. Can you say and spell your full name?

79. Can you say your full address?

80. Can you say your home or cell phone number?

81. Can you say your parents' first names?

82. What city or town are you a resident of?

83. What is the name of the area of the community that you live: a neighborhood or a village?

84. What state are you a citizen of?

85. What are communities divided into: regions or districts?

86. What is the name of the school district where you live?

87. What is the name of the leader of a school?

88. What is the name of the leader of a school district?

89. What type of a community is typically located in the countryside: rural or urban?

90. What type of a community is typically located in the city: rural or urban?

91. Do you live in a rural or an urban community?

92. What is the name of an outlying part of a city or town: a district or a suburb?

93. What is the name of the city that our community is a suburb of?

94. What is the capital of our state?

Civics – 3rd Grade

95. What is the civic term for a group of people who live in the same area and are under the same government: a county or a community?

96. What is a community also a larger part of: a global community or a national community?

97. What is the term for a person who leaves one country to permanently settle in another: immigrant or alien?

98. Is our nation a nation of immigrants or emigrants?

99. Is it good practice as a citizen to appreciate the diversity of all cultures in our nation?

100. What is the term for the practice followed among people of a particular group or place: a habit or a custom?

101. Do different cultures practice different customs and traditions?

102. What is one family custom or tradition that you have?

103. What do we follow in order to maintain order in our community, state, and nation?

104. What is the term used in which all people are treated the same: fairness, or equality under the law?

105. What is the name of the body that creates, enforces, and interprets our laws: the police or the government?

106. What is the name of the government governed by the people, where everyone is treated equally: a democracy or a liberty?

107. Is a representative democracy in which the people vote for representatives a type of republic?

108. What is the term given for the freedoms that are protected by the government: rights or responsibilities?

109. What is the term give for a citizen's duty to obey rules, laws, and the rights of others: rights or responsibilities?

110. What is the term for the person that has the rights, opportunities, and the duties of being a member of a country: a citizen or a pedestrian?

111. What is the name of the document written by our third President Thomas Jefferson and signed on July 4th, 1776 in which the 13 original colonies declared themselves free from England under King George?

112. What is the name of the document that was written in 1787 by a group of men called the "Framers" like George Washington and Ben Franklin that outlines the laws and how the government should work, and is regarded as the highest law in the land: the Declaration of Independence or the United States Constitution?

113. In which state is Independence Hall located, where the Framers met to write the Constitution: Philadelphia or Washington, D.C?

114. What is the name of the opening lines of the U.S. Constitution that begins, "We the people, in order to form a more perfect union…:" the Bill of Rights or the Preamble?"

115. What is the term for changes made to the constitution: an amendment or a revision?

116. What is the name for the first ten amendments to the U.S. Constitution that states the ten fundamental rights and liberties of all citizens: the amendments or the Bill of Rights?

117. What is the term for the rights protected by the government that include the rights of life, liberty, and the pursuit of happiness: the Bill of Rights or Inalienable Rights?

118. How many amendments are there currently to the original U.S. Constitution: 17 or 27?

119. Which amendment, added in 1791, guarantees the freedoms of religion, speech, assembly, press, and petition: the First Amendment or the Second Amendment?

120. On which day every year do Americans celebrate their independence from the British colonists under King George?

121. How many stars and how many stripes did the American flag have that represented the original number of colonies?

122. How many stars does the American flag have after the state of Hawaii was added in 1959?

123. How many horizontal stripes are there on the current American flag?

124. How would you describe the current American flag?

125. What is the term for the people who permanently settle here from another country?

126. Which group would **not** be considered immigrants: Native Americans or Latin Americans?

127. Who is the primary author of the Declaration of Independence: Thomas Jefferson or Ben Franklin?

128. What is the name of the national holiday in May in which Americans remember the people who have died for our freedoms: Memorial Day or Veterans Day?

129. What is the name of the national holiday in November in which Americans recognize the women and men who serve and have served in our armed forces: Memorial Day or Veterans Day?

130. Do all eligible citizens have the right to vote?

131. What is the minimum age that a person must be in order to vote in a public election: 18 or 21?

132. How many branches is the United States Government comprised of: three or five?

133. What are the executive, the legislative, and the judicial considered: departments or branches?

134. Do the three branches of government share the power?

135. What is the term for the ability of each branch of government to limit the powers of the other: branch equality or checks and balances?

136. What is the collective name for the two groups of people called the House of Representatives and the Senate, are stationed in Washington, D. C., and are responsible for making the laws for our country: the Assembly or the Congress?

137. How many elected members make up the U.S. Senate: 100 or 435?

138. How many elected members make up the U.S. House of Representatives: 50 or 435?

139. What is the title given to the head of the House of Representatives: the President of the House, or the Speaker of the House?

140. Which branch of the government is made up of the House of Representatives and the Senate, and is responsible for making the laws: the legislative branch or the executive branch?

141. How many national Senators does each state have: two or four?

142. What is the name of the person who is the executive leader of the United States government?

143. What is the name given to the person who is second in line to the President?

144. What is the name of the current Vice-President?

145. Which branch of the government is led by the President and the cabinet, is the leader of the Armed Forces, and has the power to veto a law: the executive branch or the judicial branch?

146. Which branch of the government is made up of Supreme Court Justices and is responsible for enforcing the laws and deciding if laws are constitutional: the executive branch or the judicial branch?

147. How many Supreme Court Justices are on the highest court: nine or twelve?

148. What is the name of the highest Supreme Court Justice: Your Honor or Chief?

149. What is the name of the place where a person goes to have their case heard when a law has been broken?

150. What is the name of the head elected official of a state: the mayor or the governor?

151. Do you know the name of the governor of our state?

152. What is the name of the head elected official of a city: the mayor or the governor?

153. Do you know the name of the mayor of our city?

154. What is the title of the head of the city police department: Lieutenant or Chief?

155. What is the title of the head of the city fire department: Lieutenant or Chief?

156. What are your responsibilities at home?

157. Is it important to have good study habits to do well in school?

158. What are some public places in our community where people work?

159. Is a museum open to the public?

160. What are some types of museums?

161. Are the library, post office, grocery store, swimming pool, and bank open to the public?

162. Can you name any private businesses in our community where people go to work every day?

163. Can you name any specific goods or services that are produced or provided in our community or in our state?

164. What are some other specialized jobs where people have to train and study in order to work in that profession?

165. What is the name of the area where people live, work, and play: a suburb or a community?

166. Can you name some civic duties of a responsible citizen in a community?

167. What is the name given to an urban area or downtown area: city or town?

168. What is the name given to a rural area of farmland: city or countryside?

169. What is the name given to the neighborhoods and communities that are located just outside of a city: suburbs or outskirts?

170. How would you describe the community you live in?

Civics – 4th Grade

171. What is the term for the set of rules and regulations set up by the government of a town, city, state, and nation: statutes or laws?

172. Does America have local, state, and federal laws?

173. What are the three levels of government: executive, legislative, and judicial, or President, House of Representatives, and Senate?

174. What is the term for the national level of government: federal or local?

175. Which level of government is in charge of the military, the coining of money, highways, passports, Social Security, income tax, and interstate commerce: state or federal?

176. Which level of government is in charge of schools, automobile registration, sales tax, and welfare: state or federal?

177. Which level of government is in charge of police and fire, zoning, roads, trash collection, voter registration, school districts, and property taxes: local or state?

178. What is the name of the document that declared the United States free from English rule?

179. What are James Madison, Alexander Hamilton, Ben Franklin, and George Washington all considered: Founding Fathers or famous inventors?

180. What is the name of the introduction to the U.S. Constitution that states: "We the People of the United States, in Order to form a more perfect Union, establish Justice, insure domestic Tranquility, provide for the common defense, promote the general Welfare, and secure the Blessings of Liberty to ourselves and our Prosperity, do ordain and establish this Constitution of the United States of America?"

181. What is the name of a city law or rule: an ordinance or a treaty?

182. What is the supreme law of the land: the United States Constitution or the Bill of Rights?

183. What is a change to the U.S. Constitution called: an addendum or an amendment?

184. What is the term for the first ten amendments to the U.S. Constitution: the Bill of Rights or the Preamble?

185. Which branch of government is made up of the Congress and makes the laws: the executive branch or the legislative branch?

186. What are the names of the two chambers that make up the U.S. Congress: The House of Representatives and the Senate, or the legislative branch and the judicial branch?

187. Where does the Congress conduct their sessions in Washington, D.C: at the U.S. Capitol, or at the White House?

188. What is the capital of the state you live in?

189. What is the name of the person elected to make laws: a candidate or a legislator?

190. Which branch of government includes the President and the cabinet, and carries out and enforces the laws: the judicial branch or the executive branch?

191. Which branch of government is made up of Supreme Court Justices that interpret the law and the U.S. Constitution: the judicial branch or the legislative branch?

192. What is the name of the policy that ensures that one branch does not have more power than another: Separation of Powers, or Checks and Balances?

193. What is the name of the policy that assigns specific duties to each branch of government, Separation of Powers, or Checks and Balances?

194. Who is the leader of the executive branch: the President or the Speaker of the House?

195. What is the name of the current President of the United States?

196. Who is the current Vice-President of the United States?

197. What is the name of the President's residence in Washington D.C?

198. Who is the commander-in-chief, the person in charge of the Armed Forces: the President or the Vice-President?

199. What is the name of the avenue where the White House is located in Washington D.C.: Pennsylvania Avenue or Philadelphia Avenue?

200. What is the name of the power a President has to reject or deny a government bill: veto power or executive power?

201. What is the name of the highest court in the United States: Head or Supreme?

202. What is the name of the person who makes an official ruling in a court: a judge or a jury?

203. What is the name of a group of people who listen to a case in a courtroom and decide whether or not a person is guilty of breaking the law: a committee or a jury?

204. What two groups make up America's legislative branch called the Congress?

205. How many members are there in the House of Representatives: 435 or 100?

206. Does the number of officials elected to Congress depend on the population of each state?

207. How many elected members are there in the U.S. Senate: 435 or 100?

208. Does the number of officials elected to the Senate depend on the population of each state, or is it currently set at two per state?

209. What is the name of the leader of the House of Representatives?

210. How long is the term of a legislator, a member of Congress: two years or six years?

211. How many U.S. Senators does each state have?

212. How long is the term of a United States Senator: two years or six years?

213. What is the name of a suggested law before it becomes a law: a bill or a proposal?

214. What is the name of a bill that has been passed by a legislature and signed by an executive?

215. What is the term for the power given to the executive branch to oppose or reject a bill?

216. What is the name of the elected person in charge of a city?

217. Do you know the name of the mayor of our city?

218. What is the name of the elected person in charge of a state: a governor or a senator?

219. Do you know the name of the governor of our state?

220. Which level of government include mayors, county executives, and aldermen: local or state?

Civics – 5th Grade

221. What is the study of the rights of others and the role of citizens: citizenship or civics?

222. What city or community are you a citizen of?

223. What is the term for the administrative divisions of states: counties or cities?

224. What county are you a citizen of?

225. What state are you a citizen of?

226. What country are you a citizen of?

227. What is the term for members of a community with rights and responsibilities to their community, or to their government: aliens or citizens?

228. What is the term for something that is due a person by law or nature: right or responsibility?

229. What is the term for the obligations of a person and the actions that person takes to meet them: right or responsibility?

230. What is the name of a government controlled by one person or a small group of people and hold absolute power: authoritarian or dictatorship??

231. What is the name of the legal process to obtain citizenship if a person is not a natural born citizen: naturalization or documentation?

232. What is the name for a group of people who settle far from home but still keep ties with their homeland: loyalists or colonists?

233. How many original colonies were there?

234. What is the name of the first written constitution of the colonies that created a "league of friendship" between the states: the Declaration of Independence or the Articles of Confederation?

235. What is the term for the freedom from the control and influence of others: sovereignty or independence?

236. What is the term for the right of a country to govern itself with complete independence: sovereignty or anarchy?

237. What is the term for a state of disorder and chaos due to the lack of rules, laws, authority and a central government: anarchy or monarchy?

238. Does Great Britain and other nations still recognize the monarchy and royal family?

239. What is the name of the document that declared the colonies free from Great Britain and signed in 1776?

240. What document includes the signatures of John Hancock, Thomas Jefferson, Samuel Adams, John Adams, and Ben Franklin?

241. In which state was the Declaration of Independence signed: Washington D.C. or Pennsylvania?

242. How many of the original thirteen colonies can you name?

243. Who is the principal writer of the Declaration of Independence: Samuel Adams or Thomas Jefferson?

244. What is the name of the government that manages the relationships among states: a central government or a national government?

245. What is the term for a written form of government: a Constitution or a Federal System??

246. What is the name for the supporters of the Constitution and of a strong national government: the Nationalists or the Federalists?

247. What is the name for the opponents to the Constitution who thought that it gave too much power to the Federal government: Anti-Nationalists or Anti- Federalists?

248. Can you name any of the "Framers" of the U.S. Constitution?

249. What is the name for the opening lines of the U.S. Constitution: the Preamble or the Bill of Rights?

250. What lines do you know of the Preamble?

251. What is meant by "domestic tranquility" as mentioned in the preamble: to have peace within the United States, or to have peace with others outside the United States?

252. Are "inalienable rights" rights that can be taken away, or rights that cannot be taken away?

253. How many articles is the U.S. Constitution made up of: seven or seventeen?

254. Does Article I of the Constitution reference the rules of the U.S. Congress in the Legislative Branch of government or the Executive Branch of government?

255. Does Article II of the Constitution reference the Legislative Branch of government or the rules for the President and Vice- President in the Executive Branch of government?

256. Does Article III of the Constitution reference the Executive Branch of government or the rules of the Supreme Court Justices in the Judicial Branch of government?

257. Does Article IV of the Constitution discuss the relationship between the states and the federal government?

258. What is the name of a change or an addition to a document?

259. What are the first ten amendments called that were added to the Constitution to protect individual rights?

260. Which amendment refers to freedom of religion, speech, press, assembly, petition and expression: the First Amendment or the Second Amendment?

261. What is the term for the rights or freedoms granted to the people by the First Amendment allowing individuals to speak, worship, assemble, organize, or petition without interference by the government: Civil liberties or Bill of Rights?

262. What is the term given for the suppression of speech through printed material or other media that might be considered offensive to some: censorship or freedom of the press?

263. What is the term that refers to the intentional spreading of lies through words: libel or slander?

264. What is the term that refers to the intentional false statement that may affect a person's reputation is are printed or published: libel or slander?

265. What is the term for the preference of an idea or point of view over another: bias or superiority?

266. What is the term given to an advertisement that is designed to promote a particular idea or issue: propaganda or bias?

267. Which amendment refers to the right to bear arms: the First Amendment or the Second?

268. Which amendment refers search and seizure: the Third Amendment or the Fourth?

269. When people choose to remain silent or not answer a question in order not to incriminate themselves, which amendment are they pleading: the Fourth Amendment or the Fifth Amendment?

270. What is the meaning of ratification: to formally approve a law or treaty or to formally approve an elected official?

271. Which amendment abolished slavery and involuntary servitude that was passed by Congress and ratified by the states in 1865: the Third Amendment or the Thirteenth Amendment?

272. Which amendment, ratified in 1868, granted citizenship to "all persons born or naturalized in the United States" and guaranteed equal protection of the laws: the Fourth Amendment or the Fourteenth Amendment?

273. Which amendment to the Constitution, ratified in 1870 but not fully taken advantage of until 1965 with the passage of the Voting Rights Act of 1965, granted African American men the right to vote: the Fifteenth Amendment or the Fifth Amendment?

274. What is the term that refers to the right of women to vote in public elections: suffrage or franchise?

275. Which amendment to the Constitution, ratified in 1920, recognized women's suffrage, granting women the right to vote: the Ninth Amendment or the Nineteenth Amendment?

276. How many amendments are there currently to the U.S. Constitution: 20 or 27?

277. What is the term for the fees that are required to be paid to local, state, and national government by people and businesses?

278. What is the term for the right of government to take private property for the use of the public in return for reasonable compensation: eminent domain, or search and seizure?

279. What is the name of the principle that states that the Federal Government will not pass laws that favor one religion over another: separation of church and state, or freedom of religion?

280. What is the name for a formal meeting attended by members of a group: a convention or a meeting?

281. What is the type of system in which the states and the national government share the power: a federal system or a national system?

282. What are the three branches of the Federal Government?

283. What is the term that refers to the ability of each branch of the government to check the power of the others: Balance of Power or Checks and Balances?

284. Which branch of the government has the power to pass laws by majority vote, declare war, borrow money, amend the constitution, confirm presidential nominations, tax, and regulate commerce: the executive branch or the legislative branch?

285. What are the two chambers of the legislative branch that make up the U.S. Congress?

286. What is the name of the part of the legislative branch where each state has two representatives: the House of Representatives or the Senate?

287. What is the name of the part of the legislative branch that is considered the "lower house" in which the number of representatives for each state is determined by the state's population and are elected by the people: the House of Representatives or the Senate?

288. What is the name of the leader of the House of Representatives?

289. Who is the President of the Senate: the Vice-President or the Secretary of State?

290. What is the role of the legislative branch of the government: to make the laws or interpret the laws?

291. What is the name for the time that the Congress meets that typically runs from January through November: a term or a session?

292. Does each house of Congress have Majority and Minority leaders?

293. What is the term for the legislative proposal that is draft of a law and must be voted on?

294. What is the name for a group of Senators or members of Congress that change or debate bills before passing them on to the executive branch: an assembly or a committee?

295. Who has the power to veto a law: the President or the Speaker of the House?

296. What is the name of the branch of government that enforces the laws, makes treaties, and commands the armed forces: the executive branch or the judicial branch?

297. Who is the leader of the executive branch?

298. Who is the Commander-in-Chief of the United States, in charge of: the Army, Navy, Marines, Air Force, and the Coast Guard?

299. Is the United States considered a Two-Party system or a Multi-Party system?

300. What is the name given for a group of citizens that share common ideas regarding how a government should work: a political party or a platform?

301. Can you name the two major political parties of the United States?

302. Which political party tends to be more conservative, and favors lower taxes and a smaller central government: the Republican Party or the Democratic Party?

303. Which political party tends to be more liberal, and favors higher taxes and more government programs and control: the Republican Party or the Democratic Party?

304. What is the political affiliation of the current President and Vice-president of the United States: Republican or Democrat?

305. Which animal is the political symbol for the Republican Party: the donkey or the elephant?

306. Which animal is the political symbol for the Democratic Party: the donkey or the elephant?

307. What is the term for the total number of people that vote for a candidate: popular vote or majority vote?

308. What is the name for the first election in which candidates for an office are narrowed down: the General Election or the Primary Election?

309. What is the name for the main election that is held to determine a winner of a political race: the Primary Election or the General Election?

310. What is the term for the group of people that are appointed by each state legislature to elect the President and the Vice-President: the electorate or the Electoral College?

311. How many of the 538 electoral votes does a Presidential candidate need to win: 250 or 270?

312. What is the term for the candidate that is the current holder of that office: the incumbent or the lame duck?

313. What is the term for an elected official who is near the end of his or her term or tenure and cannot be re-elected: incumbent or lame duck?

314. How old does a citizen need to be to be eligible to vote?

315. What day of the week are both primary and general elections typically held on?

316. What month does the U.S. Presidential election place?

317. In a presidential election, are the States that go to the Democratic candidate shaded red or blue?

318. In a presidential election, are the States that go to the Republican candidate shaded red or blue?

319. How long is the term of the President and Vice-President of the United States?

320. How many times can a United States President be re-elected?

321. What is the name of the event at the end of January every four years in which the elected President of the United States is officially sworn in: the inauguration or the assembly?

322. What is the name of the group of advisors to the President that includes the leaders of several departments including Agriculture, Commerce, Defense, Education, Health and Human Services, Homeland Security, Housing and Urban Development, Interior, Labor, State, Transportation, Treasury, Veterans Affairs, and the Attorney General: the U.S. Secretaries or the U.S. Cabinet?

323. What is the name of the speech given by the President that communicates the state of affairs of the United States: the State of the Union Address, or the American Status Report?

324. What is the name of the branch of government that interprets the laws and settles disputes between the states: the judicial branch or the legislative branch?

325. What is the name of the highest court in the United States?

326. How many Supreme Court Justices are there: nine or eleven?

327. What is the name of the lead Justice of the Supreme Court: the Chief Justice or the Head Justice?

328. Can you name the Chief Justice or any Supreme Court Justices currently on the bench?

329. What is the name for the group of citizens chosen to hear evidence and decide a case in a court of law: an assembly or a jury?

330. What is the name of the person or the institution that has had an action brought against him, her, or it in a court of law: a witness or a defendant?

331. What is the name of the person who sees an event and testifies in a court of law: a witness or a defendant?

332. What is the term for the written order that requires a person to attend court: a summons or a subpoena?

333. What is the term for the decision of a jury: a sentence or a verdict?

334. What is the name of the type of case in which a person has been accused of breaking a law: a criminal case or a civil case?

335. What is the name of the type of case in which a person has been involved in a non- criminal matter: a criminal case or a civil case?

336. What is the name given for the rights that a person is informed of when taken into custody by law enforcement that states, "You have the right to remain silent…:" Bill of Rights, or Miranda Rights?

337. What is the name of the person that defends the rights of the defendant in a court: an attorney or a defendant?

338. What is the term for an elected official in a county or state who conducts proceedings in a court on behalf of the government and its people: County Attorney or District Attorney?

339. What is the term for the chief law enforcement officer of the United States serving in the executive branch, is the head of the U.S. Justice Department, and represents the government in legal matters: Attorney General or Federal Attorney?

340. What is the term that states that government must follow the same rules and procedures, and be fair in all cases that are brought to trial: due process or trial by jury?

341. What protects a person's rights to life, liberty, and property: trial by jury, or due process of law?

342. What is the name for a serious crime such as murder, kidnapping, burglary, or passing counterfeit money: a felony or a misdemeanor?

343. What is the name for a less serious crime such as a traffic violation that is often punishable by fine: a felony or a misdemeanor?

344. What is the term for a formal charge by a grand jury: an indictment or a verdict?

345. What are guilty, not guilty, and no contest considered: court pleas, or verdicts?

346. What is the principle that states that the law applies to all, even those who govern: the rule of law, or fairness under the law?

347. What is the term for a formal request to someone in authority that is usually signed by several people: a declaration or a petition?

348. What is the term for the right of the government to take private property: eminent domain or implied powers?

349. What is the term for the unfair treatment of a certain group based on prejudice or bias: discrimination or segregation?

350. What is the term for a law at the local level of government: a policy or an ordinance?

351. What is the name for the gatherings of local citizens to discuss and vote on important issues: town meetings or assemblies?

352. What is the name of the governing body that is elected to make decisions on behalf of a school district: Board of Education, or School Board of Trustees?

353. What is the term given for a system of roads, bridges, sewers, and water in a community: infrastructure or incorporation?

354. Who is the head of the executive branch at the local level: the governor or the mayor?

355. Who is the head of the executive branch at the national level, and also has the title of commander-in-chief?

356. What are the names of the branches of the armed forces, besides the Coast Guard, that the President is in command of?

357. What is the term for the unmanned aerial vehicles, controlled by computers by remote control, used by the military to carry out dangerous operations or missions: robots or drones?

358. What is the term for a complex system of many departments and many rules: a democracy or a bureaucracy?

359. What is the term for the negotiations and relations between countries: diplomacy or commerce?

360. What are some civic duties that a citizen has?

Practice Citizenship Test

361. What is the supreme law of the land?

362. What does the Constitution do?

363. What are the first three words of the Constitution that suggests the idea of self-government?

364. What is an amendment?

365. What do we call the first ten amendments to the Constitution?

366. What is **one** right of freedom from the First Amendment?

367. How many amendments does the Constitution have?

368. What did the Declaration of Independence do?

369. What are **two** rights in the Declaration of Independence?

370. What is freedom of religion?

371. What is the economic system of the United States?

372. What is the "rule of law?"

373. What is **one** branch or part of the government?

374. Who is in charge of the executive branch?

375. What stops one branch of government from becoming too powerful?

376. Who makes federal laws?

377. What are the two parts of the U.S. Congress:

378. How many U.S. Senators are there?

379. We elect a U.S. Senator for how many years?

380. Who is one of your U.S. State Senators currently?

381. How many voting members does the House of Representatives have?

382. We elect a U.S. Representative for how many years?

383. Who is one of your U.S. Representatives currently?

384. Who does a U.S. Senator represent?

385. Why do some states have more U.S. Representatives than others?

386. We elect a President for how many years?

387. In what month do we vote for President?

388. What is the name of the President of the United States now?

389. What is the name of the Vice-President of the United States now?

390. If the President can no longer serve, who becomes President?

391. If the President and Vice-President can no longer serve, who becomes President?

392. Who is the Commander-in-chief in the military?

393. Who signs bills to become laws?

394. Who has the power to veto a bill?

395. What is the role of the President's Cabinet?

396. Can you name two secretaries in the President's Cabinet?

397. What is the role of the judicial branch of government?

398. What is the highest court in the United States?

399. How many Justices are there on the Supreme Court?

400. Who is the Chief Justice of the United States now?

401. What is one power of the federal government?

402. What is one power of the states?

403. Who is the current Governor of your state?

404. What is the capital of the state you live in?

405. What is the name of the current Speaker of the House of Representatives?

406. What are the two main political parties of the United States?

407. What is the political party of the current President of the United States?

408. Can you describe one amendment to the Constitution that describes who can vote?

409. What is one responsibility that is only for U.S. citizens?

410. Can you name one **right** that is only for U.S. citizens?

411. What are **two** rights of everyone living in the United States?

412. What do we show loyalty to when we cite the Pledge of Allegiance?

413. What is **one** promise you make when you become a United States citizen?

414. How old do citizens have to be to vote for President?

415. What are two ways that Americans can participate in their democracy?

416. When is the last day you can send in federal income tax forms?

417. When must all men register for the Secret Service?

418. What is one reason the colonists came to America?

419. Who lived in America before the Europeans arrived?

420. What group of people was taken to America and sold as slaves?

421. Why did the colonists fight the British?

422. Who wrote the Declaration of Independence?

423. When was the Declaration of Independence adopted?

424. Can you name **three** of the original thirteen states?

425. What happened at the Constitutional Convention?

426. When was the Constitution written?

427. Can you name **one** of the writers of the Federalist Papers that supported the U.S. Constitution?

428. What is **one** thing Benjamin Franklin is famous for?

429. Who is the "Father of our Country?"

430. Who was the first President of the United States?

431. What territory did the U.S. buy from France in 1803?

432. What is the name for **one** war fought by the United States in the 1800's?

433. What is the name for the U.S. war between the North and the South?

434. What is **one** problem that led to the Civil War?

435. What was **one** important thing that Abraham Lincoln did?

436. What did the Emancipation Proclamation do?

437. What did Susan B. Anthony do?

438. Can you name one war fought by the United States in the 1900's?

439. Who was President during World War I?

440. Who was President during the Great Depression and World War II?

441. Who did the United States fight in World War II?

442. What war was Eisenhower a General, before he became President of the United States?

443. What was the main concern of the United States during the Cold War?

444. What movement tried to end racial discrimination?

445. What did Martin Luther King, Jr. do?

446. What major event happened on September 11, 2001, in the United States?

447. Can you name **one** American Indian Tribe in the United States?

448. Can you **one** of the two longest rivers in the United States?

449. What ocean is on the West Coast of the United States?

450. What ocean is on the East Coast of the United States?

451. Can you name **one** U.S. territory?

452. What state can you name that borders Canada?

453. What state can you name that borders Mexico?

454. What is the capital of the United States?

455. Where is the Statue of Liberty?

456. Why does the flag have 13 stripes?

457. Why does the American flag have 50 stars?

458. What is the name of the National Anthem of the United States?

459. Who wrote the Star-Spangled Banner?

460. When do we celebrate Independence Day?

461. Can you name **two** national U.S. holidays?

462. Who said, "Give me liberty, or give me death?"

463. What are the 49th and 50th states of the Union?

464. What holiday was celebrated for the first time by American colonists?

465. What are some requirements to be eligible for President according to the U.S. Constitution?

466. What is the name of the residence of the President of the United States?

467. What is the name of the building where the Congress meets?

468. What are the colors of the American flag?

APPENDICES – Answers to Questions

APPENDIX 1: Chapter 1 – Social Studies

Pre-school

1. United States (or other)
2. Names state
3. Names city
4. English, etc.
5. Yes
6. Draws, paints, etc.
7. Piano, flute, etc.
8. July 4th
9. Names familiar holidays
10. States nationality
11. Native Americans
12. The Pilgrims
13. Thanksgiving Day
14. Teepees
15. George Washington
16. The state, the capital, etc.
17. George Washington
18. The American Flag
19. Red, white, and blue
20. Abraham Lincoln
21. The South
22. Slavery
23. Cotton and Tobacco
24. Martin Luther King Jr.
25. Yes

Social Studies – Kindergarten

26. Yes
27. Born, adopted, etc.
28. Names immediate family
29. Names relatives
30. Names city
31. Names State
32. 50
33. United States of America
34. Canada
35. Mexico
36. Different
37. Different
38. No
39. Yes
40. Yes
41. Yes
42. Hunting, fishing, and farming
43. Tomahawk, spear, etc.
44. Buffalo, deer, etc.
45. A Teepee
46. Cone-shaped
47. Tools, blankets, etc.
48. Moccasins
49. Longhouses
50. Pueblos
51. Wigwams
52. A canoe
53. Totem poles
54. States nationality
55. Different
56. States religion
57. Different
58. Yes
59. Many ethnic cultures
60. North America
61. Seven
62. Antarctica
63. A continent
64. Asia
65. Names Asian country
66. Asia
67. Africa
68. North America
69. South America
70. Antarctica
71. Europe
72. Australia
73. United States of America
74. Alaska and Hawaii
75. United States of America
76. Old Glory
77. A map
78. State
79. Yes
80. A globe
81. Pacific and Atlantic
82. North, South, East, West
83. North
84. West
85. The East
86. The West
87. North
88. South
89. Yes
90. Indians
91. Flat
92. America
93. English (Spanish), etc.
94. Names differences
95. Electricity, phones, etc.
96. One-room schoolhouse, etc.
97. Clothespins, washboard, etc.
98. First
99. Yes
100. John Adams
101. Thomas Jefferson
102. The Declaration of Independence
103. John Hancock
104. England
105. 16th
106. Lincoln
107. Teddy
108. Teddy Bear
109. Mount Rushmore
110. Names current President
111. The White House
112. Washington, D.C.
113. District of Colombia
114. Yes
115. Ballet
116. Names holidays
117. Eating turkey, etc.
118. Turkey, pumpkin pie, etc.
119. Pilgrims and Indians
120. January
121. November
122. December
123. Different

124. July 4th
125. Colors, stars, stripes
126. George Washington
127. February
128. Yes
129. January
130. Names seasons
131. Names winter holidays
132. Easter, etc.
133. Independence Day, etc.
134. Halloween, Thanksgiving Day, etc.
135. Yes
136. Yes
137. Different
138. No
139. Italian food
140. Mexican food
141. Names ethnic foods
142. Different
143. Names family similarities
144. Names family differences
145. Yes
146. Yes
147. Honesty, vote, etc.
148. Cleaning, care of pet, etc.
149. Money
150. Food, cattle, etc.
151. Work
152. Yes
153. A need
154. A want
155. The dollar
156. Names money bills
157. Different
158. Chores, etc.
159. Yes
160. A bank

Social Studies – 1st Grade

161. Explains map and globe
162. Help us locate and identify
163. Top
164. Bottom
165. To the right
166. To the left
167. Locates own city on map
168. Locates state on map
169. United States
170. Locates America in map
171. Locates North America on globe
172. 50
173. Names own state
174. Alaska and Hawaii
175. Washington, D.C.
176. Names current U.S. President
177. The White House
178. We vote
179. Names own state capital
180. Tells why own state is famous
181. Names county
182. States if attended a fair
183. Yes/no
184. States city of residence
185. Names street
186. Buildings, roads, stores, etc.
187. Farms, fields, cows, etc.
188. Population
189. Size, language, etc.
190. Size, language, technology, etc.
191. Yes
192. Democratic
193. Can cite Pledge of Allegiance
194. Star-Spangled Banner, etc.
195. Yes
196. Describes flag
197. Green, white, and red
198. Red and white
199. Tells about Mexican culture
200. Tells about Canadian culture
201. Spanish
202. English and French
203. Moose, fish, bears, etc.
204. Yes
205. Labor Day
206. Columbus Day
207. Halloween
208. Veterans Day
209. Thanksgiving Day
210. Cites cultural differences
211. Names a family tradition
212. Christmas (Hanukkah, Kwanzza, etc.)
213. Buy presents, decorate, sing, etc.
214. No
215. New Year's Day
216. Martin Luther King Day
217. Presidents' Day
218. Washington
219. Abraham Lincoln
220. St. Patrick's Day
221. Easter, etc.
222. Cinco de Mayo
223. Memorial Day
224. July 4th
225. The United Kingdom
226. States yes or no
227. Flag, tree, flowers, etc.
228. Work
229. Phone, vacation, etc.
230. Food, clothing, etc.
231. Food, shelter, etc.
232. Name U.S. coins
233. 1 cent
234. 5 cents
235. 10 cents
236. 25 cents
237. 50 cents
238. Names U.S. bills
239. Names foreign currency
240. No
241. Emergency, buy larger items, etc.
242. Traded with other goods and services
243. Yes
244. The doctor
245. A police officer
246. A fireman or firewoman
247. A dentist
248. Postal worker (mailperson)
249. A veterinarian
250. A teacher

Social Studies – 2nd Grade

251. The universe
252. The Milky Way
253. Earth
254. Names other planets
255. Oceans
256. Pacific and Atlantic
257. Yes
258. Pacific
259. Indian, Caribbean, etc.

260. Equator
261. Continents
262. Seven
263. North America (or other)
264. North America
265. To the north
266. To the south
267. No
268. Globe
269. Northern and Southern
270. Yes
271. Yes
272. Mountains, rivers, etc.
273. Yes
274. Yes
275. A capital
276. Scale
277. North, South, East, West
278. Northeast
279. Southwest
280. The east
281. The west
282. Regions
283. Divisions
284. Names region
285. Names home state
286. Names home town
287. Names home county
288. Names other counties
289. An atlas
290. A city map
291. Geography
292. The seven continents
293. Countries
294. Yes
295. North America
296. Asia
297. Yes
298. Australia
299. Africa
300. South Sudan
301. Names African animals
302. Yes
303. On a land bridge
304. Names countries of ancestors
305. States family's nationality
306. The Sahara
307. The Nile
308. North America
309. Canada
310. United States
311. Mexico
312. Central America
313. South America
314. The Andes
315. The Amazon
316. The llama
317. The Antarctic
318. Europe
319. Australia and Oceania
320. An island
321. The Indian Ocean
322. Asia
323. Emperor
324. Stars and the Universe
325. China
326. Beijing
327. Yes
328. Chinese
329. Rice, egg rolls, etc.
330. Yes
331. Silk
332. The Great Wall of China
333. Yes
334. Yes
335. Yes
336. Tokyo
337. Japanese
338. Rice, fish, sushi, etc.
339. Yes
340. A kimono
341. Shoes
342. On the floor
343. Yes
344. India
345. New Delhi
346. Hindi
347. Rice, fish, flatbreads
348. Yes
349. A sari
350. Yes
351. Names African countries
352. Swahili
353. Rice, bread, bananas, etc.
354. Giraffes, elephants, etc.
355. Africa
356. The Nile
357. The Sahara
358. Pyramids
359. Hieroglyphics
360. Papyrus
361. Pharaoh
362. Yes
363. Yes
364. North America
365. Geography
366. Yes
367. Names area of country
368. Names bordering states
369. Appalachians
370. Missouri
371. Great Salt Lake
372. The Rocky Mountains
373. Rio Grande
374. North America
375. Spanish
376. Tacos, enchiladas, etc.
377. Yes
378. Ballet Folklorico
379. Mariachi
380. Inca
381. Mexico City
382. Canada
383. Provinces
384. Territories
385. Ottawa
386. English and French
387. Fish, bacon, ham, syrup, etc.
388. Yes
389. Trout, moose, etc.
390. Yes
391. Names South American countries
392. Spanish
393. Guinea pigs, potatoes
394. Yes
395. Portuguese
396. Yes
397. Brightly colored
398. Llama, Alpaca, etc.
399. Inca
400. Names European countries
401. Yes
402. Western Europe
403. Scandinavia
404. Eastern Europe
405. The Euro
406. Europe
407. The British Pound
408. The Yen
409. The Renminbi
410. Berlin
411. German
412. Bratwurst, sauerkraut, etc.
413. Yes
414. Traditional German clothing
415. Yes
416. Yes
417. Yes
418. London
419. English
420. Yes
421. English cuisine
422. Yes
423. Yes
424. Ireland
425. Dublin
426. Yes
427. Yes
428. Paris
429. French
430. Crepes, croissants, etc.
431. Similar to us
432. Yes
433. Yes
434. Madrid
435. Spanish

436. Spanish doughnuts
437. Paella
438. Yes
439. Yes
440. Flamenco
441. Yes
442. Europe
443. Rome
444. Italian
445. Pizza, spaghetti, etc.
446. Similar to us
447. Yes
448. Yes
449. Whales, seals, and penguins
450. Bitter cold
451. Yes
452. Yes
453. Canberra
454. English
455. Yes
456. Yes
457. Koala, kangaroo, etc.
458. Yes
459. A flag
460. Red, white, and blue with stars and stripes
461. Describes state flag
462. The capital
463. District of Colombia
464. George Washington
465. History
466. Indians
467. Christopher Columbus
468. Flat
469. North America
470. Spain
471. Money
472. India
473. Spices
474. Ocean blue.
475. Niña, Pinta, and Santa María
476. Indians
477. The New World
478. The Indians
479. Yes
480. The horse
481. Diseases
482. Civilization
483. Maya
484. Pyramids
485. The Aztecs
486. The Aztecs
487. The Inca
488. Francisco Pizarro
489. Hunt and fish
490. Africa
491. Yes
492. Jamestown
493. Native Americans
494. John Smith
495. Tribes
496. The Chief
497. Names Indian tribes
498. Indian tribes
499. Pueblo
500. Longhouses
501. Plains Indians
502. Totem Poles
503. The Pilgrims
504. Religious freedom
505. Mayflower
506. Atlantic
507. Plymouth
508. The Native Americans
509. Corn
510. The Native Americans
511. Deer and pheasant
512. Wampanoag Indians
513. Thanksgiving Day
514. The Puritans
515. 13
516. Daniel Boone
517. Davy Crockett
518. Colonists
519. Near lakes and streams
520. Explains colonial lifestyle
521. No
522. Candles, oil lamps, etc.
523. Revolutionary War
524. Yes
525. Yes
526. Great Britain
527. Canada
528. The Revolutionary War
529. The Boston Tea Party
530. Thomas Paine
531. Continental
532. Declaration of Independence
533. Thomas Jefferson
534. Created equal
535. John Adams
536. 1776
537. Yes
538. 56
539. John Hancock
540. Philadelphia
541. The Liberty Bell
542. It cracked
543. Yes
544. Yes
545. Benjamin Franklin
546. John Paul Jones
547. Paul Revere
548. Sea
549. Treaty of Paris
550. The American colonists
551. U.S. Constitution
552. James Madison
553. A federal republic
554. Anarchy
555. The Bill of Rights
556. The Louisiana Purchase
557. Fifteen
558. Doubled it
559. Lewis and Clark
560. France
561. Slaves
562. Africa
563. Plantations
564. The American Civil War
565. 1861-1865
566. Abraham Lincoln
567. "Honest Abe"
568. Harriet Tubman
569. Slaves
570. Yes
571. Names monuments
572. Washington, D.C.
573. The White House
574. The President and family
575. The Statue of Liberty
576. The flag
577. A historical monument
578. Mount Rushmore

Social Studies – 3rd Grade

579. Social Studies
580. Geography
581. North America (or other)
582. Globe
583. An atlas
584. An almanac
585. Longitude
586. Latitude
587. The equator
588. Can identify places on map
589. The 7 continents
590. Oceans
591. The Pacific
592. The Arctic
593. U.S. mountain ranges
594. World mountain ranges
595. The Himalayas

596. The Andes
597. Mount Everest
598. Mount McKinley
599. Machu Picchu
600. Deserts
601. Sonoran
602. Arctic and Antarctica
603. The tropics
604. Rainforests
605. The Amazon
606. Brazil
607. The rainforest
608. Yes
609. Tropical
610. An island
611. All are islands
612. Yes
613. Hawaii
614. Hurricanes, monsoons, etc.
615. 50
616. 48
617. Alaska and Hawaii
618. Hawaii
619. Names home state
620. Names capital
621. Alabama
622. Alaska
623. Arizona
624. Arkansas
625. California
626. Colorado
627. Connecticut
628. Delaware
629. Florida
630. Georgia
631. Hawaii
632. Idaho
633. Indiana
634. Iowa
635. Kansas
636. Kentucky
637. Louisiana
638. Maine
639. Maryland
640. Massachusetts
641. Michigan
642. Minnesota
643. Mississippi
644. Missouri
645. Montana
646. Nebraska
647. Nevada
648. New Hampshire
649. New Jersey
650. New Mexico
651. New York
652. North Carolina
653. North Dakota
654. Ohio
655. Oklahoma
656. Oregon
657. Pennsylvania
658. Rhode Island
659. South Carolina
660. South Dakota
661. Tennessee
662. Texas
663. Utah
664. Vermont
665. Virginia
666. Washington
667. West Virginia
668. Wisconsin
669. Wyoming
670. Counties
671. Names county
672. Names city
673. States location of city
674. Compass rose
675. North
676. South
677. East
678. West
679. Northeast
680. Northwest
681. Southeast
682. Southwest
683. Can locate Canada
684. Provinces
685. Can locate Mexico
686. States
687. Locates U.S. on map
688. Locates Central America
689. Locates South America
690. Locates Europe
691. Locates Africa
692. Locates Asia
693. Locates Australia
694. Locates Antarctica
695. Locates the equator
696. Identifies N. Hemisphere
697. Identifies S. Hemisphere
698. Locates Pacific Ocean
699. Locates Atlantic Ocean
700. Locates Indian Ocean
701. Locates Arctic Ocean
702. Locates North Pole
703. Locates South Pole
704. A legend
705. A scale
706. A river
707. Names major rivers
708. American rivers
709. World rivers
710. The Amazon
711. The Nile
712. Fresh water
713. Salt water
714. Source
715. A tributary
716. A delta
717. Ganges
718. Nile
719. Yellow
720. Mississippi
721. Tributaries
722. A river system
723. The Mississippi
724. A drainage basin
725. The Gulf of Mexico
726. A strait
727. Bering
728. Gibraltar
729. Magellan
730. A channel
731. English
732. Yucatan
733. A reservoir
734. Lake of the Ozarks
735. Lake Mead
736. A plateau
737. Tibetan
738. Canal
739. Erie
740. Suez
741. Panama
742. Venice
743. Isthmus
744. Panama
745. Peninsula
746. Florida
747. Michigan
748. Wisconsin
749. Baja
750. Yucatan
751. Iberian
752. Italian
753. Arabian
754. Korean
755. Cape
756. Cape of Good Hope
757. Cape Cod
758. An island
759. Greenland
760. Hawaii
761. Easter Island
762. Galapagos Islands
763. Names rivers
764. China
765. Ganges
766. Delta
767. The Indus River
768. The Nile River
769. Gifts of the Nile
770. Aswan High Dam
771. Three Gorges Dam
772. The Congo River
773. The Zaire
774. The Niger

775. The Volga
776. The Danube
777. The Rhine
778. The Thames
779. Australia
780. The duck-billed platypus
781. The Amazon River
782. The Orinoco River
783. Niagara Falls
784. Both located on border
785. California
786. Florida
787. Missouri River
788. Spells Mississippi
789. Paddleboat
790. The Mackenzie
791. The Yukon
792. Canals
793. Gondola
794. Water vessels
795. Ancient history
796. Before Christ
797. "Before the Common Era"
798. "In the year of our Lord"
799. Yes
800. Before Christ
801. Greek
802. Yes
803. Greek
804. Eras
805. City-states
806. Athens and Sparta
807. Enemies
808. Sparta
809. Athens
810. Athena
811. The Acropolis
812. The Parthenon
813. Sparta
814. The Persian Wars
815. The Persians
816. The Greek
817. The Golden Age
818. Tragic plays
819. Yes
820. Sculptures
821. Three types of columns
822. Pericles
823. The Peloponnesian War
824. Greek playwrights
825. Plato
826. Aristotle
827. Homer
828. Alexander the Great
829. Alexandria
830. Olympian gods
831. The Titans
832. Zeus
833. Hercules
834. Apollo
835. Poseidon
836. Athena
837. Aphrodite
838. Greek monsters
839. Pegasus
840. Cyclopes
841. Centaurs
842. Greek
843. Olive branches
844. Olympia
845. No
846. Running and chariot racing
847. Every four years
848. Names Olympic champion
849. The Greek Alphabet
850. Alphabet
851. Greek
852. Roman
853. Seven
854. Ancient Roman
855. Yes
856. Romulus and Remus
857. Romulus
858. Yes
859. Yes
860. Roman Gods
861. Jupiter
862. Yes
863. On a peninsula
864. The Alps
865. Kings
866. A democracy
867. The Senate
868. A class system
869. Provinces
870. Latin
871. Romance languages
872. Yes
873. Carthage
874. The Phoenicians
875. Northern Africa and Sicily
876. Corsica
877. Rome
878. The Punic Wars
879. Twenty
880. Sicily, Corsica, and Sardinia
881. Spain
882. Hannibal
883. North across the Alps
884. Elephants
885. Yes
886. Rome
887. Carthage
888. Yes
889. Yes
890. Rome
891. Canals and waterways
892. Julius Caesar
893. Gaul
894. Pompey
895. Caesar
896. The Senate
897. Egypt
898. Ptolemy's sister, Cleopatra
899. Yes
900. Yes
901. Julius Caesar
902. The Battle of the Nile
903. Julius Caesar
904. Romans wanted republic
905. Stab wounds
906. Marc Antony and Octavian
907. Marc Antony
908. Octavian
909. Augustus Caesar
910. August
911. July
912. The Romans
913. September
914. October
915. November
916. December
917. Roman numerals
918. Pax Romana
919. Yes
920. Roman Peace
921. The Forum
922. The Pantheon
923. Aqueducts
924. The Romans
925. The Trevi Fountain
926. Yes
927. The toga
928. The stola
929. Bread, fish, and cheese
930. An amphitheater
931. The Coliseum
932. Chariot races
933. The Great Fire
934. Spartacus
935. Moses
936. Catholicism
937. Pompeii
938. Molten lava
939. Trajan
940. The decline and fall
941. Constantine the Great
942. Mosaics
943. Istanbul
944. The Western Roman Empire
945. The Byzantine Empire
946. The Visigoths and Germans
947. Yes

948. Justinian the Great
949. The Vikings
950. Fjord
951. Yes
952. Raiders
953. Normandy
954. Norsemen
955. A horned helmet
956. Gold and Silver
957. Monasteries
958. Viking ships
959. Longships
960. Eric the Red
961. Leif Ericsson
962. Newfoundland
963. Vinland
964. Bering Strait
965. The Inuit
966. Igloo
967. Animal skins
968. Mukluks
969. Parkas
970. Yes
971. Meat
972. Harpoons
973. Inuit Eskimo dog
974. Kayak
975. Alaska
976. Juneau
977. Land of the Midnight Sun
978. The Northern Lights
979. Yes
980. The Klondike
981. Jade
982. Yes
983. Yes
984. Oil
985. Mt. McKinley
986. Kodiak
987. Dog sledding
988. Iditarod
989. Husky
990. Sled dogs
991. Mounds
992. Anasazi
993. Adobe bricks
994. Pueblo
995. No
996. Ladders
997. Disappeared mysteriously
998. Adobe
999. The Corn Dance
1000. Kachina Doll
1001. Nomad
1002. A teepee
1003. A wigwam
1004. Buckskin
1005. Yes
1006. Moccasins
1007. Corn and buffalo meat
1008. Bow and arrow
1009. Flint
1010. Apache
1011. The Diné
1012. Longhouse
1013. The Navajo
1014. The Woodland Tribes
1015. Maize
1016. Algonquin
1017. Papoose
1018. Cradleboards
1019. Lacrosse
1020. Mud and bear fat
1021. A canoe
1022. Longhouses
1023. The Medicine Man
1024. Yes
1025. A powwow
1026. A tomahawk
1027. Totem pole
1028. Wampum
1029. A tribe
1030. A reservation
1031. Christopher Columbus
1032. 1492
1033. San Salvador
1034. Indians
1035. Spain
1036. Niña, Pinta, Santa Maria
1037. King Ferdinand and Queen Isabella
1038. Amerigo Vespucci
1039. John Cabot
1040. Conquistador
1041. Gold
1042. Hernando Cortez
1043. Vasco Nuñez de Balboa
1044. Francisco Pizarro
1045. Juan Ponce de León
1046. Rich Port
1047. The fountain of youth
1048. Florida
1049. The Gulf Stream
1050. Cuba
1051. Hernando de Soto
1052. Finding gold
1053. The horse
1054. Guns and horses
1055. St. Augustine
1056. A castle
1057. Francisco Vásquez de Coronado
1058. The Grand Canyon
1059. Río Grande
1060. Christianity
1061. Missions
1062. Smallpox, measles, etc.
1063. The Northwest Passage
1064. Henry Hudson
1065. The Netherlands
1066. Holland
1067. Scandinavia
1068. Denmark
1069. The Danish
1070. Hudson
1071. Canada
1072. Canada
1073. French and English
1074. Maple
1075. Maple
1076. Provinces
1077. Ten
1078. Provinces
1079. Territories
1080. Ottawa
1081. French
1082. Samuel de Champlain
1083. Animal furs
1084. French Canada
1085. The Rocky Mountains
1086. Yukon Territory
1087. Southern Canada
1088. Yes
1089. Fishing
1090. Seal hunting
1091. Lacrosse and hockey
1092. Exploration and Discovery
1093. France and Spain
1094. England
1095. Charter
1096. A difficult one
1097. Captain John Smith
1098. Jamestown
1099. Captain John Smith
1100. Starvation and disease
1101. The Powhatan
1102. Corn
1103. Pocahontas
1104. John Rolfe
1105. Yes
1106. The Starving Time
1107. Tobacco
1108. Women
1109. Yes
1110. Africans
1111. Slaves
1112. Pilgrims
1113. The Mayflower
1114. The Mayflower Compact
1115. Plymouth Rock
1116. William Bradford
1117. Malnutrition and exposure
1118. The Wampanoag
1119. Massasoit
1120. Squanto
1121. Thanksgiving
1122. Two years later in 1623
1123. Yes

1124. The Puritans
1125. James Winthrop
1126. Promote church teachings
1127. The Puritans
1128. Schools
1129. Harvard
1130. Roger Williams
1131. Disapprove
1132. Decreased
1133. Yes
1134. Quakers
1135. William Penn
1136. All religions
1137. Philadelphia
1138. Maryland
1139. New Netherland
1140. King Charles I
1141. Indentured servants
1142. North Carolina and South Carolina
1143. Georgia
1144. Slave trade
1145. The Quakers
1146. Religions
1147. Judaism
1148. Hebrew
1149. The Torah
1150. Adam and Eve
1151. Abraham
1152. Moses
1153. The Ten Commandments
1154. Israel
1155. David
1156. Jerusalem
1157. The Romans
1158. 1948
1159. Christianity
1160. The Old Testament
1161. Yes
1162. The Gospels
1163. Yes
1164. John the Baptist
1165. Yes
1166. Yes
1167. Gentiles
1168. Yes
1169. Christianity
1170. Christianity
1171. Yes
1172. Roman Catholicism
1173. Yes

Social Studies – 4th Grade

1174. Earth
1175. Globe
1176. Seven
1177. Pacific and Atlantic
1178. Names known continents
1179. Can read map
1180. Types of maps
1181. The equator
1182. The prime meridian
1183. Hemisphere
1184. Four
1185. Northern Hemisphere
1186. Southern Hemisphere
1187. Eastern Hemisphere
1188. Western Hemisphere
1189. The prime meridian
1190. Eastern and Western
1191. Parallels
1192. Meridians
1193. Longitude
1194. Latitude
1195. East to West
1196. North to South
1197. The prime meridian
1198. Greenwich
1199. Yes
1200. Degree
1201. 0
1202. 180
1203. The International Dateline
1204. A coordinate
1205. North of equator, east of prime meridian
1206. Can find coordinates
1207. Can identify states on map
1208. Can identify city on map
1209. Can follow building map
1210. Scale
1211. Yes
1212. A state map
1213. A city map
1214. A country map
1215. A political map
1216. A relief map
1217. A historical map
1218. A relief map
1219. A resource map
1220. A product map
1221. A road map
1222. A climate map
1223. A topographic map
1224. A relief map
1225. The Rockies
1226. Mount McKinley
1227. The Appalachian Mountains
1228. The Rockies
1229. The Appalachians
1230. Erosion
1231. Mountain state
1232. The Andes Mountains
1233. Mount Aconcagua
1234. The Inca
1235. Machu Picchu
1236. The Atlas Mountains
1237. The Eastern Highlands
1238. Mount Kilimanjaro
1239. The Alps
1240. The Alps
1241. Mont Blanc
1242. The Ural Mountains
1243. Mount Fuji
1244. The Himalayas
1245. Mount Everest
1246. Mount Everest
1247. Less oxygen
1248. The Rockies and Appalachians
1249. Yes
1250. Mid-Atlantic
1251. The Midwest
1252. The Pacific Northwest
1253. Rocky Mountain
1254. New England
1255. South Atlantic States
1256. The Southwest
1257. Canada
1258. Mexico
1259. Alaska and Hawaii
1260. A relief map
1261. Channel
1262. A strait
1263. A delta
1264. A prairie
1265. A plateau
1266. A mesa
1267. A cliff
1268. A canyon
1269. The Grand Canyon
1270. A basin
1271. A cape
1272. Cape Cod
1273. A gulf
1274. The Gulf of Mexico
1275. The Persian Gulf
1276. A bay
1277. A desert
1278. The Sahara
1279. Antarctica
1280. The Mojave
1281. The Atacama
1282. The Arabian
1283. A peninsula
1284. An isthmus

1285. A fjord
1286. A lake
1287. A river
1288. Names famous lakes
1289. Huron, Ontario, Michigan, Erie, and Superior
1290. Great Salt Lake
1291. Amazon, Nile, etc.
1292. Missouri, Mississippi, etc.
1293. Rio Grande
1294. The Amazon
1295. The Nile
1296. The Yellow
1297. The Yangtze
1298. The Ganges
1299. The Volga
1300. The Danube
1301. The Rhine
1302. The Seine
1303. The Thames
1304. The Mississippi
1305. A tributary
1306. Tributaries
1307. Delta
1308. North America (or other)
1309. Names continents
1310. Asia
1311. China
1312. Antarctica
1313. Europe
1314. Scandinavia
1315. The British Isles
1316. Africa
1317. Asia
1318. South America
1319. Provinces
1320. North America
1321. French and English
1322. States
1323. North America
1324. Spanish
1325. 48
1326. Alaska and Hawaii
1327. Hawaii
1328. Alaska
1329. Arizona
1330. New Mexico
1331. Oklahoma
1332. Utah
1333. Wyoming
1334. Idaho
1335. Washington
1336. Montana
1337. South Dakota
1338. North Dakota
1339. Colorado
1340. Nebraska
1341. Nevada
1342. West Virginia
1343. Kansas
1344. Oregon
1345. Minnesota
1346. California
1347. Wisconsin
1348. Iowa
1349. Texas
1350. Florida
1351. Michigan
1352. Arkansas
1353. Missouri
1354. Maine
1355. Alabama
1356. Illinois
1357. Mississippi
1358. Indiana
1359. Louisiana
1360. Ohio
1361. Tennessee
1362. Kentucky
1363. Vermont
1364. Rhode Island
1365. North Carolina
1366. New York
1367. Virginia
1368. New Hampshire
1369. South Carolina
1370. Maryland
1371. Massachusetts
1372. Connecticut
1373. Georgia
1374. New Jersey
1375. Pennsylvania
1376. Delaware
1377. Texas
1378. Rhode Island
1379. Washington D.C.
1380. District of Columbia
1381. The Atlantic
1382. The Pacific
1383. Canada
1384. Mexico
1385. Names bordering states
1386. Names bordering counties
1387. Yes
1388. The American Flag
1389. Thirteen
1390. The Pledge of Allegiance
1391. Betsy Ross
1392. The Liberty Bell
1393. The Bald Eagle
1394. The Statue of Liberty
1395. The Declaration of Independence
1396. The United States Constitution
1397. The Star-Spangled Banner
1398. Flags, birds, songs, etc.
1399. Mount Rushmore
1400. Roosevelt
1401. Washington, D.C.
1402. The White House
1403. Virginia
1404. The Washington Monument
1405. Iwo Jima
1406. Niagara Falls
1407. National Parks
1408. Names states' monuments
1409. Yes
1410. Ancient history
1411. Prehistory
1412. Mesopotamia
1413. Iraq
1414. Mesopotamia
1415. The Tigris and Euphrates
1416. A class system
1417. Babylon
1418. Hammurabi
1419. Mesopotamia
1420. Yes
1421. Cuneiform
1422. Mesopotamia
1423. Sumerians
1424. The Assyrians
1425. The Sumerians
1426. The seed plow
1427. 60
1428. Ziggurats
1429. The Hanging Gardens
1430. The Middle Ages
1431. Medieval
1432. The peasants
1433. Serf
1434. The Barbarians
1435. Byzantine
1436. Constantinople
1437. The Huns
1438. Attila
1439. Stirrups
1440. The Vandals
1441. The Visigoths
1442. The Angles
1443. The Saxons
1444. Dark Ages
1445. Christianity
1446. The Pope
1447. Judaism
1448. Monks
1449. Nuns
1450. Charlemagne
1451. Feudalism
1452. Nobility, church, and commoners
1453. The king
1454. The vassal
1455. The lord
1456. A fief
1457. Yes
1458. Knights
1459. A serf

1460. A castle
1461. A minstrel
1462. A jester
1463. Croquet
1464. A page
1465. A squire
1466. The Canterbury Tales
1467. A knight
1468. To sew, weave, and spin
1469. Jousting
1470. Chivalry
1471. Yes
1472. Yes
1473. A guild
1474. An apprentice
1475. A journeyman
1476. A master
1477. Yes
1478. Yes
1479. A strong kingdom
1480. England
1481. William the Conqueror
1482. Yes
1483. William II
1484. Yes
1485. Yes
1486. Yes
1487. Gave up land to France
1488. Counts, dukes, lords, and earls
1489. The Magna Carta
1490. A Parliament
1491. Black Death
1492. The Hundred Years' War
1493. Joan of Arc
1494. Yes
1495. The Byzantine Empire
1496. World religions
1497. Islam
1498. Mecca
1499. Kaaba
1500. Dome of the Rock
1501. Medina
1502. Hijra
1503. A Mosque
1504. The Grand Mosque
1505. The Prophet's Mosque
1506. Jihad
1507. The Quran
1508. The Five Pillars of Islam
1509. Yes
1510. Yes
1511. The Alhambra
1512. Córdoba
1513. Yes
1514. The Crusades
1515. Arabic numerals
1516. The Moors
1517. Africa
1518. Sahara
1519. Atlas
1520. Savanna
1521. The Congo
1522. Africa
1523. Egypt
1524. Pharaoh
1525. Yes
1526. Yes
1527. Second
1528. The Vizier
1529. Yes
1530. Dynasty
1531. Yes
1532. Upper and Lower Egypt
1533. King Menes
1534. Memphis
1535. Thebes
1536. Cairo
1537. Giza
1538. Pyramid of Khufu
1539. The Great Pyramid of Giza
1540. The Great Sphinx
1541. To guard the temples and tombs
1542. 240 feet long
1543. The nose
1544. Erosion
1545. Pillar
1546. Nefertiti
1547. King Tutankhamen
1548. Ramses II
1549. The cobra goddess
1550. The Valley of the Kings
1551. Howard Carter
1552. Paintings
1553. The Book of the Dead
1554. Vandals
1555. Mummification
1556. Yes
1557. Decimal system
1558. Hieroglyphics
1559. Consonant sounds
1560. Scribes
1561. Scribes
1562. The Rosetta Stone
1563. Farmers
1564. Yes
1565. Necklaces
1566. Mud bricks
1567. Bread
1568. The Egyptians
1569. The Persians
1570. The Kingdom of Kush
1571. Alexander the Great
1572. Ptolemaic
1573. Cleopatra
1574. The Valley of the Kings
1575. The Nile
1576. A tributary
1577. Yes
1578. Papyrus
1579. Papyrus
1580. Papyrus reeds
1581. Reed boats
1582. The camel
1583. A caravan
1584. Papyrus
1585. No
1586. A chariot
1587. West African Empires
1588. Mansa Musa
1589. Griots
1590. 54
1591. Africa
1592. Malaria
1593. One billion
1594. Charles Darwin
1595. Sudan
1596. Mt. Kilimanjaro
1597. Cape of Good Hope
1598. The Suez Canal
1599. The Aswan Dam
1600. Anwar Sadat
1601. Ivory Coast
1602. The Nile and the Congo
1603. The Sahara and Kalahari
1604. Yes
1605. The savanna
1606. Elephants, zebras, giraffes, etc.
1607. Elephant
1608. Elephants, giraffes, lions, etc.
1609. Kenya
1610. The cheetah
1611. African languages
1612. 2000
1613. Yes
1614. Arabic
1615. Islam
1616. Ramadan
1617. Madagascar
1618. Masks
1619. Drums
1620. Nelson Mandela
1621. Apartheid
1622. Muammar Gaddafi
1623. Yes
1624. Kwanzaa
1625. "The Lion King"
1626. Asia
1627. 48
1628. Vatican City
1629. Russia
1630. China
1631. Dynasties
1632. Qin Shi Huang
1633. Yes
1634. The Great Wall of China

1635. Terracotta
1636. Han Dynasty
1637. Yes
1638. Yes
1639. Confucius
1640. Civil service
1641. Yes
1642. Schools
1643. Silk
1644. Yes
1645. Birds and flowers
1646. Clothing
1647. Upper class
1648. The Silk Road
1649. Trade and commerce
1650. Yes
1651. Buddhism
1652. Tang
1653. Trading
1654. A camel
1655. Woodblock printing
1656. A book
1657. Gunpowder
1658. Porcelain
1659. Poetry
1660. Confucianism
1661. Tea
1662. Toilet paper
1663. Paper
1664. The Great Wall
1665. After
1666. Magnetic compass and iron plow
1667. Books
1668. Yes
1669. Rice
1670. Tall pagodas
1671. Mongolia
1672. Gobi
1673. The Chinese
1674. The abacus
1675. Beijing
1676. Merchant associations
1677. Marco Polo
1678. The Silk Road
1679. Ming
1680. Porcelain pottery
1681. White
1682. Blue
1683. China
1684. Silk scrolls
1685. Calligraphy
1686. The Three Perfections
1687. Lacquer
1688. Landscapes
1689. The Great Wall
1690. The longest
1691. The wheelbarrow
1692. Grand Canal
1693. The Forbidden City
1694. Imperial Palace
1695. 24
1696. Before
1697. India and Africa
1698. Religions
1699. Nepal
1700. Yin and Yang
1701. Feng Shui
1702. The Yellow and Yangtze
1703. The dragon
1704. Imperial power
1705. The New Year
1706. Chopsticks
1707. Bamboo
1708. The Giant Panda
1709. China
1710. Two
1711. An animal
1712. The Himalayas
1713. Mt. Everest
1714. K2
1715. China
1716. The People's Republic of China
1717. Hong Kong
1718. Communist country
1719. Beijing
1720. Tiananmen
1721. Shanghai
1722. Mandarin
1723. Seven
1724. Yes
1725. Symbols
1726. Chinese
1727. Shoes
1728. Lion and Dragon Dance
1729. Kung Fu
1730. Zodiac
1731. Christopher Columbus
1732. The Age of Discovery
1733. The 1600's
1734. Great Britain
1735. The French and Indian War
1736. The Seven Years War
1737. Taxes
1738. "No taxation without representation"
1739. The Stamp Act
1740. Protested and boycotted British products
1741. The Colonial Congress
1742. The Sons of Liberty
1743. The Townshend Acts
1744. Protested and rebelled
1745. The Boston Massacre
1746. The Boston Tea Party
1747. The Intolerable Acts
1748. The First Continental Congress
1749. Patrick Henry
1750. "Common Sense"
1751. Thomas Paine
1752. Patriots
1753. Founding Fathers
1754. Loyalists
1755. Lexington and Concord
1756. Yes
1757. Paul Revere
1758. William Dawes
1759. Lanterns
1760. Redcoats
1761. "The Redcoats are coming."
1762. Lexington and Concord
1763. Yes
1764. Minutemen
1765. Yes
1766. Muskets
1767. Lexington
1768. Still uncertain
1769. The Americans
1770. Boston
1771. Lt. Colonel Francis Smith
1772. Captain John Parker
1773. Bunker and Breeds
1774. Took place on Breeds Hill
1775. British
1776. The whites of their eyes
1777. The British
1778. Land and freedom
1779. The Second Continental Congress
1780. George Washington
1781. The eagle
1782. 5,000
1783. Thomas Jefferson
1784. July 4, 1776
1785. July 4th
1786. 56
1787. John Hancock
1788. Yes
1789. Yes
1790. The National Archives
1791. Yes
1792. Money and land
1793. Delaware
1794. An American flag
1795. June 14th
1796. Yes
1797. 50
1798. The American flag
1799. Saratoga
1800. France
1801. France
1802. Yes
1803. Benedict Arnold
1804. Valley Forge
1805. Yorktown
1806. The Treaty of Paris

1807. The American Revolution
1808. Yes
1809. The Articles of Confederation
1810. Shays' Rebellion
1811. The Virginia Plan
1812. The Federalist Papers
1813. The Bill of Rights
1814. The Constitutional Convention
1815. Executive
1816. Judicial
1817. Legislative
1818. The Connecticut Compromise
1819. The House and the Senate
1820. Two
1821. 100
1822. Number based on population
1823. 435
1824. The Three-Fifths Compromise
1825. 20
1826. The U.S. Constitution
1827. The Preamble
1828. Checks and balances
1829. Yes
1830. 1790
1831. An amendment
1832. The Bill of Rights
1833. The First Amendment
1834. Yes
1835. The President
1836. The governor
1837. Names state governor
1838. The mayor
1839. Names city mayor
1840. Taxes
1841. Yes
1842. President Lincoln
1843. George Washington
1844. Martha Washington
1845. John Adams
1846. Cabinet
1847. Yes
1848. Secretary
1849. 15
1850. Secretary of State
1851. Yes
1852. Yes
1853. Thomas Jefferson
1854. Alexander Hamilton
1855. Four
1856. Two
1857. Yes
1858. Democratic-Republican
1859. Federalist
1860. Democratic-Republican and Federalist
1861. Republican and Democrat
1862. New York City
1863. Washington, D.C.
1864. The White House
1865. Mount Vernon
1866. The U.S. Capitol
1867. John Adams
1868. Jefferson
1869. Abigail Adams
1870. Thomas Jefferson
1871. France
1872. Louisiana
1873. Napoleon Bonaparte
1874. The Louisiana Purchase
1875. Lewis and Clark
1876. Two years
1877. Kept detailed journals
1878. James Madison
1879. The War of 1812
1880. USS Constitution
1881. The Capitol
1882. The Treaty of Ghent
1883. The Battle of New Orleans
1884. James Monroe
1885. Yes
1886. The South
1887. The North
1888. Abolitionists
1889. The Missouri Compromise
1890. The Monroe Doctrine
1891. John Quincy Adams
1892. Andrew Jackson
1893. Transfer Indian land
1894. The Indian Removal Act
1895. The Trail of Tears
1896. Reformer
1897. Dorothea Dix
1898. Horace Mann
1899. Lucretia Mott and Elizabeth Stanton
1900. Amelia Bloomer
1901. Sojourner Truth

Social Studies – 5th Grade

1902. Geology
1903. Earth
1904. Atmosphere
1905. Lithosphere
1906. Hydrosphere
1907. Tropics of Cancer and Capricorn
1908. Equator
1909. Equator
1910. Northern Hemisphere
1911. Southern Hemisphere
1912. Colder
1913. The prime meridian
1914. Greenwich Meridian
1915. The International Dateline
1916. The date
1917. Yes
1918. Sunday
1919. Friday
1920. Yes
1921. Latitude
1922. Longitude
1923. Longitude
1924. 0 degrees longitude
1925. Coordinates
1926. Mason-Dixon Line
1927. The Arctic Circle
1928. Polar ice cap
1929. Antarctic Circle
1930. Tropic of Cancer
1931. Tropic of Capricorn
1932. The tropics
1933. Climate zones
1934. Very hot
1935. Very cold
1936. Moderate
1937. Frigid
1938. Rotation of the Earth
1939. Rotation and Revolution
1940. Yes
1941. Summer
1942. Winter
1943. Winter
1944. Summer
1945. The opposite
1946. The same
1947. Solstice
1948. June 21st
1949. December 21st
1950. Equinox
1951. The passage of time
1952. 1000
1953. 100
1954. 10
1955. 365 ¼
1956. February 29th
1957. Leap day
1958. The Egyptians
1959. Julius Caesar
1960. The Gregorian calendar

1961. 30
1962. 7
1963. Saturday and Sunday
1964. 24
1965. 60
1966. 60
1967. Sundials
1968. Yes
1969. The prime meridian
1970. 24
1971. The United States
1972. Central
1973. Mountain
1974. Pacific
1975. Eastern
1976. Names time zone
1977. Yes
1978. Noon
1979. Standard
1980. Daylight Savings Time
1981. A.M.
1982. P.M.
1983. Midday
1984. A.M.
1985. P.M.
1986. Yes
1987. Yes
1988. Cartographers
1989. Projections
1990. Gerardus Mercator
1991. Yes
1992. Pacific and Atlantic
1993. Lakes
1994. Yes
1995. Yes
1996. Salty
1997. Africa
1998. South America
1999. Asia
2000. Salty lakes
2001. Names lakes
2002. Huron, Ontario, Michigan, Erie, and Superior
2003. Political
2004. Relief
2005. A relief map
2006. Names world rivers
2007. Mississippi, Missouri, etc.
2008. A relief map
2009. Names mountain ranges
2010. Relief map
2011. Names world deserts
2012. Seven
2013. Canada, U.S. and Mexico
2014. 50
2015. Five
2016. The Northeast
2017. New England
2018. Northeast
2019. Southeast
2020. Midwest
2021. West
2022. Southwest
2023. Divisions
2024. Pacific Alaska Region
2025. Great Plains
2026. Great Lakes
2027. Rocky Mountain
2028. Pacific
2029. Mid-Atlantic
2030. Southeast
2031. Southwest
2032. Northeast
2033. Hawaii
2034. Alaska
2035. Names home state
2036. Names bordering states
2037. Counties
2038. A city
2039. Chicago
2040. Detroit
2041. New York
2042. Los Angeles
2043. Denver
2044. Boston
2045. New Orleans
2046. San Francisco
2047. Philadelphia
2048. St. Louis
2049. Pittsburgh
2050. Paris
2051. Jerusalem
2052. Wizard of Oz city
2053. Town
2054. Urban
2055. Rural
2056. Suburban
2057. Identifies community
2058. Residents
2059. The town square
2060. Yes
2061. The Zócalo
2062. Trafalgar Square
2063. Piazza San Marco
2064. Tiananmen Square
2065. Main Market Square
2066. Times Square
2067. St. Peter's Square
2068. The Plaza Mayor
2069. Red Square
2070. The Little Mermaid
2071. Motherland Calls
2072. David
2073. The Olmecs
2074. Great Sphinx
2075. Christ the Redeemer
2076. Moai Statues
2077. Stonehenge
2078. The Statue of Liberty
2079. The CN Tower
2080. The Space Needle
2081. Tallest buildings
2082. Big Ben
2083. The Leaning Tower of Pisa
2084. The Eiffel Tower
2085. The United States Capitol
2086. St. Paul's Cathedral
2087. Santa Maria del Fiore
2088. The Pantheon
2089. St. Peter's Cathedral
2090. The Taj Mahal
2091. St. Basil's Cathedral
2092. The Brooklyn Bridge
2093. The Sydney Harbour Bridge
2094. London Bridge
2095. The Golden Gate Bridge
2096. Ponte Vecchio
2097. Vietnam Veterans Memorial
2098. The Berlin Wall
2099. The Western Wall
2100. The Walls of Babylon
2101. The Great Wall of China
2102. Plymouth Rock
2103. The Blarney Stone
2104. The Rock of Gibraltar
2105. The Rosetta Stone
2106. Yes
2107. Egypt
2108. Japan
2109. Italy
2110. Australia
2111. Australia
2112. China
2113. Switzerland
2114. Ireland
2115. Israel
2116. Canada
2117. United States
2118. Iceland
2119. Peru
2120. England
2121. "Uncle Sam"
2122. Asia
2123. The Middle East
2124. The Far East
2125. Eastern Europe
2126. Western Europe
2127. The British Isles
2128. The United Kingdom
2129. Scandinavia
2130. The Netherlands
2131. The Hague
2132. Holland
2133. English
2134. Dutch
2135. Danish
2136. Danish
2137. Swedish

2138. Norwegian
2139. Belgian
2140. Dutch
2141. Irish
2142. French
2143. Spanish
2144. Portuguese
2145. Portuguese
2146. German
2147. Italian
2148. Swiss
2149. French, German, and Italian
2150. German
2151. Polish
2152. Greek
2153. Latin and Italian
2154. Hebrew and Arabic
2155. Mandarin Chinese
2156. Spanish
2157. English
2158. Hindi
2159. Arabic
2160. French and English
2161. Spanish
2162. None
2163. Names languages spoken
2164. States nationality
2165. Yes
2166. Names civilizations
2167. Maya, Aztec, and Inca
2168. Mexico and Guatemala
2169. Mexico
2170. Peru
2171. City-states
2172. Yes
2173. A king
2174. Yes
2175. Tikal
2176. Teotihuacan
2177. Gods
2178. Perform sacrifices
2179. The Yucatan
2180. Chichen Itza
2181. 365
2182. The Maya
2183. Pyramids
2184. A snake
2185. Kukulkan
2186. Itzamna
2187. Yes
2188. Yes
2189. The Maya
2190. Chac
2191. Calendars
2192. Three
2193. Simultaneously
2194. The Long Count
2195. Codices
2196. The Maya
2197. Hieroglyphics
2198. Zero
2199. Twenty
2200. Dots and bars
2201. Yes
2202. King, noble, commoner
2203. Yes
2204. Subsistence cultivation
2205. Maize
2206. Chocolate
2207. Cacao beans
2208. A cenote
2209. The nobles
2210. The commoners
2211. A rubber ball
2212. The hands
2213. The losing side
2214. Yes
2215. Stone
2216. Yes
2217. A codex
2218. A stela
2219. Popol Vuh
2220. Yes
2221. No
2222. Plaster
2223. Obsidian
2224. The Mayan nobles
2225. The Quetzal
2226. Classic
2227. Yes
2228. Yes
2229. The 1500's
2230. The Aztec
2231. Eagle on cactus with snake
2232. Tenochtitlan
2233. City-states
2234. Causeways
2235. When attacked by enemy
2236. The Templo Mayor
2237. Near the Temple
2238. At Tenochtitlan
2239. The Emperor
2240. Powerful Aztec Emperors
2241. Yes
2242. High level
2243. Yes
2244. Honoring the Sun
2245. Sacrifices
2246. Human blood
2247. Serpents and Jaguars
2248. Huitzilopochtli
2249. Tlaloc
2250. Quetzalcoatl
2251. The family
2252. Nahuatl
2253. Nahuatl
2254. Yes
2255. Chinampas
2256. Maize
2257. Popcorn
2258. To cook and sew
2259. Yes
2260. Different
2261. The nobles
2262. Cocoa beans
2263. Chocolatl
2264. An aqueduct
2265. Yes
2266. Honoring their gods
2267. The Aztec Calendar
2268. Poetry
2269. Yes
2270. Glyphs
2271. Codex
2272. Yes
2273. The Aztec Calendar
2274. Two
2275. Festivals and ceremonies
2276. Herbs
2277. An advantage
2278. Spain
2279. Smallpox
2280. Hernán Cortés
2281. Tenochtitlan
2282. Mexico City
2283. The Inca
2284. Nazca
2285. The Andes
2286. Yes
2287. Yes
2288. Yes
2289. Sapa Inca
2290. Inti
2291. Cuzco
2292. 11,000 feet above
2293. Yes
2294. Quechua
2295. Farming the land
2296. Yes
2297. Stonemasons
2298. Yes
2299. Rope suspension bridges
2300. Llamas
2301. Alpaca
2302. They created terraces
2303. Yes
2304. Potatoes
2305. Yes
2306. Colorful tunics and dresses
2307. Adobe huts
2308. Taxes
2309. The children of nobles
2310. Mark religious occasions and crops
2311. Coca leaves
2312. Machu Picchu
2313. Hiram Bingham

2314. Francisco Pizarro
2315. Gold
2316. Conquer Inca and claim gold
2317. The Spanish
2318. Pizarro
2319. Europe
2320. Portugal
2321. Christopher Columbus
2322. Ferdinando and Isabella
2323. The Americas
2324. China
2325. Niña, Pinta, and Santa Maria
2326. The Santa Maria
2327. San Salvador
2328. Indians
2329. The horse
2330. Four
2331. Yes
2332. October 12th
2333. Columbus, D.C., etc.
2334. Amerigo Vespucci
2335. Yes
2336. Vasco de Gama
2337. Pedro Cabral
2338. Portuguese
2339. Cannons
2340. Ferdinand Magellan
2341. Discover route to Asia
2342. The Strait of Magellan
2343. Names of five ships
2344. Cape of Good Hope
2345. The Pacific
2346. Four months
2347. Killed in a battle
2348. 18
2349. The Dutch
2350. Trade monopoly
2351. The Old World
2352. Colonies
2353. Thirteen
2354. Yes
2355. The natives
2356. Sugarcane
2357. Transatlantic slave trade
2358. Sugar, coffee, and cotton
2359. Africa
2360. Gold and Angolan Coasts
2361. Triangular Trade
2362. The Middle Passage
2363. Jamestown
2364. Twelve million
2365. Yes
2366. Arabic
2367. Latin
2368. Renaissance
2369. 1300-1600
2370. Age of Discovery
2371. Yes
2372. The Ottoman Empire
2373. The end
2374. Humanism
2375. Humanities
2376. Florence
2377. The teachings of philosophers
2378. Medici
2379. Renaissance artists
2380. Michelangelo
2381. Leonardo da Vinci
2382. An Italian scientist
2383. The Scientific Method
2384. Galileo
2385. The pendulum
2386. Astronomy
2387. Earth and planets orbit Sun
2388. Johannes Kepler
2389. Dante
2390. A Renaissance architect
2391. Leonardo da Vinci
2392. The *Mona Lisa*
2393. Michelangelo
2394. Raphael
2395. Renaissance artists
2396. Masaccio
2397. Yes
2398. Yes
2399. Renaissance
2400. Yes
2401. Yes
2402. Machiavelli
2403. Catholic
2404. Music and dance
2405. Yes
2406. Yes
2407. Ballet
2408. Madrigal
2409. The violin
2410. The printing press
2411. Johannes Gutenberg
2412. The Gutenberg Bible
2413. The Northern Renaissance
2414. Martin Luther
2415. Reformists
2416. Protestants
2417. The Reformation
2418. A Protestant
2419. Christianity sub-divided
2420. Ignatius of Loyola
2421. King Henry VIII
2422. The Church of England
2423. Elizabethan Era
2424. The monarch and nobility
2425. A Protestant Church
2426. Puritans
2427. Divided
2428. Its theatre
2429. Famous theatres
2430. William Shakespeare
2431. Plays
2432. Plays
2433. 14
2434. Both nobles and spectators
2435. Sent own ships to claim riches
2436. Yes
2437. The Spanish Armada
2438. Sir Francis Drake
2439. The English
2440. Yes
2441. Yes
2442. Second to sail
2443. 44 years
2444. Virginia
2445. James I of Scotland
2446. The King James Bible
2447. Jamestown
2448. Yes
2449. Without a Parliament
2450. Yes
2451. Massachusetts
2452. The English Civil War
2453. The Parliament
2454. Oliver Cromwell
2455. Enforced Puritan rules
2456. Bring back monarchy
2457. Charles II
2458. A Catholic King
2459. William and Mary
2460. The Glorious Revolution
2461. The Bill of Rights
2462. Yes
2463. Yes
2464. Ivan the Great
2465. Ivan the Terrible
2466. Peter the Great
2467. Catherine the Great
2468. Yes
2469. Japan
2470. Monsoon, typhoons, and tsunamis
2471. "Land of the Rising Sun"
2472. Yes
2473. Feudalism
2474. The top
2475. Below
2476. Samurai
2477. Farmers, artisans, and merchants
2478. Buddhism
2479. Buddha
2480. Yoga
2481. Yes
2482. Gardens
2483. Claude Monet
2484. Shintoism
2485. Renaissance
2486. The Colonial Period

2487. West
2488. The Appalachian Mountains
2489. Yes
2490. Northwest Territory
2491. Daniel Boone
2492. The Wilderness Trail
2493. Yes
2494. The Louisiana Purchase
2495. Lewis and Clark
2496. An interpreter
2497. The fur trade
2498. Yes
2499. Pioneers
2500. Mormons
2501. Gold
2502. The Gold Rush
2503. Prospectors
2504. Panning
2505. Boom towns
2506. Ghost towns
2507. Montana
2508. Wagon trains
2509. Weather, rivers, and diseases
2510. The Oregon Trail
2511. During the Gold Rush
2512. Log homes
2513. The frontier woman
2514. The frontiersman
2515. The frontier children
2516. Summer and winter
2517. Spring and autumn
2518. Pioneers
2519. Posed threat to crops and homes
2520. John Deere
2521. The Native Americans
2522. Outhouses
2523. Log and adobe
2524. With notches
2525. Mud
2526. Yes
2527. Manifest Destiny
2528. Texas
2529. The Mexicans
2530. Davy Crockett and Jim Bowie
2531. "Remember the Alamo"
2532. The Republic of Texas
2533. 1845
2534. The Mexican-American War
2535. James K. Polk
2536. Mexico City
2537. The Treaty of Guadalupe Hidalgo
2538. Fifty percent
2539. Los Niños Heroes
2540. Yes
2541. Yes
2542. North
2543. South
2544. Slavery
2545. Opposed slavery
2546. The North
2547. The South
2548. The Mason-Dixon Line
2549. The Missouri Compromise
2550. Abolitionists
2551. Harriet Beecher Stowe
2552. The Dred Scott Decision
2553. The Lincoln-Douglas Debates
2554. The Southern States
2555. Abraham Lincoln
2556. Secede the Union
2557. The Confederate States
2558. Against slavery and strong government
2559. Jefferson Davis
2560. The American Civil War
2561. The Battle of Fort Sumter
2562. The Battle of Shiloh
2563. "Stonewall" Jackson
2564. The Confederate States
2565. Jefferson Davis
2566. Robert E. Lee
2567. Robert E. Lee
2568. Richmond
2569. Ulysses S. Grant
2570. "Unconditional Surrender" Grant
2571. 15-25
2572. Yes
2573. "Yankees"
2574. "Rebels"
2575. Blue
2576. Grey
2577. Muskets and rifles
2578. A knapsack
2579. The Union Blockade
2580. Were first ironclad ships
2581. To set someone free
2582. The Emancipation Proclamation
2583. Five days after
2584. Yes
2585. The Underground Railroad
2586. Canada
2587. Conductors
2588. Stations
2589. Harriet Tubman
2590. Pickett's Charge
2591. The Battle of Gettysburg
2592. Lincoln's Gettysburg Address
2593. "Four score and seven years ago"
2594. Twenty
2595. Yes
2596. Sherman's March to the Sea
2597. Yes
2598. The Union
2599. The Union
2600. Lee surrendered to Grant
2601. Yes
2602. The American Civil War
2603. Assassinated
2604. Ford's Theatre
2605. John Wilkes Booth
2606. His leg
2607. Twelve days
2608. A Museum
2609. Andrew Jackson
2610. Reconstruction
2611. Bring Confederate states back
2612. Largely destroyed
2613. Rebuilding the South
2614. Union troops
2615. Yes
2616. "The Veto President"
2617. Impeach him
2618. Not-guilty
2619. Black Codes
2620. 13th, 14th, and 15th
2621. Yes
2622. The Union
2623. Carpetbaggers
2624. The Freedmen's Bureau
2625. Yes
2626. The Ku Klux Klan
2627. Yes
2628. The 20th Century
2629. West
2630. The "Wild West"
2631. The Homestead Act
2632. A sod house
2633. Cowboys
2634. A round up
2635. A cattle drive
2636. Yes
2637. A ten-gallon hat
2638. Cowboys
2639. The Rodeo
2640. A harmonica
2641. Gunfighters, bandits, and outlaws
2642. "Buffalo Bill"
2643. Annie Oakley
2644. The Pony Express
2645. The telegraph
2646. The Transcontinental Railroad
2647. Yes

2648. The American Frontier
2649. Alaska
2650. Gold
2651. Yes
2652. Yes
2653. Yes
2654. For Westward expansion
2655. Land rights
2656. Clara Barton
2657. George Washington
2658. Names current President
2659. Names current First Lady
2660. Former Presidents
2661. Former First Ladies
2662. Famous aviators
2663. Famous nurses
2664. Famous inventors
2665. Famous reformers
2666. Famous entertainers
2667. Famous frontiersmen
2668. Names famous American
2669. United States of America
2670. Mexico
2671. Puerto Rico
2672. The Dominican Republic
2673. Cuba
2674. Costa Rica
2675. Guatemala
2676. El Salvador
2677. Nicaragua
2678. Panama
2679. Venezuela
2680. Ecuador
2681. Columbia
2682. Bolivia
2683. Argentina
2684. Paraguay
2685. Uruguay
2686. Chile
2687. Peru
2688. Brazil
2689. Iceland
2690. England
2691. Ireland
2692. Scotland
2693. Germany
2694. Poland
2695. Italy
2696. Portugal
2697. France
2698. Monaco
2699. Canada
2700. Australia
2701. New Zealand
2702. Spain
2703. Morocco
2704. Egypt
2705. Israel
2706. Saudi Arabia
2707. Dubai
2708. Afghanistan
2709. India
2710. Nepal
2711. Thailand
2712. Vietnam
2713. The Philippines
2714. Japan
2715. Kenya
2716. Tanzania
2717. South Africa
2718. Austria
2719. Switzerland
2720. Greece
2721. Belgium
2722. Denmark
2723. The Netherlands
2724. Sweden
2725. Finland
2726. Norway
2727. Russia
2728. China
2729. The United States
2730. Names countries

APPENDIX 2: Chapter 2 – Civics

Pre-School

1. Yes
2. Yes
3. Names school rules
4. Names home rules
5. Names current President
6. Police officer, firemen, etc.
7. Yes
8. Yes
9. Names businesses
10. Mail letters, etc.
11. Place to manage money, etc.
12. Put out fires, rescue, etc.
13. Enforce laws, safety, etc.
14. Yes
15. The police
16. Yes
17. To educate; for learning
18. Yes
19. Yes
20. Yes
21. A community
22. Yes
23. Names town
24. Names home state
25. United States (or other)
26. Yes
27. Yes

Civics – Kindergarten

28. Policemen, crossing guards, etc.
29. Teachers, principal, etc.
30. Yes
31. Yes
32. Yes
33. States responsibilities
34. The grocery store
35. The post office
36. The library
37. The bank
38. Names different jobs
39. Police cars or vans
40. Fire trucks, etc.
41. Boat, car, plane, train, etc.
42. For order and safety
43. The Golden Rule
44. Yes
45. Yes
46. Yes
47. For order and safety
48. Government
49. Police officers
50. Fine or jail
51. Yes
52. Yes
53. Yes
54. Describes flag
55. A symbol
56. Yes
57. The Pledge of Allegiance
58. Star-Spangled Banner, etc.
59. Yes
60. National Anthem, etc.
61. Yes
62. Suggests community project

Civics – 1st Grade

63. Civics
64. Walk, listen, etc.
65. Yes
66. Yes
67. The government
68. Fine, jail, etc.
69. Yes
70. Lifeguard
71. Teachers, principal, etc.
72. Yes
73. Yes
74. Yes
75. Vote
76. An election
77. Yes

Civics – 2nd Grade

78. Says and spells name
79. Cites address
80. Cites phone number
81. Says parents first names
82. Says hometown
83. A neighborhood
84. Names home state
85. Districts
86. Names school district
87. The principal
88. The Superintendent
89. Rural
90. Urban
91. Says type of community
92. A suburb
93. Names closest city
94. Names state capital

Civics – 3rd Grade

95. A community
96. A global community
97. Immigrant
98. Immigrants
99. Yes
100. A custom

101. Yes
102. Names family custom
103. Laws
104. Equality under the law
105. The government
106. A democracy
107. Yes
108. Rights
109. Responsibilities
110. A citizen
111. The Declaration of Independence
112. The U.S. Constitution
113. Philadelphia
114. The Preamble
115. An amendment
116. The Bill of Rights
117. Inalienable Rights
118. 27 Amendments
119. The First Amendment
120. July 4th
121. Thirteen
122. Fifty
123. Thirteen
124. Describes flag
125. Immigrants
126. Native Americans
127. Thomas Jefferson
128. Memorial Day
129. Veterans Day
130. Yes
131. 18 years old
132. Three
133. Branches
134. Yes
135. Checks and Balances
136. The Congress
137. 100
138. 435
139. The Speaker of the House
140. The legislative branch
141. Two
142. The President
143. The Vice-President
144. Names Vice-President
145. The executive branch
146. The judicial branch
147. Nine
148. Chief
149. A court
150. The governor
151. Names state governor
152. The mayor
153. Names city mayor
154. Chief
155. Chief
156. Cites responsibilities
157. Yes
158. Library, store, etc.
159. Yes
160. Art, historical, etc.
161. Yes
162. Names private business
163. Names goods and services
164. Teacher, doctor, etc.
165. A community
166. Obey laws, vote, etc.
167. City
168. Countryside
169. Suburbs
170. Describes community

Civics – 4th Grade

171. Laws
172. Yes
173. Executive, legislative, and judicial
174. Federal
175. Federal
176. State
177. Local
178. The Declaration of Independence
179. Founding Fathers
180. The Preamble
181. An ordinance
182. The U.S. Constitution
183. An amendment
184. The Bill of Rights
185. The legislative branch
186. The House and the Senate
187. The U.S. Capitol
188. Names state capital
189. A legislator
190. The executive branch
191. The judicial branch
192. Checks and Balances
193. Separation of Powers
194. The President
195. Names current President
196. Names current Vice-President
197. The White House
198. The President
199. Pennsylvania Avenue
200. Veto power
201. Supreme
202. A judge
203. A jury
204. Senate and the House
205. 435
206. Yes
207. 100
208. Two per state
209. The Speaker
210. Two years
211. Two
212. Six years
213. A bill
214. A law
215. Veto
216. A mayor
217. Names city mayor
218. A governor
219. Names state governor
220. Local

Civics – 5th Grade

221. Civics
222. Names community
223. Counties
224. Names home county
225. Names home state
226. United States (or other)
227. Citizens
228. Right
229. Responsibility
230. Dictatorship
231. Naturalization
232. Colonists
233. Thirteen
234. The Articles of Confederation
235. Independence
236. Sovereignty
237. Anarchy
238. Yes
239. The Declaration of Independence
240. The Declaration of Independence
241. Pennsylvania
242. Delaware, Massachusetts, etc.
243. Thomas Jefferson

244. A national government
245. A Constitution
246. Federalists
247. Anti-Federalists
248. Jefferson, Madison, Franklin, etc.
249. The Preamble
250. Cites Preamble
251. Peace within United States
252. Cannot be taken away
253. Seven articles
254. The Legislative Branch
255. The Executive Branch
256. The Judicial Branch
257. Yes
258. An amendment
259. The Bill of Rights
260. The First Amendment
261. Civil liberties
262. Censorship
263. Slander
264. Libel
265. Bias
266. Propaganda
267. The Second Amendment
268. The Fourth Amendment
269. The Fifth Amendment
270. Formally approve a law
271. The Thirteenth Amendment
272. The Fourteenth Amendment
273. The Fifteenth Amendment
274. Suffrage
275. The Nineteenth Amendment
276. 27 Amendments
277. Taxes
278. Eminent domain
279. Separation of Church and State
280. A convention
281. A federal system
282. Legislative, Executive, and Judicial
283. Checks and Balances
284. The legislative branch
285. House and Senate
286. The Senate
287. The House of Representatives
288. The Speaker of the House
289. The Vice-President
290. To make the laws
291. A session
292. Yes
293. A bill
294. A committee
295. The President
296. The executive branch
297. The President
298. The President
299. A Two-Party system
300. A political party
301. Republican and Democrat
302. The Republican Party
303. The Democratic Party
304. States party in office
305. The elephant
306. The donkey
307. Popular vote
308. The Primary Election
309. The General Election
310. The Electoral College
311. 270
312. The incumbent
313. Lame duck
314. 18
315. Tuesday
316. November
317. Blue
318. Red
319. Four years
320. Once
321. The inauguration
322. The U.S. Cabinet
323. State of the Union Address
324. The judicial branch
325. The Supreme Court
326. Nine
327. The Chief Justice
328. Names Court Justices
329. A jury
330. A defendant
331. A witness
332. A subpoena
333. A verdict
334. A civil case
335. A civil case
336. Miranda Rights
337. An attorney
338. District Attorney
339. Attorney General
340. Due process
341. Due process of law
342. A felony
343. A misdemeanor
344. An indictment
345. Court pleas
346. The rule of law
347. A petition
348. Eminent domain
349. Discrimination
350. An ordinance
351. Town meetings
352. Board of Education
353. Infrastructure
354. The mayor
355. The President
356. Army, Navy, Air Force, Marines
357. Drones
358. Bureaucracy
359. Diplomacy
360. Names civic duties

Practice Citizenship Test

361. The Constitution
362. Defines government and basic rights
363. We the People…
364. A change to the Constitution
365. The Bill of Rights
366. Speech, religion, press, assembly
367. 27 amendments
368. Declared freedom from Britain
369. Life, liberty, pursuit of happiness
370. One can practice any religion
371. Capitalistic or market
372. No one is above the law
373. Legislative, executive, or judicial
374. The President
375. Checks and balances
376. The Congress
377. The House and the Senate
378. 100
379. 6 years
380. Names state Senator
381. 435 members
382. Two years
383. Names U.S. Representative
384. All of the people
385. Because of the state's population
386. Four years
387. November
388. Names current President
389. Names Vice-President
390. The Vice-President
391. The Speaker of the House

392. The President
393. The President
394. The President
395. Advises the President
396. State, Defense, Energy, etc.
397. Interprets laws and Constitution
398. The Supreme Court
399. Nine
400. Names current Chief Justice
401. Print money, declare war, make treaties
402. Schools, police, fire, land zoning, etc.
403. Names current Governor
404. Names state capital
405. Names current Speaker
406. Republican and Democratic
407. Names Presidential party
408. Any citizen can vote, age 18, etc.
409. Vote, jury duty
410. Vote, run for federal office
411. Speech, worship, bear arms, etc.
412. The flag and America
413. Obey laws, loyalty, serve nation, etc.
414. At least 18
415. Vote, join civic group, run for office, etc.
416. April 15th
417. At age 18
418. Religious freedom, economic opportunity
419. Native Americans
420. Africans
421. High taxes, no self-government
422. Thomas Jefferson
423. July 4, 1776
424. Delaware, Massachusetts, Virginia, etc.
425. Founding Fathers wrote Constitution
426. 1787
427. James Madison, Alexander Hamilton
428. Inventor, diplomat, Postmaster General, etc.
429. George Washington
430. George Washington
431. The Louisiana Territory
432. 1812, Civil, Mexican-American
433. American Civil War
434. Slavery, states' rights
435. Freed slaves, preserved Union
436. Freed the slaves
437. Fought for women's rights
438. World Wars I, II, Korean, Vietnam, Gulf
439. Woodrow Wilson
440. Franklin Roosevelt
441. Germany, Japan, and Italy
442. World War II
443. Communism
444. Civil Rights Movement
445. Fought for civil rights and equality
446. Terrorists attacked
447. Cherokee, Navajo, Sioux, etc.
448. Missouri or Mississippi
449. The Pacific
450. The Atlantic
451. Puerto Rico, Guam, Virgin Islands
452. Montana, Michigan, New York, Alaska
453. California, Arizona, Texas
454. Washington, D.C.
455. Liberty Island in New York Harbor
456. Represents 13 original colonies
457. One star for each state
458. The Star-Spangled Banner
459. Francis Scott Key
460. July 4th
461. Christmas, Thanksgiving, etc.
462. Patrick Henry
463. Alaska and Hawaii
464. Thanksgiving
465. Natural born, 35 years old, etc.
466. The White House
467. The U.S. Capitol
468. Red, white, and blue

Bibliography

"Ducksters: Education Site for Kids and Teachers." *Ducksters: Education Site for Kids and Teachers*. N.p., n.d. Web. Accessed 2014. http://www.ducksters.com.

"ENCHANTED LEARNING HOME PAGE." *ENCHANTED LEARNING HOME PAGE*. N.p., n.d. Web. 10 Accessed 2014. http://www.enchantedlearning.com.

"Fact Monster from Information Please." *Fact Monster: Online Almanac, Dictionary, Encyclopedia, and Homework Help*. N.p., n.d. Web. Accessed 2014. http://www.factmonster.com.

Grade Level Help at Internet 4 Classrooms." *Grade Level Help at Internet 4 Classrooms*. N.p., n.d. Web. Accessed 2014. http://www.internet4classrooms.com.

Hirsch, E. D. *What Your First grader Needs to Know: Fundamentals of a Good First-Grade Education*. New York: Doubleday, 1991. Print.

Hirsch, E. D. *What Your Third Grader Needs to Know: Fundamentals of a Good Third-Grade Education*. New York: Doubleday, 1992. Print.

Hirsch, E. D. *What Your Fourth Grader Needs to Know: Fundamentals of a Good Fourth-Grade Education*. New York: Doubleday, 1992. Print.

Hirsch, E. D. *What Your Fifth Grader Needs to Know: Fundamentals of a Good Fifth-Grade Education*. New York: Doubleday, 1993. Print.

Hirsch, E. D., and John Holdren. *What Your Kindergartner Needs to Know: Preparing Your Child for a Lifetime of Learning*. New York: Doubleday, 1996. Print.

Hirsch, E. D. *What Your Second Grader Needs to Know: Fundamentals of a Good Second-Grade Education*. Rev. Ed. New York: Dell, 1998. Print.

Hirsch, E. D., and Linda Bevilacqua. *What Your Preschooler Needs to Know*. New York, NY: Bantam Dell, 2008. Print.

"K-12 Curriculum." *Cedarburg*. N.p., n.d. Web. June 2014. http://www.cedarburg.buildyourowncurriculum.com/public/Landing_Grades.aspx.

"Make an Amazing Timeline in Minutes." *Preceden: Timeline Maker & Timeline Generator*. N.p., n.d. Web. Accessed 2014. http://www.preceden.com.

"Native Indian Tribes." *Warpaths2piecepipes*. N.p., n.d. Web. Accessed 2014. http://www.warpaths2piecepipes.com.

"Typical Course of Study." *Typical Course of Study*. N.p., n.d. Web. 10 July 2014. http://www.worldbook.com/typical-course-of-study.

BIBLIOGRAPHY

"Online Dictionary | Thesaurus." *Online Dictionary*. N.p., n.d. Web. Accessed 2014. http://www.onlinedictionary.com.

"Practice Math & Language Arts." *IXL Math and English*. N.p., n.d. Web. Accessed 2014. http://www.ixl.com.

"The Great Idea Finder - Celebrating the Spirit of Innovation." *The Great Idea Finder - Celebrating the Spirit of Innovation*. N.p., n.d. Web. Accessed 2014. http://www.ideafinder.com.

"Top Ten Lists at TheTopTens." *Top Ten Lists at TheTopTens*. N.p., n.d. Web. Accessed 2014. http://www.thetoptens.com.

"Touropia - Travel, Tours and Top Tens." *Touropia*. N.p., n.d. Web. Accessed 2014. http://www.touropia.com.

"Wikepedia.com." *Wikepedia.com*. N.p., n.d. Web. 30 Accessed 2014. http://www.wikepedia.com.

www.ingramcontent.com/pod-product-compliance
Lightning Source LLC
Chambersburg PA
CBHW080048280326
41934CB00014B/3249

* 9 7 8 0 9 8 6 0 8 0 1 7 3 *